AGING AS A
SPIRITUAL JOURNEY

AGING AS A SPIRITUAL JOURNEY

Eugene C. Bianchi

CROSSROAD · NEW YORK

Grateful acknowledgment is made to the following for permission to reprint previously published material:

Lines from "Mr. Flood's Party" are reprinted with permission of Macmillan Publishing Co., Inc. from *Collected Poems* by Edwin Arlington Robinson. Copyright 1921 by Edwin Arlington Robinson, renewed 1949 by Ruth Nivison. Lines from *Sonnets to Orpheus* by Rainer Maria Rilke, translated by C. E. Macintyre, are reprinted with permission from the University of California Press. Lines from "You, Andrew Marvell" by Archibald MacLeish are from *New and Collected Poems 1917–1976* by Archibald MacLeish. Copyright © 1976 by Archibald MacLeish. Reprinted by permission of Houghton Mifflin Company. The excerpt from "Shadows" from *The Complete Poems of D.H. Lawrence,* Collected and Edited by Vivian de Sola Pinto and F. Warren Roberts, is reprinted with permission of Viking Penguin Inc., Laurence Pollinger Ltd., and The Estate of Frieda Lawrence Ravagli. Copyright © 1964, 1971 by Angelo Ravagli and C. M. Weekley, Executors of The Estate of Frieda Lawrence Ravagli. Lines from the poems of W. B. Yeats—"The Circus Animal's Desertion," "In Memory of Eva Gore-Booth and Con Markiewicz," "What Then," "Sailing to Byzantium," "The Apparitions," and "Death"— are reprinted with permission of Macmillan Publishing Co., Inc. from *Collected Poems of W. B. Yeats.* Copyright 1928, 1933 by Macmillan Publishing Co., Inc., renewed 1956, 1961 by Bertha Georgie Yeats. Copyright 1940 by Georgie Yeats, renewed 1968 by Bertha Georgie Yeats, Michael Butler Yeats, and Anne Yeats. Also reprinted by permission of M. B. Yeats, Anne Yeats and Macmillan London Limited. Excerpts from "Ash Wednesday" and "The Love Song of J. Alfred Prufrock" in *Collected Poems 1909–1962* and from "Little Gidding" in *Four Quartets,* both by T. S. Eliot, are reprinted by permission of Harcourt Brace Jovanovich, Inc., copyright © 1943, 1963, 1964 by T. S. Eliot, copyright 1971 by Esme Valerie Eliot. Also reprinted by permission of Faber and Faber Ltd.

1984

The Crossroad Publishing Company
370 Lexington Avenue
New York, N.Y. 10017

Printed in the United States of America

Library of Congress Cataloging in Publication Data

Bianchi, Eugene C.
  Aging as a spiritual journey.

  Includes bibliographical references.
  1. Aged—Religious life.   I. Title.
BV4580.B485   1982   248.8′5   82-17103
ISBN 0-8245-0486-0
ISBN 0-8245-0622-7 (pbk.)

CONTENTS

AGING AS A
SPIRITUAL JOURNEY

INTRODUCTION

These preliminary reflections attempt to establish a general framework for a spirituality of aging. In the last two decades a large body of literature, in the form of both empirical investigation and theoretical analysis, has focused on the personality changes, traumas, and potentials of individuals in midlife and later maturity. It is almost as though the social disciplines, psychology especially, have arrived at a kind of middle age of their own. Prior to the 1960s, most of the pioneer work among psychiatrists and psychologists concentrated on childhood and its ramifications in later life. While this orientation remains very important, close attention to the problems of older people constitutes a relatively recent phenomenon. Theologians have only begun in very limited ways to address the mounting research on aging. Voices within and outside the community of religion scholars urge such a dialogue. Noting that a recent and otherwise very complete handbook on aging lacks any article on religious or ethical dimensions, a commentator at a national convention on aging advocates serious discussion about spiritual dimensions.[1] A well-known pastoral counselor exhorts theologians to explore the impressive corpus of writings on aging in the social and psychological sciences before theologizing on the subject.[2]

The religious basis for these particular reflections on aging is Christian, in a broad sense, with occasional excursions into Judaism and into eastern religions. I have also been particularly influenced by Jungian psychology. This way of understanding the life cycle focuses on an inward dialogue between the conscious ego and the deep psyche, that is, the unconscious realm of archetypical images. For Jung, this dialogue, sometimes an upsetting dialectic, is a characteristic and necessary happening for persons in midlife who care about psychospiritual development. Moreover, a close interplay exists between the scriptural and the Jungian perspectives. For example, a core biblical theme is that of confronting one's finitude (death) with a spirit of trusting faith. The Beatitudes demonstrate this letting-go in faith that paradoxically opens the seeker to the experience of new spiritual horizons. In an analogous way, the Jungian approach to the unconscious calls for a kind of "psychological faith" through which the ego allows itself to encounter and be led by inner forces that transcend its complete control. The Shadow archetype, for instance, represents the dark energies (among which are finitude, death, limitation) that must be faced and assimilated in the journey toward greater personal wholeness.

Yet this book also departs from the Jungian perspective, which tends to focus intensely on the intrapsychic realm. In this regard, the biblical outlook, with its ethos of social responsibility, acts as a corrective to excessive introspection. We will argue that the inward conversions of midlife and elderhood have a vital significance bearing on worldly issues of peace, justice, and ecological sanity.

The basic theme of this work is that persons in midlife are called to make their lives more contemplative within the context of active, worldly endeavors. Those in elderhood are summoned to fuller participation in the great concerns of humanity. These goals for midlife and elderhood run against the grain of contemporary technological society, which tends to make contemplation impossible or unwanted among the middle-aged, and forces the old into individualistic pursuits at the periphery of the social order. We will return to this theme at the end of the following discussion about the method of our inquiry, and the rest of the book will attempt to refine and develop it as fundamental to a spirituality of aging.

The method of this essay on aging is both dialogical and dialectical in a cross-cultural context. Dialogue implies both learning and sharing. Much of the work done on midlife transitions, for example, presents data, proximate interpretations of the data, and further speculation on where the data leads. From this material, the theologian learns about a crucial phase of the human life cycle. As he or she reflects on the psychosocial language in which middle-age problems and potentials are treated, a theologian sees analogies and relationships to religion, and wishes to share these insights awakened in the encounter between diverse fields. The symbolic mode of expressing reality proper to religion enters into a *dialogical* exchange with other approaches to aging. But the method is also *dialectical* in that the theologian establishes a style of both yes-and-no-saying. (An example of this dialectic follows shortly in a discussion on stage-theory approaches to the aging process.) A dialectical method also means that the theologian will criticize positions and assumptions arising from religion.

The phenomena of aging, as recorded by many observers, are studied from a theological perspective—that is, as they pertain to matters of spiritual growth and meaning. Some of the phenomena of aging are indeed objective, but many others are subjective in at least two ways. There are the subjective assessments of middle-aged and older persons about their own experiences. Furthermore, the theological commentator adds his or her own subjective slant to the topic. What is important as far as method is concerned is an acknowledgement and awareness of this objective-subjective blend or synthesis in the treatment of the material. Such a methodology differs consciously from that of the strictly sociological observer, who attempts to restrict analysis to an interpretation of empirical data according to well-established measuring techniques in the social sciences. We take cognizance of empirical studies, but seek to incorporate them into a larger interpretive whole.

Furthermore, aging as a subject of inquiry is relative and changing; as a dynamic process it is variously affected by culture and by a person's past and present experiences. While some constants seem to pertain to the aging process, its qualities are not absolute or fixed. Moreover, I am a middle-aged man writing about a topic that relates closely to my own existence. Even as I write about midlife or later maturity, I am a person reflecting, feeling, choosing as one personally immersed in the subject. In other words, a twenty-year-old or a ninety-year-old would discuss middle age with less personal involvement; no doubt, the outcome of the youthful and the elderly person's analysis would differ in important ways from that of a middle-aged commentator.

Another aspect of the book's method is its blending of cultural, psychological, social-science, and theological elements in the course of the chapters. Some readers may prefer to know exactly which hat the author is wearing in a particular section. Is he speaking from cultural observation, from social-science research, or from theological reflection? Although empirical research on aging will undergird some of the commentary, the book is not intended as an empirical study. Nor do the interview chapters reflect rigorous social-science methodology; rather, they serve a kind of illustrative and corroborative function for the whole argument.

But a more important question is that of the validity of "blending" the viewpoints of different fields. First of all, we must be aware of which perspective we are working from at a given moment. This will be done explicitly throughout the book, or will be clear from the references to works in various fields. But the most appropriate response to this question of the validity of a "blending" method is to affirm its value. A cross-disciplinary approach to aging naturally moves an investigator toward holistic thinking about the topic, toward trying to grasp with an interlinking integrity. This holistic vision is precisely what a theological reflection on aging *should* attempt, especially because we hope to elaborate a spirituality intrinsic to the aging process itself.

In addition to these reflections on method as such, it is important to place our reflections in the context of the much-discussed stage theories of the aging process. Many recent works on aging, especially since the formulation of Erik Erikson's "life stages" theory, describe chronological phases from childhood to old age. Each phase or stage manifests certain characteristics and calls for particular tasks to be accomplished before the stage is successfully negotiated. Erikson and most of his followers strive to avoid rigid understandings of the stages, as though everyone proceeds through them at a similar rate. Moreover, the multistage writers temper their doctrines by pointing out that an individual may evince a mélange of traits, some characteristic of his or her age cohort and some more appropriate to previous phases.

The multistage authors also declare that broad empirical investigation confirms (sometimes to the surprise of the investigators) the truth of a particular stage description or hypothesis. This declaration is meant to discourage the suspicion that the data was cleverly made up to fit preestablished categories. R. Gould and D. Levinson provide examples of chronological staging; the former lists four stages from sixteen to forty-five; the latter presents six five-year stages between thirty and sixty.[3] J. and L. Davitz describe a ten-year period between forty and fifty that follows a pattern of intense crisis around forty-five and successful resolution near fifty.[4]

These and other writings on midlife offer excellent material that will supply a basis for reflection in later sections of this essay.

However, these stage theories appear too fixed, hierarchical, and prescriptive. Perhaps the main difficulty in these approaches is an underlying linear system of thinking based on scientific rationality. In the perspective of W. Barrett, these stage theorists suffer from the invasion and limiting influence of technique.[5] A hypothetical goal for a certain life stage is assumed, that is, an ideal kind of personality development; then the stages to reach the goal are indicated. In this approach, the method of the natural sciences is transferred into the human arena. The hypotheses are tested in order to arrive at laws of human development. When this shift is made, there is a danger of mystifying the data, that is, manipulating it into patterns of reality that are determined by the relative truths of a particular era and culture.

In contrast to these linear stage theories, H. Katchadourian concludes that life phases cannot be dealt with outside of historical and cultural contexts.[6] And B. Neugarten stresses the point that context, not chronology, is crucial for understanding personality variations in aging.[7] Attention to social contexts within a given culture would look to family and other societal variables causing diverse outcomes in middle age. The Grant Study underlines this point in a convincing way.[8] Moreover, people in nonwestern and less industrialized environments show a different range of development in time periods that correspond to what is known in the West as middle age.[9]

A more satisfactory approach to the life cycle consists of recognizing major phases such as childhood, youth, middle and old age, while at the same time allowing for as much variation as possible in any of the periods. Within this framework, one can speak of traits and tasks for a given time span without fixing these factors in a tightly bound progression. This procedural choice, moreover, implies more than an arbitrary decision about grouping data on aging. A theological concern guides this judgment about conceptual frameworks. The theologian is leery of the scientific, linear tendency to turn description into prescription. Although the specific-stage scholars proclaim their descriptive intentions and nonnormative use of data, it is not hard to detect a prescriptive element in their work.

A Jungian approach to aging provides a mixture of freedom and structure more amenable to the reality of the aging process. Jung speaks about an ascendant and descendant curve in the life cycle.[10] He refers to a morning and afternoon of life, each with different agendas. For the most part, midlife transition summons a person to greater inwardness in the individuation process. Midlife especially may call for a kind of flexible compensation out of keeping with the dictates of stage theories. For example, a passive youth may demand an assertive middle age; a contemplative youth may need an active, worldly midlife for compensatory development. In his last days, Socrates obeyed a dream summons to write poetry, possibly as a mode of counterbalancing a life given to dialectical argument and philosophical speculation.

It is not that closely defined stage theories are wrong or useless. They can serve as tentative artifacts in the search for meaning in aging. But in their linear-scientific-appearing form, they predict and "prove" too much. Their rationalist bias needs to be countered by a more imaginative, intuitive, and attentive style. This might be termed a religious method of approaching the data—one that invites mystery and mysticism to challenge the sole rule of scientific technique, with its proclivity for accuracy and control.

The mental picture of an ascendant and descendant curve, however, might translate too simply into ascendant-positive, descendant-negative. This simplistic imagery needs to be corrected at the outset, lest it distort the understanding of the aging process. The notion of an ascendant and descendant curve derives primarily from a physical analysis of aging. There is gradual slowing down and deterioration of the biological organism from early midlife to old age. In this context of decline toward death, the curve indicates negative, and even fearsome dimensions. Certain religious systems attempt to discount bodily deterioration by resorting to extreme forms of mind control or to descriptions of the afterlife that remove the negative and tragic sting from death. These mind-over-matter and easy-passage-to-the-next-life attitudes impoverish the growth potential of aging. They fail to see that serious confrontation with the bodily limits of mortality, with all its emotional impact, can be part of the catalyst for human transformation in middle and later adulthood. Moreover, a facile interpretation of the first part of life as an ascendant period furthers an already exaggerated glorification of youth in a death-denying culture.

Life-curve imagery, therefore, must be pictured in a figurative, as well as physical sense. On one level, the symbolism of an ascendant and descendant slope portrays positive aspects of its "downward" incline. To descend indicates a movement toward death and away from an existence constrained by superficial ambitions and relationships. Middle and late adulthood present opportunities for combining the physical descent or gradual organic diminution with a spiritual *ascent.* The latter, as we shall see, demands a delicate balance between a healthy acceptance of physical decline and a search for more satisfactory and humane experiences. The potential for this spiritual ascent, moreover, indicates more than individual development alone; it also promises a reform of social relationships toward a more sharing and just society.

On yet another level, a symbolic interpretation of ascent and descent invites us to imagine the life curve intersected all along its course by an upward and downward line. Youth, midlife, and elderhood bring the experience of ascendant and descendant factors. Illness, disappointment, depression, and failure are not reserved to the later periods of life; neither are spiritual experiences of wonder, love, courage, and selflessness unknown to the young. Thus the ascendant and descendant modes of aging offer numerous occasions for growth. The aging experience itself can become consciously religious in the events of each day through all life stages.

The major theme of the whole work can be understood within the curve-of-life imagery. Midlife and elderhood fall for the most part into the downward slope. Given the previous corrections of "downward," we will argue that a spirituality for middle age calls for a turning inward, for a deeper contemplative life. Such spirituality stands against the tide of our culture, which drives the middle-aged to compete externally with all the ardor of youth. The contemplative orientation does not mean that persons in midlife are to abandon active pursuits and enter monasteries. But in keeping with the needs and temperaments of individuals, a more meditative life in middle age, whether it is expressed in traditional religious or modern psychological idiom, becomes crucial for meeting the challenges and realizing the potentials of this life phase. In the chapters on elderhood, we will argue that a spirituality of aging invites older persons to engage more actively in the world. Again, this worldly emphasis for elders runs against the cultural current that tends to shunt older people to the outer eddies of life's stream. Yet it is not any sort of activity that we propose for elders; rather, they are summoned to return to the centers of decision making with the universal concerns that arise from the acquired wisdom of their experience of aging.

This last point connects the spirituality of midlife with that of elderhood. For unless the inner conversions of middle age take place, there is little hope that elderhood will advance beyond the growing despair and selfish concerns attached to gradual decline. Conversely, elders who are able to return to the centers of life with new wisdom become role models for younger persons, but especially for the middle-aged, who often see the proximate approach of their later years as a threat to their human integrity and worth. Not only are there important consequences for personal growth in this interplay between midlife conversions and elderly wisdom, but crucial socioethical results are also at stake for the wider community. For with inward spiritual changes come transformed attitudes toward such matters as dominant power or enabling power, possessiveness or sharing, tribalism or universalism. The four chapters on challenges and potentials in the later stages of life are complemented by two chapters of interviews with thoughtful elders. In many ways their reflections illustrate the above themes about midlife and elderhood. Among these interviewees, the development of values in the aging process points toward a creative elderhood in and for the world.

I hope that these thoughts on aging will help others to reflect personally on the perils, as well as the spiritual promise of growing older. Luke's gospel underscores this hope: "And Jesus advanced in wisdom, and age, and grace with God and men" (Luke 2:52, Douai Bible, 1582).

I
MIDLIFE:
THE CHALLENGES

> In the middle of the journey of our life
> I came to myself within a dark wood
> Where the straight way was lost.
> (Dante, *Inferno* I: 1–3)

As a middle-aged man, I write about midlife. Youth is now a memory that I can only partially recall, knowing that even in the recalling I am selectively remembering, and also imbuing the memory with middle-aged thoughts. Old age is, for me, a matter of projective imagination; it is a time that I would like to live well, but the last part of the life span also awakens in me fears of physical or mental decline, and the ultimate anxiety about my death. About midlife I am more focused; yet even concerning this age, self-deception may blight my understanding. I may be too close to it to gain perspective; or I may be weighted under by excessive perspective gained from the extensive literature on middle age. Have I merely incorporated the assessments of others without experiencing for myself the realities of midlife? This kind of questioning is valuable, but not for any sure answers that will be forthcoming. Rather, the constant testing of my own experience against the literature on the topic may provide a litmus for at least partial authenticity.

Shakespeare's Regan said of her father, King Lear, "Tis the infirmity of his age; yet he hath ever but slenderly known himself." Perhaps I can avoid such comments in old age if I dwell now on the problems of midlife. But I want to ponder the losses and potential gains of middle age as a theologian, that is, as one who looks for the spiritual or transcendent aspects intrinsic to the experiences of this period. Middle age can be broadly defined as that portion of the life span from about forty to sixty years of age. What do I find to be intrinsically religious about experiences that psychologists and social scientists discuss in another idiom? Is it merely a matter of words, of idiom? It would hardly be worth the effort to do this commentary if a religious understanding of aging phenomena added only another terminology to describe these experiences. My premise, on the contrary, is that religious reflection enlarges the meaning of the languages of other fields, raising the possibility of transcendent understanding. Such religiousness is implied by Levinson when he speaks of the inward growth of a person in midlife: "His spirituality may take the form of an explicit religious doctrine, but often he tries to free himself from formal doctrine in order to attain a personal understanding of what it means to be human."[1]

Since being human, in the fullest sense, is to explore the spiritual dimensions of life, the great human questions that challenge the aging person are profoundly, intrinsically, religious issues.

Challenges to Identity and Worth

Whether consciously perceived or known only indirectly, through unconscious impulses, the central issue of middle age is the loss of youth; other losses stem from this one.[2] Among these losses experienced in middle age, a sense of physical decline, coupled with loss of youth, affects most people. Although health may continue to be good during this period, the tell-tale signs of aging appear. A man's physical energy is diminished to a certain degree; he cannot run as fast or as far as he used to, and it takes him longer to recover from aches and fatigue. A look in the mirror is even more indicative of organic change: gray hair, new lines etched in his face, and possibly added weight at the waist. For a woman, the transition to age forty brings similar signs of physical transformation. The prospect of approaching menopause offers striking confirmation that her body is entering a new phase. Mental powers are still strong, but in some areas, such as memorization, abilities are lessening. This experience of physical change provokes a special kind of distress in a culture that has formed a social conspiracy to make youth last a lifetime.[3] The media constantly insist that true worth attaches to the vitality and beauty of youth. This culture factor takes on great importance in influencing individual and group attitudes toward becoming middle-aged. Many of the negative reactions that we are about to consider are accentuated by the accepted social conception of midlife.

The key theological issue in the negative responses to midlife changes has to do with the experience of individual and social brokenness. The word "experience" is key in the last sentence because mere notional knowledge (as a twenty-year-old might have of middle age) does not possess the poignancy or felt reality of knowing in a bodily, personal way. The experience of brokenness, that is, of the limitation and precariousness of human existence, constitutes a primordial understanding of the traditional religious concept of sin. Indeed, sin is usually defined in terms of the destructiveness of unethical conduct. But sin, in this sense, is secondary to the prior experience of brokenness. This more fundamental condition leads to the destructive behavior usually called sin. Of course, the existential encounter with the broken human condition in one's own flesh is not the only way to come to a knowledge of sin. Younger persons know in a cognitive way that life is often askew, contradictory, and even vicious. Middle age, however, through its encounter with physical decline, offers a personal and deeply internal awareness of the context of human brokenness, which the traditional language of Christianity called "original sin."

This keener perception of the downward slope, in the sense of both physical decline and moral ambiguity, is intimately related to an awareness of finitude and death. Yet the word "awareness" may be misleading. More often, it is an indirect or concealed awareness of death through various forms of denial, which can foster destructive styles of life in middle age. Many reactions to becoming middle-aged are mechanisms for "beating time," for refurbishing childhood illusions of omnipotence.[4] Through social conformity or seemingly rebellious actions, many in midlife make a secret pact with the world in order that childhood fears of annihilation might not return. R. Gould sharply underlines the resurgence, in midlife, of infantile illusions of safety in the face of evil and death. Just as children play certain parlor games with parents to be assured of their protection, so forty-five-year-olds repeat, in novel ways, the patterns of childhood, as if safety could last forever in the face of destructive powers.[5] Thus the middle-aged person is forced, both consciously and unconsciously, to respond to an acute realization of personal death. Whether mortality is faced directly and worked through to new levels of appreciation, or whether it is hidden and denied by escape mechanisms, it becomes central to the midlife turning point in personality organization.[6] We begin to measure our lifetime from the distance to the end rather than from birth. Thus the key loss, that of youth, is closely tied to the sense of one's mortality.

E. Jaques stresses the centrality of death-awareness in a widely quoted discussion of the midlife crisis.[7] During this stage of development, we are challenged to transcend youthful attitudes toward death, in which we disguise it as an external force to be controlled or as a blight that idealism will overcome. According to Jaques, the artist approaching midlife moves from precipitate to sculpted creativity by contemplating and incorporating the tragic, death-prone dimension of life. G. Vaillant, on the other hand, questions the notion that fear of death is a pivotal principle in middle age. Vaillant, reflecting on the longitudinal Grant Study, underscores the turmoil of reawakened childhood instincts and a more honest capacity for dealing with lingering pain.[8] Yet we might respond to Vaillant by tracing the resurgent instincts of abandonment and annihilation. Suffice it, at this point, to link sin, as a primordial experience of brokenness, with this threat of extinction. I sometimes marvel at the bravery of my middle-aged peers who tell me they have no fear of death. Nevertheless, I soon take courage that my conviction about death-fear may be justified when I see these same people religiously jogging up hills and going to health-food stores.

In light of the link between loss of youth and awareness of death, we can understand why the middle-aged respond negatively to their lot. Negative responses, in this context, are those which hinder or arrest development toward the deeper reaches of being human. These responses, themselves influenced by familial and cultural factors, are not without meaning. They become the dodges and compromises, the defense mechanisms that provide occasions for working through the challenge toward more successful patterns of aging. To some extent, we all experience them in midlife. They form part of the forest, savage and dense, through which Dante had to be guided. Thus the major areas of loss in middle age—physical decline, role threat, sexual-relational problems, and the diverse negative reactions that ensue—have a dual aspect. They may prevent psychospiritual growth or they may become the purgatorial or "pathologizing" environment through which fuller "soul-making," as J. Hillman terms it, can result. They are Avernus of Virgil's *Aeneid:* "Down to Avernus the descent is light. But thence thy journey to retrace, there lies the labor, there the mighty toil by few achieved."[9] Our first task is to confront and own our negative reactions to the sense of threat evoked by the signs of physical decline.

In reflective moments of middle age we encounter, in an experiential way, our finiteness. As the lines of age become etched on our faces, we know, in a very personal way, that we are contingent, not absolute, beings. The realization of our contingency through physical or mental limits helps us "pierce the armor of functionality."[10] In a technological society, where virtually everything is measured by ascertainable productivity, we are defined by our functions. A quasi-absoluteness attaches to functionality, in the sense that we are what we do; we are identified by contributions to family and society. Although these exist wherever there are civilizations, when the awareness of personal contingency dawns, we know that we are expendable, merely temporary actors on the stage of social history. We tend to avoid the experience of contingency because it brings dread to the surface of consciousness. Yet, as Kierkegaard knew from his own life story, dread, anxiety about our precarious situation, suspended as we are over the chasm of nonbeing, can also be the turning point toward a more significant journey. Thus a sense of personal contingency, of the confinement of our own existence, is often recognized in signs of physical decline from the idealized person of youth.

One midlife reaction to the menace of physical decline is hyperactivity.[11] Our highly competitive culture conditions us, males especially, to run all the harder when we are challenged. Thus many deny the effects of age by stepping up the tempo of their involvements. They seek to prove their physical stamina by playing an extra set of tennis or running a few more miles. We cannot but wonder about the rationale of middle-aged men driving themselves with strenuous sports, such as handball and jogging, even in inclement weather. It is difficult to believe that the body needs this kind of conditioning (or punishment). While studies show that good physical health is a crucial factor for maintaining emotional balance in midlife, hyperenergetic activity may also be a symptom of our attempt to escape gnawing fears of mortality and finitude.[12] Yet running from these fears only assures and magnifies them.[13] Frenetic activity can also include increased engagement with job or career. Work can be a vital dimension of our creativity and personal unfolding, but it can also become a place to hide from our fears through repetition of the familiar. To some degree, we are all subject to the Freudian defense mechanism of repetition-compulsion. But the hectic pace in the work world for many in midlife indicates an attempt through repeated action to stave off the anxiety of physical decline and preserve a semblance of order and control.

If hyperactivity is one side of the middle-aged response to threat, hypoactive embracing of decline is the other. Some begin to "act old," curtailing their interests and involvements for motives ranging from hypochondria to alleged boredom with life. By acting old, these persons seek to avert the need for a change in their self-image.[14] They dramatize their decay by putting on weight, walking more slowly, and complaining of physical problems. It is almost as though they were begging society to acquit them, with good conscience, of the mandate to grow through the new and fearsome awarenesses of midlife. Psychosomatic illnesses and hypochondria abound, especially among women, since society more easily allows the female to claim illness as an attribute of the "weaker sex." Hypochondria, in the middle-aged, represents a fear of going forward, of grappling with the task of retracing one's journey and shaping a new self-image adequate to the challenge of this stage of life. It may also connote an arrest of religious development, as a person rests content with past achievements.[15] An eschatological or futurist orientation essential to religious transformation is lacking.

Eschatology is not future-thinking that postpones living in the present for some all-recompensing heaven, another form of escape from the challenge of the present. Rather, the eschatological or future-oriented attitude of genuine religiousness finds a source of hope and enthusiasm for the present through our faith that an ultimately benevolent God invites us forward to be and to create at every phase of the life span. It is a great error in our culture to ascribe a future only to youth; it reveals a lack of faith, a moribund eschatology. That the aging and, perhaps especially, the very old have a future is both a crucial awareness for true spirituality and a needed corrective for our prevalent conception of futureless aging.

The Psalmist echoes true eschatology: "I will walk in Yahweh's presence in the land of the living" (Psalm 116). I *will* walk—a future orientation; in Yahweh's presence—the benevolent ambience; in the land of the living—as physical death comes nearer, the terrain is ever more that of the living. Too often in the aging process we settle for reminiscing rather than creating new memories. To recollect is to gather together past experiences of success or failure as stepping stones for new ventures. To reminisce is to flee the present and live again in the past. "Living in the past," however, also has value as a vicarious reliving of past events. Reminiscence is misused when it becomes a refuge for a life of passive drifting, a surprisingly frequent phenomenon in middle age. Whether we react to the threat of decline by exaggerated activity or passivity, the underlying attitude is one of fear, resentment, and disdain. Such a person conceals a fright-laden resentment of the prowess and promise of the young. At the same time, we tend to harbor a disdainful anger toward those in old age.[16] The elderly remind us of our own not-too-distant plight. As we see what happens to aged family members, neighbors, friends, and associates, we envision ourselves too soon in their place. Humans live toward the future, the realm of expectations. Our expectations about old age frighten us.

Hyperactivity and hypoactivity, as responses to the startling awareness of our aging in midlife, point to the deeper issue of the personal meaning of time. To the young, time seems relatively endless; short of some life-threatening event, it is almost impossible for the young to imagine their own deaths. Freud's notion about the inability of the unconscious to cope with personal death and Jung's insight about the unconscious's lack of fearful interest in one's own death seem especially true of children and young adults. To them life appears endless; choices proliferate; if one path does not suit, another can be tried. In midlife this carefree sense of time ceases, at least for those who are alert to the changes of their inner clocks. Qoheleth tried to preach such a message to the young: "And remember your creator in the days of your youth, before evil days come . . . before sun and moon and stars grow dark. . . ." (Eccles. 12:1–2). But this ancient sage seemed to know that young people will "follow the promptings of [their] hearts and the desires of [their] eyes" (Eccles. 11:9). For the young cannot grasp, in an experiential way, that time is not on their side. They know only in a conceptual way "the day when those who keep the house tremble and strong men are bowed; when women grind no longer at the mill because the day is darkening at the windows" (Eccles. 12:3). But those in midlife can read these lines with personal references. Time is short: so many projects to start or to finish, so many longings to fulfill, faults to set straight.[17]

The curtailing of time fosters a sense of restlessness and subliminal anxiety that forms one of the principal pains of this period. Yet we must experience as deeply as possible the shortening of our life span as the necessary prelude to fashioning a new understanding of time. Such a new understanding breaks through the cultural myth that aging can be seen only as a linear progression. A nonlinear way of looking at time will be discussed later in the discussion of the *puer-senex* archetypes as immediately present to all ages, as a legitimate way of detemporalizing the life span. The chief point to underline here, however, is that we must seriously enter into the experience of the sands slipping away in the hour glass of our lives. This discomforting feeling of the unstoppable dimming of the light, the numbering of breaths, must be embraced until it hurts. Otherwise our possible responses will remain intellectual thoughts, not contemplated, internalized, soul-gripping realities. The "answer" will be no answer to us, in the depths of our beings, because the questions were only conceptualized, and put at a distance by mental gymnastics so that they could not touch our exposed, vulnerable egos.

Thus the young remind the middle-aged of the passing of time and the irreversible loss of youth in a culture that treasures youthfulness so highly. The old offer a preview of further losses in physical abilities and in social stature. A good example of this in-between state, with its negative feelings and consequent guilts, can be observed in the relation of the middle-aged to their teenage children, on the one hand, and to their elderly parents on the other. Yet even this fear and disdain call for recognition within the middle-aged individual. By denying or cloaking these unpleasant reactions, the first stage of growth beyond them is lost. Without owning our negative feelings, moreover, guilt becomes free-floating, its sources unclarified. Such guilt further paralyzes the personality, or impels it into futile compensatory gestures.

The issue of guilt deserves reflection in this context. The earliest guilt formation, the basis for all subsequent feelings of remorse, attaches to a child's ambivalent relationship to parental figures. The parents are both loved and hated, obeyed and resisted, praised and maligned, in the normal process of childhood ego development. Guilt feelings are an inevitable consequence of such interactions. How can we be justified in opposing, disliking, even wishing evil to those who love and nurture us? Yet, however well we have managed to repress, or to forget, these early transactions, the guilt mechanism has begun. Guilt is at once a part of our brokenness, the tragic ambiguity of being human, our "original sin" (from the Adam and Eve tale of opposition to the loving source) and, at the same time, in its better sense, the font of our conscience, the quickening of responsibility for justice and gratitude. During the middle and later years a heightened awareness of guilt recurs. After the time of youthful striving, when the ego has managed to forget its guilts in order to seek the goals of self-identity and social success, the repressed guilts return. Now they are blended with fresh guilts arising from reflection on self, work, and others. Have we made unworthy choices about our own development? Have we chosen our careers for ulterior motives? Do we use them humanely? How have we hurt our immediate family and friends?

When the pace of life slackens and the moments become more meditative, questions like these beset the middle-aged. The underlying sense of anxiety and guilt frequently relates to hurts sustained in life. Sometimes these are the hurts of childhood, suppressed in the years of ego development, but now returning for attention in middle age. Sometimes the injuries to our own self-esteem arise from later events built on earlier traumas. With the actual loss of youth come cracks, symbolized by facial wrinkles, in an earlier identity structure through which we either denied the earlier hurts or blamed them on others. We may turn to more harmful strategies, blaming ourselves for injuries and deficiencies in ways that lead to depression. The Latins called this *acedia*, a kind of depressed self-paralysis in which zest for life has fled. Memories of hurts and shortcomings flood in. At first we oscillate between sadness and anger, which, when directed outward, gives us at least some energy to temporarily stem depression. Yet this process, so difficult during a midlife crisis, is a necessary stage in moving toward a deeper healing of our memories of hurt and guilt. These painful events constitute a call inward to discover the resources for healing in our own depths and/or in a newly prayerful encounter with religious tradition in its forms of divine healing presence.

For many persons in midlife, therefore, basic self-identity is called into question. The ego, that cluster of traits by which we know ourselves and which we have striven in youth to shore up as distinct and unique, is shaken and endangered by unforeseen forces in the aging process. The roots of this menace to the self lie in an awakening sense of personal mortality manifested by the loss of youth. The physical awareness of this process is only part of the story; psychological doubts about our abilities, values, and goals also assault the personality. Many of these doubts arise from new challenges in the workplace or in interpersonal relations, areas that we shall soon discuss. But a good portion of the anxiety about identity and worth stems from a direct critique of the psychological props of our younger years. The dreams of youth seem illusory. We had embraced the romantic cultural promise that all would be well if we obeyed the rules of family and society. Thus it is not just the death of the bodily self that frightens us, but the mortality of these illusions, the myths by which we lived. Joseph Campbell and others emphasize that myths are crucial for ordering and energizing our life patterns. In midlife, however, many of the youthful myths that sustained our life's direction become inadequate. The psychological dimension of middle-age crises could rightly be described as the demise of personal myths by which the self understood its identity and presented itself to the world. The death of key myths creates a vacuum, a no-man's-land where anxieties intensify for want of directional signals.

This trauma of identity in the middle years is a form of existential alienation that eastern religions regard as a necessary harbinger of a new level of spiritual integration.[18] Western traditions refer to this phenomenon as the "dark night of the soul" or entrance into the "cloud of unknowing," where previous securities are undermined. Although this experience can lead to what Arasteh labels "final integration," there is no automatic assurance that such spiritual integrity of the personality will result. Moreover, we must question the notion of a *final* integration itself, if it is understood as a state of psychospiritual equilibrium achieved in this life. Such supreme balance is probably just another illusion, or even an occasion of spiritual pride. Rather, all integration, whether connected with God or the *Tao,* will be partial fulfillment, ever inviting the soul to search for deeper truth and participation. But more to our point, the disintegration of the self often experienced in midlife becomes the necessary deconstruction of the personality prerequisite to a dawning reintegration. This rhythm of descent and ascent fills our great literature from Gilgamesh to Jesus, from Dante to T. S. Eliot.

From a psychological standpoint, Jung described the need for this existential alienation as arising from a too rigid or one-sided formation of the personality in young adulthood. The "muscular," linear, voluntaristic ego of youth has built its deceptively strong house on the sands of social conventions and immediate needs for acceptance. From the Jungian perspective, the youthful ego must be willing, at some point in its development, to clear away the sands of illusion and find itself suspended over the abyss of the unconscious. Here again, the encounter is fearsome, anxiety-producing, alienating. But it is a necessary process if we hope to break through to greater wholeness through the reconciliation of opposites in the psyche. Only when the full polarity of opposites, conscious and unconscious, interior and exterior, repressed and expressed, personal and collective, is experienced by the personality, can it build on deeper spiritual moorings. This is what Simone Weil called "grace and gravity" in the title of one of her books. Only when we feel the full weight, heaviness, ponderousness of our alienated (from previous illusions) human situation, can grace lift us to a new place. Yet to identify with our gravity in the sense of physical and mental mortality is painful. Augustine knew this when he proclaimed, *"pondus meum, amor meus"*[19]: In the frightening heaviness of our mortality is paradoxically the seed of redemption and the ability to be loving in and through that deadliness.

The crisis of the self in midlife is particularly accentuated in our culture, which prizes so highly the very elements most threatened in this changing time. Our self-worth is strongly measured by society in terms of material attainments, social roles, and in general, productivity. Overall, this constitutes a functional view of persons: We are what we do; we have social being or selfhood by producing.

There is nothing intrinsically wrong with this. Humans have always evaluated others, to some extent, according to their accomplishments. We are, in some ways, what we do. That is, we mold our self-definition partially by the contributions we make to the wider community. This becomes problematic when there is virtually no other yardstick for measuring self-worth in our culture. Outside of a few loving relationships with parents, intimates, or friends by whom we are accepted unconditionally for being ourselves, society judges us almost exclusively by concrete achievements. In this context, Van Kaam discusses the midlife crisis as a struggle between a functionally determined self and one defined by a transcendental dimension.[20]

Van Kaam describes the midlife crisis as a transcendence in which the disclosure of our finiteness "pierces the armor of functionality."[21] It is only through confrontation with our radical contingency that we come to understand that the transcendent dimension forms the core of our selfhood. But this lesson is not learned without suffering, because the personal experience of contingency engenders dread. We realize, perhaps for the first time, our contingent aloneness in the universe. Nothing can restore our former illusory sense of absoluteness, not belongings or friends, or acceptance and attainment in the world of work. An illness or disability may remind us of our contingency; elderly parents or associates confirm the decline that awaits in a relatively short time. A twenty-year time span seems brief when one is fifty, compared to how it appeared at thirty. Time periods seem to shorten geometrically with the passing of years. To the fifty-year-old, thirty was only a distant yesterday; to the thirty-year-old, being ten years old seems a very long time ago. The hastening pace of time underscores the acute sense of personal contingency provoking a midlife crisis that can lead to a breaking-in of transcendent experience.

The paradox of this experience of transcendent potential through immersion in radical contingency is striking. When the disclosure of our finiteness pierces self-definition through functionality, we can then return to a deeper appropriation of our core selves. It is only when our self-definition through accomplishment is profoundly relativized that we can reach a turning point in self-understanding that opens the soul, in trusting faith, to an absolute benevolence. In this process, previous traditions, motives, and goals are also relativized. It is as though the Spirit in our spirits had to shatter the encrusted patterns of the past to free us for new awareness and choices. When I think about these paradoxical things, I marvel at the importance of midlife anxiety, and even dread, for deepening our spiritual life. When I participated in the Spiritual Exercises of Ignatius Loyola in my younger years, these paradoxes were certainly present in many meditations. At that time I probably could have written an essay about this topic. But I did not understand the subject in an experiential mode, in a way that truly grips the soul. It has been only in midlife, through a series of personal crises, coupled with the growing awareness of my aging, with its sense of limits and contingency, that the paradoxical process of self-transcendence has dawned for me in a concrete way.

During this same period of my life, I came to appreciate the paradox of self-continuity through discontinuity in Jungian psychology and therapy. To some extent, Jung based his whole psychological enterprise on midlife crises. For it was during this period of the life span that the inadequate, one-sided self-definitions of his clients began to collapse. In the Jungian paradigm, the ensuing distress and anxiety signaled the in-breaking of unconscious content that had been repressed or neglected. The primordial images or vectors of psychic energy, which he referred to as archetypes of the deep psyche, were challenging the ego's overly defensive structuring of the personality. The personal path of these vectors from the unconscious was through the symbolic language of dreams and fantasy. It was also broadcast in myth and metaphor, or great literature and art.

This whole therapeutic process, by which the conscious ego develops by gradually encountering psychic depths, is founded on paradoxical discontinuity. For it is only when the conscious self becomes open to the discontinuous, to that which is not of its limited fashioning, that it can find healing. The unconscious elements sometimes radically and painfully challenge the ego's self-definition. Yet it is by means of such discontinuity that the little self, or ego, in Jungian terms, can discover a deeper continuity with the core Self at the center of the psyche. The Jungian metaphors have the advantage of personalizing the process of individuation by rooting it in the actual clash of images within the personality. This psychological system is not *the* spiritual method for dealing with the middle-aged self in crisis, but it is *a* spiritual or religious design, in the broad sense, for grappling with these issues.

In his fifties, Leo Tolstoy experienced and expressed (in *My Confession*) an intense crisis, which proved to be a major turning point in his life. To all outward appearances he had achieved prosperity and fame. Tolstoy boasted of his beloved family and ever-growing estate. At that time he was highly respected by neighbors and friends, and had already attained renown for his great novels *War and Peace* and *Anna Karenina.* Yet in the year 1879, in the midst of a brilliant career, he published these remarks: "I felt that what I was standing on had given way, that I had no foundation to stand on, that that which I lived by no longer existed, and that I had nothing to live by."[22] In part, this desolation came from an intense encounter with his own mortality, in light of which all his accomplishments seemed futile. He would later express the same theme in *The Death of Ivan Ilyich,* portraying a character who, when faced with death, recognized that his previous life had been dedicated to unworthy goals. In *My Confession*, Tolstoy wrote of himself:

> The truth was that life was meaningless. It was as though I had just been living and walking along, and had come to an abyss, where I saw clearly that there was nothing but perdition. And it was impossible to stop and go back, and impossible to shut my eyes, in order that I might not see that there was nothing ahead but suffering and imminent death—complete annihilation.[23]

This passage expresses perfectly a keenly felt midlife trial. Tolstoy had moved through his earlier life with the ardor and purpose of youthful energies. As a "healthy, happy man" he faces his own ultimate finitude; with an artist's sensitivity, he, like the poet Eliot, knows he cannot "turn again." Moreover, it was impossible now for him to shut his eyes to his fate. Only by staying "drunk," that is, drugged by the seemingly endless course of youth, could he avoid facing his cruel reality. "The moment he sobered up, he could not help seeing that all that was only a deception."[24]

This sense of deception also projected Tolstoy into a religious crisis. He felt that God had played a "stupid, mean trick" on him by bringing him along the path of life only to meet the destruction of self and of all he held dear.[25] Resentment toward God is still another aspect of the midlife crisis, especially for those who believe that a benevolent deity will protect them against life's vicissitudes.[26] This is a type of unconscious pact that many of us make with the divine: In exchange for living basically good, worthy lives, according to the rules of church and culture, we expect some kind of external guarantee of immunity from life's tragedies. Yet it is precisely this midlife dilemma of naked, undeceptive finitude that inspired Tolstoy to search for a new religious meaning, distinct from that of the Orthodox church in his nation. Again, he grappled with the task of middle age, that of developing his own religiousness by listening, not only to external tradition, but also to his internal spirit in the face of death. In his quest for a Christian religion by which he might live, Tolstoy rejected the oppressive violence that he observed in his society, derived insight from the simplicity of the peasants, and became a forerunner of modern prophets of nonviolence, including Gandhi, whom he influenced.

A similar experience of a midlife crisis, with its sense of contingency, discontinuity, and paradox stands out in T. S. Eliot's "Ash Wednesday." The poet opens his verses with a statement of a time past and irretrievably gone: "Because I do not hope to turn again. . . . / Desiring this man's gift and that man's scope / I no longer strive to strive towards such things / (Why should the aged eagle stretch his wings?)." He does not hope to return to the strivings of younger years because he realizes the ineluctable passage of time, moving irreversibly onward: "Because I know that time is always time / and place is always and only place / And what is actual is actual only for one time. . . ." The past can be illuminating, but it is irretrievable; there is discontinuity between then and now. The poet does not dwell on what has transpired in order to find resources for courage. Rather, he renounces the past: "I renounce the blessed face / And renounce the voice / Because I cannot hope to turn again." Yet in the renunciation arise, paradoxically, resources for reshaping the self: "Consequently I rejoice, having to construct something / Upon which to rejoice." This is reminiscent of Kierkegaard's description of Abraham in *Fear and Trembling*, who chose, in obedience, to sacrifice his past, Isaac, the child of time-bound flesh who, before the renouncing, also embodied Abraham's hope of progeny. Yet, as Kierkegaard perceived, in the very faith-inspired renunciation a new future was paradoxically given back to Father Abraham, the Knight of Faith. After the testing there is a new hope and a new self: Abraham became the spiritual father of many peoples.

Renunciation of the hope that is based on what has been is enveloped in pain and dread. The poet knows the movement to a "higher dream," to constructing something on which to rejoice, can only be realized "through a bright cloud of tears, the years, restoring / With a new verse the ancient rhyme. Redeem / The Time. Redeem / The unreal vision in the higher dream. . . ." Again, there is no easy solace as the seer risks in midlife a transit to a completely different way of self-definition. The new dream of how life can be hangs suspended between birth and death: "This is the time of tension between dying and birth / The place of solitude where . . . dreams cross / Between the rocks." Even after the renunciation, there is no unfailing assurance from the human vantage point. We may still be deceived if our presumed new wisdom is based only upon a finite calculation, on clever ways of mesmerizing ourselves to believe that wishing will make it so. No, we must continue to move in the valley of treacherous rocks. Thus the poet prays to a feminine reflection of divinity, to his guiding anima-figure: "Blessed sister, holy mother, spirit of the fountain, spirit of the garden, / Suffer us not to mock ourselves with falsehood /. . . . Teach us to sit still / Even among these rocks."

The crisis of the self in midlife, as seen in the lives of many persons, manifests certain common traits. These characteristics are not experienced by all in the same way or in the same sequence. Many people do not even recognize abrupt changes in middle age that could be classified as midlife crises. For a variety of reasons, such as the demands of economic survival or general contentment in a career, some people report no distinct period of turmoil. Yet these "smooth evolvers" relate important changes, and even traumas, in their middle years.[27] They may never have clustered these changes so as to recognize a full period of upheaval, or they may have experienced the significant events in such a gradual and extended way that the impact of a crisis phase was minimized. Yet certain common aspects of the midlife crisis are apparent in their challenged self-understandings.[28]

One characteristic reported by those who have undergone midlife upheaval is the unexpected and almost foreign dimension of the challenge. They do not choose to enter a period of reflection or serious self-renewal. Whether the crisis creeps up on them or is suddenly hurled at them depends on a variety of circumstances. In the case of Tolstoy, the critical happenings seemed to break through from his own unconscious, from interior sources, while his outward life appeared happy and prosperous. For others, the catalyst of crisis may be an external event such as the loss of a job, a death in the family, a divorce, or an illness. The trial period may also be associated with a change of place; this move, either distant or relatively near, uproots us from the familiar and the routine. When our environment of safety and support is withdrawn, the self's equilibrium is shaken. Yet, whether the provocation be inner or outer, or a combination of the two, it is experienced as a foreign intrusion. From a psychological viewpoint, this otherness of the catalytic events implies an upsetting of the ego control and rational planning characteristic of early adulthood. It is as though deeper elements in the psyche were demanding attention, aided by external perturbations. From a theological perspective, the alien thrust of the provocation connotes the presence of grace, which often arrives amid upsetting circumstances. The religious person will not find the crisis any easier in its intensity, but in the otherness of its coming, he or she will recognize the unmerited and unexpected gift of grace.

Another group of traits in the midlife crisis occurs on the emotional level, with a reversal of values and goals. One's basic sense of meaning in life is challenged. Emotional dimensions of personality suppressed or repressed in the pursuit of a career and the building of a family now rise painfully to the surface of consciousness. This is the context of Freud's "return of the repressed," which calls for various forms of healing attention. It is also reminiscent of the Renaissance notion of *ricorso,* the circular motion of inner and outer reality by whose returning patterns greater unity is achieved in self and world. Jung underlined the emotional impact of the midlife upheaval:

> Instead of looking forward, one looks backward . . . one begins to take stock, to see how his life has developed up to this point. The real motivations are sought and the real discoveries are made. . . . But these

insights do not come to him easily; they are gained only through the severest shocks.[29]

Under the pressure of the "shocks," the usual forward-looking motion, the linear, ego-dominated progression, is arrested. Again, the line of attention curves backward, returns to ask neglected questions. Who am I aside from my social roles? Where am I going in life? What do I really want? What can I truly attain? This detachment from the conventional forward motion of life causes a new sense of loneliness, of being cut off from the normal sources of consolation. We feel emotionally at sea, drifting without a rudder or wind in the sails.

At the heart of this emotional trauma is the beginning of a reversal of values and goals. Jung speaks of the afternoon of life bringing "the reversal of all the ideals and values that were cherished in the morning."[30] This reversal, or turning back, may at first glance seem to contradict T. S. Eliot's "I do not hope to turn again." But, in fact, the psychologist agrees with Eliot: Jung does not expect to return to things as they were, to desiring "this man's gift and that man's scope," to the values of younger years. Such a going back would be merely a repetition of the youthful search for ideals. True reversal implies a kind of Hebrew *teshuba*, or turning, in which the faithful Israelite turns away from destructive involvements and turns toward Yahweh to learn new spiritual counsels. The reversal of values and goals is also akin to the Christian concept of conversion or *metanoia*. It is a change of heart, a turning around of the self, through which we can begin to understand differently what we have always seen.

Challenges of World and Work

Another set of challenges, which often evokes negative responses in midlife, revolves around losses pertaining to career and role changes. For many, self-image and self-esteem derive from the world of work. Youthful dreams of success encounter the disillusioning reality of middle-age attainments. The scenario for success may have been linked to monetary attainment, prestigious excellence in one's field, or some form of political notoriety. Usually the dream combines a number of elements, including success in building friendship, intimacy, and a family. Although this affective area impinges on job issues, it merits separate discussion in the following section. For many, disillusionment with career achievements prevails whether they are adjudged, by themselves or others, as successes or failures in their job roles.[31]

Those who have not reached their career goals tend to blame external circumstances or poor job choices early in life. This disillusionment may lead to a resigned coping, a dull going through the motions. Because of family needs, lack of education, or lack of personal vision and courage, they settle into years of half-life in their careers. They are increasingly affected by a kind of enervating apathy. Sometimes they become cynical toward institutions or supervisors, often manifesting traits of avoidance and passive aggression.[32] The cynic avoids acting upon the problem and expresses moderate anger without risking his or her job in the eyes of authorities.

Others, of lesser achievement, may be tormented by insecurities and self-depreciation, but manage to conceal these feelings by doggedly trying to prove themselves to others. Yet this same compulsion to be acknowledged by others as superior may be simultaneously accompanied by the unspoken conviction that they have gone as far as they ever will on the career ladder. This inconsistency between inner feeling and outward expression inclines such individuals toward desperation, if not actual despair. Resistance to change, a quality noted in some elderly persons, has its origins mainly in middle age. The world narrows as one learns to adjust to an unsatisfactory routine. Change is seen as a threat to hard-won securities.[33] Those who achieved the projected success of their youth, or even surpass it, can experience another kind of disillusionment. Earlier goals, with their privileges and prestige, fail to satisfy; career attainment does not bring the satisfaction that was anticipated in earlier days. The middle-aged minister, for example, may gain a certain stature in the congregation, but a new awareness of irrelevance or ineffectiveness calls into question the original motivations of his calling.[34]

Moreover, many persons judged successful in middle age have become overachievers. They are enveloped by the job, unable to escape from its ceaseless demands. Their whole personal identity becomes associated with their job roles, while other aspects of their personalities, which could bring joy, are neglected or suppressed.

For both underachievers and overachievers, however, the negative potentials of midlife depend heavily on cultural conditioning and expectations. Indeed, the negative reactions to the losses of midlife are dictated as much by social mandate as by personal choice.[35] This social dimension of aging must be kept in mind at every stage of our discussion; beyond the physical and personal aspects of aging, attitudes toward growing older are overtly or subtly influenced by collective expectations or requirements. It has even been claimed that the problems of middle age are not intrinsic to that phase of life, but rather are a consequence of environmental conditions.[36] While such social determinism seems excessive, the societal environment of attitudes and expectations regarding aging remains crucially important.

To understand how deeply occupation contributes to identity in our culture, we have only to observe the extreme trauma that loss of a job causes to a middle-aged person. In addition to the economic threat to self and family, job loss profoundly shakes the worker's sense of self-confidence and self-esteem. For many, life's meaning depends on their jobs; when jobs are lost the significance of existence is in jeopardy.[37] Other middle-aged persons are victimized by retaining jobs that have become unrewarding, either because of mistaken career choices in the first place or because the worker has outgrown the job's potential. They cling fearfully to that one handle that allows them to define themselves, however unsatisfactorily, by what Studs Terkel calls a perverted work ethic.[38] Numbed and tired, they hold on while "a strange alchemy is at work: the gold that may be found in their unexamined lives is transmuted into the dross of banal being."[39] In a certain way, the loss experienced by these midlife hangers-on may be greater than that of actual job loss. Upon the loss of a job, people are forced to reconsider, not only a series of job options, but also what kind of work would contribute most in the middle years to personal development.

Thus the challenge and the real losses related to work, with or without a job, merit much reflection in midlife. We sell people short; many more than we think may be looking for a calling, rather than a mere job, which may prove too small for the human spirit.[40]

The social impact on career expectations has been especially strong for the middle-aged woman in recent decades. She is caught between a generation of younger women who are encouraged to follow professional paths and an older cohort of women whose lives were more traditionally structured around their roles as wives and mothers. Today's forty-year-old woman may face a diminishing maternal role as her children become independent, and at the same time, face the difficult prospect of entry or reentry into the world of employment. With such a late start, she finds it hard to move beyond the lower rungs of a career ladder.[41] Her long absence from the competitive arena may double her sense of insecurity and dim her confidence about future potentials.

Such a woman may be further stressed by a mate who appreciates the added income to the family, but expects the woman to do the double duty of job and housework. Or she may be married to a man whose male image depends on his being the sole financial support of the family. A study from the sixties indicates that many women who embraced conventional mothering roles became depressed when the last children left the household.[42] This depression is aggravated if mothers are not encouraged to redirect their energies in satisfying ways. In such situations, women are often willing and able to seek careers, but find themselves stymied by intense opposition at home.

Middle-aged women who have worked outside the home for most of their adult lives tell another story about sexism and obstacles to advancement in a male-dominated culture. It is significant that Freud and Erikson demonstrate a male bias in reference to the place of work in adulthood. For Freud, a mentally healthy man was one who could both love and work. Erikson tends to apply his categories of intimacy and generativity with a male focus. For him, female adulthood is defined less by participation in the world of work than by the cultivation of "inner space." These observations, especially in a time of changing roles for men and women, warn us to be leery of psychological ideologies. How easy it is to accept the status quo as the essential and necessary pattern for a particular gender. Yet all these liabilities and sufferings, with their possible consequences, must be grasped existentially if a deeper midlife spirituality is to be fashioned. Only when feelings and attitudes are faced honestly can the balancing of male and female traits within each of the sexes be achieved.[43]

The issue of power and self-definition underlies many difficulties with work roles in middle age. As labor has become more specialized in our advanced technological society, high degrees of particular competence are at a premium. Value to the tribe, and therefore self-image, is molded by the stature derived from specialized functions. Persons in midlife often feel greater societal pressure to be able to exercise competence in ways that enhance their own sense of identity and contribute to the common good. Studies indicate that men in midlife rate their "life satisfaction" in direct proportion to their stature and performance on the job.[44] We can expect this phenomenon to become increasingly common among women, too, as they seek professional roles outside the home. Until recently, women have been more interested in interpersonal and social rewards in the work place than in status and power. Here again, however, we must be cautious in ascribing gender-specific motives for working. Indeed, women have long avoided censure and received social approval for not competing in "masculine" enterprises for "masculine" reasons.

A dilemma arises for many in midlife, however, when they realize the need and value of exercising power, but experience the disillusionment with work roles that is so often the lot of both the seemingly successful and the unsuccessful. This contradiction results, to a large extent, from the way power is understood and employed in our culture. While it is crucial for psychic well-being that persons exercise their power or creative potential in assertive, even aggressive ways, modern culture has blighted our understanding of life-enriching power for mid-life.[45] Our prevalent notion of power continues to be one of efficiency and dominance. This is more appropriate to younger people, who are learning the skills of mastery over external things. The young also tend toward a power of dominance and control over persons, because their own identities are insecure and their role in society is not assured.

In midlife, however, continuing exercise of the power of dominance and control becomes counterproductive. The illusion that work roles under the aegis of such power will stave off the threat of death is shaken by the realities of aging. R. Gould argues that middle-aged adults in our culture seek to use their work as a pact of immunity against death.[46] It is as though we could become invulnerable through the exercise of power connected with external wealth and stature. Yet the magic balm of work only dulls the pain associated with midlife awareness; it makes the ache controllable, but does not allow a breakthrough to a healing kind of power. That would require a transformation of our understanding of power, and consequently of work, in middle age. To achieve this metamorphosis of power and identity requires a spiritual renewal that is especially appropriate to middle age. The style of dominant power, related to the ascendant curve of life, must give place to an interiorized and serving power based on a spirit of faith.

Challenges to Intimacy

Middle-aged persons experience losses other than the physical decline at the end of youth and problems related to work roles. They also encounter threatening challenges in the area of intimacy and family. Freud's thumbnail rule for mental and emotional health was the attainment of some measure of success in the two areas of love and work. Crisis in the love dimension was acutely expressed by E. Bergler more than two decades ago.[47] Most of the literature since his book appeared repeats the theme of the middle-aged man leaving or "betraying" his wife and family in pursuit of younger women. Bergler's psychoanalytic explanation of such conduct as the outcome of psychic masochism is a dubious explanation, which tries to cover far too much ground. Nevertheless, his insight into a fundamental motive for such exploits remains sound: The middle-aged male attempts to defy time by proving his potency and desirability.[48] He realizes that the sands are spilling quickly in the hourglass of his life and believes that a new love affair will rejuvenate his vitality. Workplace and home life may contribute to these ventures in romance. The job may have become routine and lost its allure, or younger colleagues may be threatening his position, which has reached a plateau without prospect of advancement. He needs to feel powerful and wanted. Career successes in midlife can also provoke romantic episodes: The younger woman feels important by drawing closer to the older, successful man who, in turn, becomes convinced that a person should not have his activities curtailed by sexual conventions.

Life at home may further incline him toward extramarital affairs. His middle-aged wife cannot compete in youthful attractiveness with younger women in an American culture that accentuates the cult of young female beauty. Moreover, the wife, knowing his foibles and vulnerabilities, may not treat him with the deference accorded by the admiring young woman. Husband and wife may have grown apart over the years, their patterns of communication devolving to practical matters of household maintenance. Emotional needs go unmet and no environment exists for the expression of deeper hopes and fears. Long-suppressed bitterness and resentment over the state of their marriage may have closed the doors to healing dialogue. Or perhaps friendship has died through indirect bickering and accusatory fighting that has alienated the spouses. The home scene may be further troubled by disputes with teenaged children or by the seeming freedom or permissiveness of the younger generation. Several students of middle age have noted the similarities of adolescent and midlife crises. In both periods a new search for identity unfolds: youth seeking a first adult independence and identity, the middle-aged person searching for new personal meaning at the high noon of life.[49]

A son-father relationship activates the Oedipal struggle in reverse for the midlife parent. He may feel threatened in his manhood and turn elsewhere for its confirmation. As a member of the generation in the middle, he feels cheated when he observes the easier sexual behavior allowed among the young. Pressed by the feeling of lessening time in life, he may rush into sexual relations "before it is too late." The impulse to experiment is further stimulated by fear of losing sexual potency. When he compares his sexual performance with the standards of his youth, he notices his physiological decline. Such cultural stress has been placed on orgasmic performance in sex that he often lacks the assurance arising from mature sexuality, with its ability to create a deeper loving exchange without the quantifiable exploits of youth. Impelled by the promptings of the noonday devil, he pursues sex less for itself than for reassurance that he is not losing his identity through aging.

Others respond to the sexual challenge in midlife by fleeing through intensified absorption in work or substitute diversions. This passive, or evasive, reaction to the problem may be more detrimental to transformation in middle age than the Don Juan pattern. Sexual escapades may permit the middle-aged man to experience changes in sexuality, impelling him toward a new sexual identity. On the other hand, the passive escapist dulls his capacity for experiencing the anxiety of loss that sets the stage for personality growth in midlife.

The middle-aged woman also undergoes challenges to her sexuality that may disturb the spousal relationship. His extramarital interests, coupled with her own realization of physical aging, may conspire to lessen her sense of attractiveness and worth. Faced with this situation, she may retreat into a kind of asexual motherliness or dowdy matronhood, seeking to discount or avoid the problems. Or she may become involved in extramarital affairs in order to confirm her own sense of value and desirability. Less encumbered by the inhibitions of girlhood training and more physically attuned in her thirties and forties to her own sexual needs and potentials, she may find her partner unsatisfying. This is especially true if he has taken the route of sexual routine or avoidance. She may feel more acutely the "empty nest syndrome" as children leave home and sense the loneliness of suburban isolation. Fears of divorce, linked with economic insecurity and loneliness, add to the turmoil of midlife for a significant number of women. Thus the zone of intimacy for men and women in midlife presents a volatile mixture of personal and cultural factors.

The intimate relationship offers a vital, watershed opportunity for destructive or creative responses to midlife changes. Religious progress will be fostered through new styles of commitment and communication between men and women, or it will be stunted by negative reactions to these challenges. The losses of midlife should not be minimized. It is difficult to say farewell to youth, with the looming prospect of aging and death; disillusionment about career goals and disappointments in the zone of intimacy are genuine sufferings for the middle-aged. Yet, as Anne Morrow Lindbergh notes, the middle period of life shows traits that are wrongly interpreted as signs of decay: discontent, restlessness, doubt, despair, and longing.[50] She realizes that many do not climb above the midlife plateau; they prefer to deny or escape the paradoxical signs that presage both life and death: "Anything rather than stand still and learn from them. One tries to cure the signs of growth, to exorcise them, as if they were devils, when really they might be angels of annunciation."[51] These angels announce the possibility of "a new stage in living . . . free at last for spiritual growth."[52]

II

MIDLIFE:
THE POTENTIALS

The previous chapter examined some of the principal challenges facing persons in middle age. In this section, we shall consider the same problem areas in order to discover potentials for spiritual growth usually ignored or hidden within the challenges themselves. It is a kind of alchemical process whereby what seem to be negative or base elements in this phase of life become, in reality, the material for a transformation of spirit. Our approach will be a theological-spiritual reflection on literature drawn mainly from psychology and the social sciences. This method is based on the premise that the theologian's task is not to impose foreign categories on midlife investigations, but rather to elicit from the studies themselves openings to transcendent or religious perspectives. It is a question of an angle of perception or a formal focus that does not distort the data, but draws from it views that may have been neglected or gone undetected by the legitimate endeavors of other disciplines.

The theory of our approach was neatly summarized by G. Elliott, in her reflective essay written in the mid–1930s about women over forty. She suggested that religion should gather up, not substitute for, life experiences.[1] We have considered the losses of midlife under the rubrics of personal or physical decline, career challenges, and tensions in intimacy. When the sources are viewed from the standpoint of gains and potentials, they seem to group naturally under similar headings of self (personal), world (career-work), and others (friendship and intimacy). Although these three aspects are closely intertwined, there is an advantage of expository clarity in concentrating on one theme at a time.

Potentials for the Developing Self

The threatened self in midlife is poised on the verge of an opportunity for a new inwardness. One of the best known researchers on personality change in midlife, B. Neugarten, emphasizes this "inner-orientation" in her various writings.[2] She characterizes it as a passive mastery of the environment, in contrast to the active strivings of youth. She observes middle-aged persons to be more reflective about their inner needs, taking stock through deepened introspection. There is a natural tendency to restructure ego processes from self-definition toward self-synthesis. The orientation toward self-definition in youth includes more aggressive efforts to define oneself over against the world and others. Paradoxically, however, younger people also show a greater need for external authorities or mentors and for a sense of acceptance by others. In contrast, self-synthesis means becoming one's own mentor and finding a fuller acceptance from within the self.

To achieve these ends, one must be willing to take the inward path. Unfortunately, many are prevented from following it by social demands, as well as by fear of the road's unknown turns. The demands of making a living and coping with familial or civic responsibilities weigh heavily on the middle-aged. Many of these external circumstances are valuable as a kind of reality testing against an escapist or self-congratulatory spirituality. Moreover, worldly responsibilities can foster the development of care and commitment. But the preponderant conditioning of technological culture opposes the inward journey as a threat to the ethos of man-the-producer. The contemplative life is thought to be opposed to the full-time energy required for productive purposes.

Yet all the great religions encourage their followers to pursue inner values and prayerful reflection. Hinduism, in its classic form, structures the stages of life to encourage the busy householder to seek deeper spiritual wisdom in midcareer. The movement from the second to the third phase of life calls for a distancing from everyday affairs in order to participate in various disciplines (yogas) that dispose the human spirit to richer insight and experience. Buddhism, in its Mahayana form, invites not only monks, but also lay persons, to break the rhythms of daily involvements with retreats for meditation. It is a pattern of withdrawal for the sake of reentry into the secular order, a cadence of distancing through contemplation that permits clearer discernment for the inner expansion of the self, as well as wiser decision-making in human affairs.

Although Christianity has not traditionally stressed spiritualities appropriate for specific life stages, there seems to be significant disparity in how one is "in Christ" at different times. The clearest statement of this difference in early Christianity comes from Paul: "When I was a child, I spoke like a child, I thought like a child. . . ." (I Cor. 13:11). Some maintain that the popular Christian tradition, until the fairly recent advent of the psychological era, did not dwell on, or expand the issue of distinct phases of religious life. Yet the monastic tradition and its lay counterparts have always distinguished phases of spiritual growth that correlate to some extent with age differences. Furthermore, trying to preach the whole gospel to everyone, regardless of life-phase differences, results in serious pedagogical problems. A good case may be made, for example, that the spirit of the Beatitudes, a central text of Christianity, is more appropriate for midlife than for youth.

The Beatitudes demand a reversal of faith akin to the conversion or *metanoia* of middle age. A confrontation with personal finitude and self-delusions, characteristic of midlife, seems a necessary prerequisite for embracing the evangelical revolution of the Beatitudes. Because Christianity has been popularly preached as a religion of youthful imitation of, and loyalty to, the heroic Christ, commentators like G. Stanley Hall have depicted it as a faith adequate only for youth.[3] Nevertheless, it is likely to be counterproductive to ask young people to relinquish their ego-striving precisely when they are in the stage of building a strong identity. Younger persons are more likely to profit by imitating the ego-enhancing aspects of a strong Christ figure who demands effort and self-sacrifice in pursuit of ideals. Preaching meekness and humility to vulnerable egos can lead to dangerous self-deprecation and later rejection of traditional religion for Nietzschean reasons, that is, because it promotes weakness and subservience.

If it can be argued that the spirit of the Beatitudes is more appropriate for midlife, Christianity would then call for a deepening of the inner spiritual life during this period. The middle-age confrontation with finitude and self-delusions provides an environment for assimilating into one's personal life the teaching that the kingdom of God is within. It is not that the Christian scriptures insist exclusively on the inward life of the individual; the gospels consistently urge believers toward social justice and charity. But the theme of the inward kingdom seems to be essentially related to external, social commitments. For the depth and motivational purity of these outward engagements will depend on how fully one has cultivated the inner spirit. The internalizing of religion in Christianity has, moreover, an intrinsic excellence of its own, apart from its role in social responsibility. To understand that the kingdom of God is within each seeker frees a person from excessive obligation to outward observances and institutions. Embracing of the inward kingdom also enriches one's personal communication with God. Middle age is a uniquely appropriate time for this conversion toward a more contemplative existence.

The literature on middle age in psychology and the social sciences underlines the point of inwardness or introspection in ways that relate to the teachings of religions. The social sciences do not describe or advocate religious modes of living out the inward impulse. Nor should they, given the intent and limits of their fields. The work of some psychologists like D. Levinson leads one to the threshold of explicitly religious concerns without crossing over into spirituality. Levinson speaks of the task of turning inward in midlife in an almost Jungian vein.[4] The key point, however, is not the difference of content between religion and psychology on the meaning of the inner journey; rather, the main issue is the intrinsic continuity between the psychological and the religious calling in middle age.

Certain contemporary writings about middle age give the impression that the inward journey is initiated almost automatically. This erroneous notion may result from accepting stage theories of universal application. These theories too readily assume that individuals follow patterns determined by the age group into which they fall. But a more realistic assessment of individuals in midlife refutes such facile assumptions. In addition to the cultural obstacles to the inward quest, the journey itself is elusive and forbidding. It ordinarily requires some guidance, especially in the early phases. Many persons today find guides along the arduous first steps in counselors or therapists, who help their clients confront defensive mechanisms and other emotional hindrances that become especially burdensome in midlife. Such therapy can be very important in laying the groundwork for further spiritual development, which requires the often painful remedy of self-knowledge on intellectual, affective, and unconscious levels. This therapeutic work can also help to open a person to the deeper existential challenges to be met on the inward path.

A first challenge on the inner road in middle age is the confrontation with personal finitude. Jaques, as we have seen, speaks of it as the disturbing realization of personal mortality. R. Gould refers to it as the mastering or rechanneling of childhood passions surrounding the infantile sense of omnipotence.[5] The child transfers an early, but quickly lost, feeling of omnipotence to parents; attachment to them will provide safety and stave off threats to survival. This fantasy lies dormant, as a kind of reserve assurance, during the youthful struggle to establish an identity in the areas of intimacy and career. Awareness of finitude in middle life, of a radical lack of omnipotence or everlastingness, either in oneself or in others, gives the lie to the silent assurance of childhood. Moreover, the hurts of childhood, variously masked by youthful strivings, reassert themselves in the midlife turmoil.[6] Again, the unavoidable grasp of one's finitude makes it impossible to continue the illusion that the hurts of childhood will be fully healed.

Progress along the inner route of spirituality, therefore, requires a willingness to travel as a wounded seeker. No quest for power, whether proffered by the latest guru, by the market place, or by political life, will serve as an adequate balm to the injuries of childhood. For the latter are fundamentally inseparable from the condition of finitude. Life cannot be guaranteed against the unknown. An experiential awareness of this reality in middle age has been called a "graduating from mendacity."[7] We all harbor the lie that parents, teachers, employers, or the state will somehow "make it all right." If these powers fail, surely human love and divine presence will quiet the revived terrors of finitude. It is precisely at this point in the lie that religion paradoxically enters. For neither friends, lovers, nor God will relieve us of the painful meeting with our own finitude. Tragically, a form of ersatz religion, all too readily embraced in our time, pretends to grant this assurance. By accepting this or that savior or by performing certain rituals and disciplines within an elite group, we are promised absolution from the terror of our own extinction.

The message of authentic religiousness, however, is strangely paradoxical. The way inward is not by a comfortable, circuitous route around this ultimate fear, but by moving into and through it in faith. Dante had to journey through the *Inferno* on his spiritual pilgrimage. Yeats, in midlife, grasped this profoundly religious insight when he wrote: ". . . Now that my ladder is gone, / I must lie down where all ladders start, / In the foul rag and bone shop of the heart."[8] The ladder of assurance or the ladder of success, as a way to overcome finitude, must collapse before the spiritual venture can begin. Both Job and Jesus portray, in what by the standards of past millennia might be termed midlife, the experience of authentic religion. Job, in final faith, and without comfort, confronts the nadir of mortality; Jesus in Gethsemane "sweats blood" at the prospect of his death.

This encounter with personal finitude as a portal to the inward journey relates not only to physical death, but also to the demise of meaning and value. The systems of meaning constructed in youth are usually buffeted seriously, if not destroyed, in midlife. Levinson describes the need to "modify the dream" of youth in middle age.[9] Those who cling to the dreams of youth against the reality of midlife tend to lull themselves into a life of illusion. Yet beneath the veneer of false hopes, the gnawing truth of self-deception consumes the spirit. Such persons resign themselves to a superficial existence, exchanging the arduous road toward death for a quiet life of routine. They miss, therefore, taking advantage of the unique opportunity that midlife offers for deeper growth. Since the egos of the middle-aged are less constricted by the narrow demands of youth,[10] such persons relinquish a final chance to break their self-imposed bonds of youth.[11] These ties keep them defensively evading the encounter with finitude, that singular portal to deeper realms. Others are destroyed by the death of meaning and worth in middle age. Even physical and mental health can decline when earlier hopes fade. Yet the religious response to the death of meaning calls for more than Levinson's "modifying the dream." It frequently demands that we abandon the deathless dream of youth and allow it to be replaced by a new vision, tempered by finitude.

This does not mean that the religious response is always discontinuous with one's earlier hopes. In a true sense, grace builds on nature; one's earlier projections and plans ordinarily contain aspects that can be subsumed into midlife religiousness. But such spirituality demands a more complete transformation of the dream because the projections of youth are, of necessity, tainted by illusion and self-deception. The reason for such illusion is the radical need for assurance or self-confidence characteristic of young persons. Childhood fears of extinction on the physical level, or abandonment (that is, nonacceptance) on the social level are so deeply influential that the visions of youth are seriously flawed. This is true in romantic daydreams of a fully satisfying love life, as well as of career projections of success. These dreams have their purpose, of course, as the necessary scaffolding for building the precarious ego-identity of youth. Yet such dreams tend to be one-sided, in the Jungian sense, focusing on the needs of a self-centered, striving ego. The archetypical voices of the deep psyche, which frequently oppose conscious ego in order to integrate it into a richer personality, are not truly awakened in the younger years.

Although we think of the dreams of youth as limitless, they are, in truth, too narrow and confined. They are restricted because they are only on the surface or horizontal. Their fantasies move mainly along a straight line toward establishing a family, pursuing a successful career, and achieving related goals. Because the young, for the most part, have not confronted the deepest limits of the finitude of self, their dreams are not as apt to enable the soul to penetrate the realms of the unknown, the zone of mystery and mysticism whence mature religion and psychospiritual growth proceed. Camus, with youthful vigor, spoke of living only with what he knew, as if such existential bravado ennobled the human spirit. On the contrary, it is by multiplying contacts with the unknown that our dreams delve vertically into the wellsprings of existence and soar into the sometimes frightening spaces of authentic religion.

By midlife, the chastened self is ready for the religious journey. The philosopher William Barrett has spoken beautifully about the nature of real religion, calling it the deepest part of ourselves, that center of yearning, acceptance, and rebellion, that locus of simultaneous despair and aspiration.[12] It was this kind of religiousness, at once difficult and profoundly personal, that Whitehead referred to when he wrote, "Apart from the religious vision, human life is a flash of occasional enjoyments lighting up a mass of pain and misery, a bagatelle of transient experience."[13] This region of religion is usually not reached by the projections of young dreams. For it is a paradoxical experience in which the Latin maxim holds sway, *ignotum per ignotius,* finding the unknown through that which is even more unknown. This enigmatic statement may be better understood through examples from psychology and religion.

For Jung, the great dilemmas revealed in the dream imagery of one's unconscious processes, images already mysterious, are known, in as much as they can be, by the even more unknown forces of the archetypes that inhabit our deepest unconscious. Transposed to another idiom, this means that to live by faith is to walk not necessarily against reason, but beyond it. It is the full exercise of reason, as a combination of mind, will, and emotion, that leads us to the door of the unknown, that uncrossable threshold of personal finitude. Yet it is faith, an even more mysterious phenomenon, that beckons us beyond the entrance of the unknown to risk, fashion, and experience a more comprehensive unity of life. Thus the dreams of middle age, when its crises are faced, must not only modify the dreams of youth, but transform them in a more radical way.

Interestingly enough, however, in midlife the method of transforming the dreams of youth resembles that of a *bricoleur,* a tinkerer or handyman, rather than the style of a master planner. The latter style reflects the energy and active organization of youth, whose reasoning power orchestrates stages on the path to desired goals, however limited these may be. The *bricoleur* understands the limits of both his tools and of science for his enterprise in depth. He tries to fit together the various pieces of his life experiences in different juxtapositions, realizing that the unity and fuller meaning of the mosaic will come from sources within, yet beyond him. Rather than engaging in an activity of mastery and control, the *bricoleur* tries to perceive and to blend with the odd parts, letting them reveal their own directions for building a new self.

In the perspective of D. Bakan, youth emphasizes the "agentic" dimension of knowledge for external mastery and individual separateness.[14] The agentic dreams of youth, while valuable for earlier periods, lead to an intense malaise in midlife unless they are changed to allow the development of what Bakan calls "communion." Communion implies a movement away from separate individualism and external action toward union with nature and other persons. It is a movement of greater unity through the coalescence of love. From this viewpoint, as from the Jungian, the dreams of youth need a more radical and disquieting alteration than the mere modification proposed by Levinson. Spiritual inwardness, through confrontation with personal finitude, is a closed path for those who are exclusively immersed in the agentic realm throughout midlife. In some ways, middle-aged persons will be greatly involved in seemingly agentic pursuits because they are in leadership roles in various careers by this time. But the movement from the agentic to the communal does not mean a lessening of efficiency or active participation. Rather, the change lies in the attitude inspiring these involvements. Is the work important mainly as a tool for personal ambition, for the enhancement or survival of the separate ego? Can we let go sufficiently of the separate, controlling ego to understand ourselves as servants of wider purposes, of communal needs? This switch of the internal orientation by which we perform tasks demands a serious conversion away from the habits of youth. It is not attained without a change of heart similar to the act of religious faith.

The religious sense of conversion or *metanoia* is linked in a particularly important way to the midlife turning from ego to self-awareness, in Jung's language, or from the agentic to the communal, in Bakan's. A chief goal of religion is to foster the transition from one dimension to the other, as well as the fuller blending of both. But this process of conversion calls for a wide-ranging and often painful death and rebirth of meaning and value. It also involves the risk of faith, the transcending of human psychological remedies, in the quest for new meaning. Faith, in the context of the midlife conversion to deeper existence, does not equate with a particular belief system, although it can be expressed in that way. Faith, for middle-age conversion, means that one takes a different stance or set of attitudes toward life from those usually assumed in youth.

In general, this posture of faith implies an experiential awareness of one's limitations and weaknesses, both psychological and

ethical. Such an awareness of limits need not lead to apathy or resignation; rather, it should engender a more honest activity that is
less possessively self-interested and more comprehensive in its altruism. In addition to a recognition of limits, faith in midlife consists of a "letting go," a release of the omnipotent ego that must be
protected at all costs. The middle-aged person who has progressed a
reasonable distance beyond the defensive fears of childhood knows
in a newly personal way that death will visit him or her. The release
of faith, therefore, is at the deepest level a letting go of personal
selfhood into the care of a benevolent reality greater than the self.
The broad term "benevolent reality" is used purposely to allow for
the widest possible context of meaning. The deity implied by benevolent reality may be personal or impersonal, directly expressed or
subtly implied by a person's attitude and conduct. This spirit of
faith pervades every dimension of the discussion on the gains and
potentials of midlife, under all three categories of self, world, and
other. Each point stems from it, or relates to it, either implicitly or
explicitly.

To confront finitude with faith in midlife also requires the cultivation of a contemplative attitude. The opposite attitude to contemplation was described by J. Maritain as a desperate activism that
poorly cloaks despair.[15] Maritain was commenting on American activism, but his point might be extrapolated to the activism inherent
in all technological cultures. Maritain was quick to add, however,
that the American spirit of idealism in great undertakings disguised
the desire for a more contemplative mode of life. But a kind of desperate activism becomes a cause of particular concern for those in
midlife, because, unlike the young, the middle-aged know more
acutely the limits of activity, and they have a glimpse of the possibilities of contemplation. R. Bellah attributes a lack of responsible
adulthood to the overwhelming of the contemplative spirit by self-
centered activism.[16] Without contemplation, according to Bellah, a
people falls into the destructive stance of "kill and survive"; with a
contemplative experience people are more willing to "die and become." These contrasts are taken from a recent work of E. Erikson,
who further explains:

> But there is the other, the transcendent, effort at insuring salvation
> through a conscious acceptance of finiteness . . . instead of a compe-

tition for the world's goods, it seeks human brotherhood and self-denial.[17]

These lines seem to paraphrase a biblical observation that because no one ponders in his heart the land is laid waste. The possibilities for the exercise of wisdom and charity are greatly diminished when identity is achieved in a culture through the activism of individualistic striving. The result of such uncurbed activism often devolves into the Hobbesian condition of the war of all against all.

The attitude of "kill and survive" is, on one level, common to humans who maintain their existence by killing animals for food. Yet, in a more metaphorical but very real sense, the same hunter mentality carries over into the destructive violence that affects the lives of individuals and groups. Whether the violence is the overt kind, in wars, street crimes, and terrorism, or the more subtle variety of structural-institutional injustice, the driving force in its maintenance is the "kill and survive" frame of mind. Survival, the battle against death, physical and psychological, becomes the primary motive for action. Whatever is perceived as threatening must be destroyed. This drive is as primitive as ancient blood sacrifices to placate the gods. Animals or humans were offered in sacrifice so that the individual and the tribe would escape death.

It may seem exaggerated to apply such a violent penchant to the cultural activism of technological society; nevertheless, beneath the thin veneer of decorum and respectability, these very impulses frequently work toward destructive ends. It is not activity itself in human affairs that is at fault. To be active is to participate in divine energies; as Pascal noted, "Our nature consists in motion; complete rest is death."[18] Rather, it is the motive for activity, when one is driven by the selfish survival mentality alone, that contributes greatly to violence in society.

To be sure, the young have no monopoly on such selfish activism; yet it is more natural to them because of the demands for activism in establishing their unique identities and securing their vocational niche in the world. It would amount to an undesirable elitism among older persons to claim that youth cannot turn inward, that the young are bent only on dominant power. Such an error would be tantamount to saying that young persons cannot be nonviolent. This assertion has been frequently disproved by the nonviolent activities of the young in many modern movements. Moreover, the young can begin to learn contemplative ways. The main point of these reflections, however, is that the young are not naturally inclined toward inwardness, and toward the exercise of enabling power, because of the assertive, ego-building demands of early adulthood.

One of the tasks of midlife, therefore, with the highest potential for individual and social wellbeing, concerns the reversal of the "kill and survive" attitude into that of "die and become." This turnabout is another way of addressing a central element in midlife spirituality. The components of this reversal, or conversion, are interrelated: contemplation, finitude, nonviolence. If we listen to its rhythms, midlife disposes us to the contemplative moment. Its message is, in part, to slow down, to listen to deeper impulses, to question the hectic pace of youth. Indeed, contemplation brings us face to face with the reality of personal finitude. "Die and become" first finds meaning as a series of little dyings to the psychic mechanism we maintain at great spiritual cost. We gradually enter into our finitude by accepting personal mortality, by willing and working that others may live. "Die and become" calls into question our youthful desires for the wealth and dominating power that would garrison us about with protection against extinction.

Indeed, "die and become" requires a deep act of faith, for there is no obvious assurance that such becoming will be life-enhancing. At the heart of this faith is the vision of a less violent commerce among peoples. The hope for nonviolent communities rests squarely on enough persons going through this interior revolution. From a Christian point of view, it constitutes the heart of the gospel, the evangelical reversal proclaimed in the Beatitudes. This evangelical revolution does not render the believer weak or inactive before the social tasks of justice and reconciliation. Rather, the new spirit, based on faith, lessens selfish activism and increases the possibility for genuine community-building. Yet beyond these social consequences of the spirit of the Beatitudes, we need to ask about the meaning of contemplation for the growth of the self in midlife.

For the great majority of middle-aged people in advanced technological cultures the idea of contemplation seems remote and unattractive. The life of meditation is associated with withdrawal to monasteries or the strange postures and breathing of yoga. For some, formal spiritual retreats from the daily routine or the use of the techniques of meditation have proven useful. Through these exercises a measure of inner quiet and deep reflection balances the hectic pace of modern life. But many more persons are dissuaded from this route by fear of what seems exotic; moreover, these same persons often discount their own capacity for a meditative existence. Too often, the church has convinced them that only great saints and mystics have such abilities, a notion reinforced by the tendency of contemporary eastern movements to lionize this or that holy man as one who possesses the key to the secrets of living.

In fact, middle age offers one of the richest periods for growth in meditative interiority. The confrontation with finitude demanded during this transition can dispose individuals to contemplative experiences that enhance physical and spiritual integration of personality. This spirit of contemplation is not easily developed, however; it is not a state of mind achieved by crash formulas or a few directives from a guru. Ignatius Loyola, who promoted among members of his order the ideal of "a contemplative in action," understood the rigors and deceptions connected with living as an active contemplative. Despite the difficulties, however, it is just this type of meditative involvement that most recommends itself to the contemporary person in middle life.

The middle-aged person can adapt many aspects of the contemplative tradition to an active daily regime. In the West, mysticism has been closely associated with such major contemplative figures as Teresa of Avila and John of the Cross. Most people perceive such spirituality in monastic settings and styles as different in kind from anything that lay people can experience. This perception of the extraordinary otherness of the great mystics has hindered many from taking steps toward the contemplative life. Yet in recent decades, eastern forms of meditation have enabled many people to appreciate their own potential for the inward journey. Some of the physical disciplines of hatha yoga, notably the body postures and breathing exercises, aid in calming, centering, and disposing one for contemplative prayer. Time can be found during the day for moments of meditative reflection. With some practice, these quieting, insightful moments can even be fused with active pursuits. The language of contemplation can be religious in traditional ways or it can employ other idioms to lead to deeper reflection. Poetry, mantras, dance movements, painting or sculpting, quiet walking in beautiful surroundings—these and many other factors can stimulate the contemplative experience.

A brief look at some of the characteristics of the contemplative experience noted in religious traditions reveals the appropriateness of an inward journey for the midlife transition. In general, there is in meditation a gradual movement away from active reasoning (often a beginning phase) toward a prayer, or state of simplicity, in the soul. As we have noted, the journey beyond active, controlling ego-consciousness to the deeper reaches of one's spirit is very help-ful in the midlife transition. This more passive, listening attitude of contemplation allows us to break through ego facades, experience genuine feelings within, and begin to unify self and world. At some point in the process, what has traditionally been called "infused contemplation," or the prayer of silence, may occur. This can be described as an experience of emptiness or void, but it is not a mere absence of reality. Rather, the quiet emptiness is sometimes filled with calming peace and richness, which allows the broken strands of our existence to be mended and old wounds to be healed. But this mending and healing are not voluntary acts of reason; they are gifts from a force within and beyond ourselves.

Still another facet of the contemplative experience is what mys-tics have called the "dark night of the soul." This experience of suf-fering is marked by aridity of spirit, confusion, and desolation. Med-itation seems useless and tedious; the soul feels devoid of God's presence and consolation. The contemplative is tempted to aban-don the whole enterprise. Nevertheless, with perseverance, a new level of peace, now chastened and more subtle, enters the soul. This rhythm of painful enlightenment resembles, in Jungian terms, the encounter between ego and unconscious; when the archetypi-cal images of the deep psyche confront the self-image of rational consciousness, disruptive suffering occurs. It is noteworthy that Jung identified this process in the psychological disturbances of middle-aged persons. The encounter with one's finitude in midlife, whether experienced in the dark night of contemplation or in the idiom of Jungian psychology, is an event at once illuminating and painful.

Contemplation also enables one to enjoy a vision of unity be-tween self and world, as well as within the self. This unification is not a rational process of the calculating intellect; rather, it is a unity of enlightenment granted to the soul apart from the ordinary discrimination of subject and object. Yet the self is not totally lost or submerged in this emerging unity; it is, rather, a unity within diversity, in which the contemplative self feels united with a wider reality, yet remains distinct as a critical, responsible person. During midlife many persons begin to sense, in an acute way, the fragmentation within their own lives, as well as the seemingly unresolvable distinctions and oppositions in the world. The contemplative process is a way of moving, in a nonmanipulative fashion, toward inner and outer reconciliation of alienated opposites. It allows us to stand momentarily at the "still-point of the turning world," to know, in a healing mode, that beyond brokenness is a potential for wholeness.[19] These experiences do not provide an easy balm for life's wounds, in the sense of Bonhoeffer's "cheap grace." It is not that something different is seen, but, as Jung suggests, that one sees differently. We must note that this "seeing" is not only an intellectual grasp, but a vision that can profoundly alter the way in which we walk the earth.

In a concise discussion of the meditative experience, R. Pannikar explores other traits of the contemplative person.[20] Such a one learns to focus on the meaning and the excellence of the present event rather than postpone life, as it were, to a time of future achievements or benefits. The present act itself becomes valuable, not just a future product. Such an orientation could be extremely helpful to middle-aged persons in our society, who are driven from inner, as well as outer compulsions, to concentrate almost exclusively on future attainments. The contemplative is also more appreciative of interpersonal intimacy than of exterior possessions. Intimacy is understood here in the sense of the broadest spectrum of friendship toward the natural and human worlds. This cultivation of the present and the intimate leads to greater peace within the self. We are not pulled in myriad directions; rather, we can more readily discover the still-point within which the self is refreshed and centered again.

Solitude is a requisite condition for developing a spirit of contemplation. S. Hiltner and R. Howe underline this dimension in their discussion of a midlife spirituality.[21] Solitude must be distinguished, however, from both loneliness and isolation. Loneliness implies being cut off from desired friends. In a sense, it can be the negative road leading to solitude. When one begins to go through midlife turmoils, loneliness rises as part of the detachment that we necessarily experience, even from those who have been closest to us. This darker side, which inclines us toward solitude, cannot be written off as an aberration, as something we should get over quickly by an act of will. Nor should the pain of midlife loneliness be dulled by that frantic search for company or for distracting diversions so characteristic of western ways. From loneliness the midlife seeker can gradually discover the positive path toward creative solitude, the experience of aloneness. It is, however, easier for us to risk and to cherish radical aloneness for developing the aging self if we have previously benefited from nurturing relationships.[22]

Aloneness is not the same as isolation, although a certain amount of separateness and private time is crucial for solitude. Nor is aloneness an escape from facing the world as an aging individual. It can be found in the midst of a crowd or in the normal engagements of life. Solitude, whether in aloneness or in company with others, is a feeling of letting one's self be, without forcing or controlling events. It has a passive dimension, in which the self alone, peacefully and temporarily, releases the compulsion to control, with its attendant anxiety. Another aspect of contemplative solitude is its unitive or integrating perspective. In a paradoxical way, the solitary self, when the need for control and defense are relaxed, senses its ability to blend or unite with nature and other persons. Without denying the dangers and destructiveness of the world, the solitary self associates with the benevolent energies of the universe. Solitude of this kind has affinities with prayerfulness and faith.

Solitude fosters faith as an act of releasing the walled-off self into communion with a benevolent and sustaining reality that pervades all things. In moments of aloneness, the unfettered imagination encourages communion with all that is nonself. Such imagining is not only the fictive or fanciful activity often associated with the word "imaginary." Rather, it signifies imagination as the wellspring of intellectual and moral development. It is the poetic experience of passing through mere means to an experience of meaning. In an era dominated by the scientific mentality, W. Barrett notes that we too readily sacrifice meaning for the sake of technical means.[23]

These techniques or means seek to reduce all things to universal common denominators, principles and laws that can be empirically measured. Thus, means are stressed over meaning and the universal measurable over pluralism of knowledge and experience. The scientific and technological revolutions of the last two centuries have been so dominant (and in many ways so rewarding) that we fail to recognize how completely our sense of reality is shaped by them. The very brilliance of these revolutions blinds us to their limits. The new questionings of middle age provide a singular occasion to cultivate the meditative solitude that creates an ambience for reaching through and beyond the scientific mind-set. In contemplation, we permit the rule of order and control, so much a part of the technological ethos, to be relaxed. We allow our spiritual selves to flow unitively into nature and other persons.

This demands an attitude of faith because it goes beyond empirical knowing to the experience of wider meaning. Such a contemplative attitude uncovers a new level of unity transcending that oneness that merely strives to reduce reality to material, quantifiable elements. Contemplative meditation in solitude engenders a deeper form of unity, which cherishes pluralism and spiritual meaning. Since it transcends the reductionism of technology, the contemplative stance allows one to enjoy the unity in remarkable diversity that is characteristic of personal and social realms, as well as those dimensions of nature that inspire beauty. Important byproducts of contemplative solitude, mentioned here only in passing, include a new potential for creativity in the scientific area and an increased ethical sensitivity. A number of leading scientists have underscored the value of contemplation for unexpected breakthroughs in knowledge. New levels of uniting with nature and others through meditative silence can bring to light our deeper unfulfilled desires and inspire a greater sense of universal care and commitment.

The cultivation of contemplative solitude in midlife leads to either a renewal or a beginning of prayerfulness. Prayer has become an unfortunately maligned term in many circles today. Both early childhood training and church practices concerning prayer frequently instill a distorted understanding that is later rejected altogether or continued in a mindless rote form. Prayer, in the popular imagination, is mainly petition, with occasional vocal statements of praise. In its more debased interpretation, prayer is seen as the superfluous act of a childish psyche, which seeks blessings and rewards from a parental, even capricious, God.

This view flies in the face of the technological person, whose civilization emphasizes self-confidence and terrestrial limits. The Father-in-the-sky, as recipient of prayers, affronts our more Promethean attitude, because this parental deity conjures up the threats and beguilements experienced in childhood from our own parents. Moreover, the reductionistic penchant of technological culture stimulates a growing doubt about the usefulness of prayer, as words addressed out of fear or insecurity to a nonexistent deity. It is important to grasp this partial case against prayer (one could also criticize the explicit language of much formal prayer) that is overtly or subconsciously made by many persons today. For it stands in the way of attaining an authentic spirit of prayerfulness, which is a vital component of life-enriching solitude for middle-aged people.

In contrast to the bleak, but all too common, picture just sketched, we can consider prayer as a way of dwelling at the core of our being. Prayer can be expressed in praise, petition, or thanksgiving, but in a more fundamental sense it is a listening in faith. This contemplative mode of listening implies a lively passivity, a receptive awareness. It is a stance of faith because it originates from those deepest longings and perplexities that are not subject to rational control and planning. It touches a profound part of our souls, our religious zone, that uncertain center of yearning, acceptance, and rebellion, simultaneous despair and aspiration.[24] This contemplative listening brings us into dialogue with the alluring, yet threatening, mystery of death. Thus the middle-aged person, already sensitized to his or her mortality, could be a prime candidate for a life of prayerfulness. Through prayer, a gradual transformation of heart and will takes place whereby a person attains greater freedom in reference to personal death.

Those who experience such freedom through prayer know that it is the result neither of moral Pelagianism nor of Skinnerian conditioning. It is, rather, a sense of receiving a gift from God in the depths of the self. This freedom of prayer is not a limitless liberation, without restraints. The fears, limitations, and perplexities of mortality remain, but they are strangely altered; in and through these restraints a new zest for life and an appreciation of its precari-

ousness arise. Prayer in this sense allows the aging person to cultivate his or her own religious vision. Such a vision may well build
upon one or more religious traditions, but it attains a stamp of personal uniqueness. This seems to conform to A. N. Whitehead's unusual definition of religion as what a person does with solitude.[25]

Facing finitude with a prayerful spirit opens the way for the middle-aged person to develop a flexibility on both mental and emotional levels. It is important to consider the matter of flexibility, because midlife is also the time when many persons become more
rigid in their attitudes. William James spoke of fixity of personality
occurring as early as thirty: "in most of us by age thirty, the character has set like plaster, and will never soften again."[26] We may have
worked hard to establish a safe niche in life; change threatens to
upset this realized security. Moreover, the future no longer seems
an unlimited period for adaptation and new beginnings. We know
we are aging when we count our days from the end rather than the
beginning of life. As a result, we tend to hold tenaciously to ideologies and practices that promise security for our own personal
boundaries. The literature on middle life urges flexibility as a task
or goal. For example, R. Peck places mental and emotional flexibility as an ideal attainment of this period.[27]

J. Feibleman coins an unusual term, "standpointlessness," as an
optimal trait of midlife. "Standpointlessness" is not vacillating in-
decision, which would hardly be a sign of maturity. Rather, it represents an ability to shift subjectivity at will to another person or object.[28] Such a flexible person may indeed have strong convictions
and commitments, but he or she is able to bracket or suspend personal motives in order to enter empathically into the thoughts and
feelings of another. This ability corresponds to the polarity between
attachment and separateness that Levinson notes as one of the
tasks of midlife individuation.[29] We are well aware of the extremes
of separateness, manifest most profoundly in schizophrenia, as a
tragic aberration in human development. But the artist's separateness, and yet empathic identity with the subject points to the kind
of flexible distance intended by Levinson.

Yet to attain such empathetic flexibility calls for developments in
the personality that are either explicitly religious or implicitly so,
that is, of traits that are in a continuum with religious existence.
For religiousness, in its mature form, entails a twofold movement in

the depths of the personality. There is, first, the ability to accept one's finitude and release some of the defenses erected to secure personal survival at any cost. This defensiveness, which is the hall-mark of rigidity, is the opposite of the "letting-go" of faith. To be mentally and emotionally flexible, even at a time when one's vulnerabilities are most exposed, is a religious activity. Indeed, it implies a freedom from the self's needs or compulsions and a form of trust in a benevolent reality beyond the self that can help us negotiate a broken or seemingly intransigent situation.

The movement in the soul toward freedom from self-protective rigidities is but one side of the polarity. A second movement of religiousness in depth is a freedom for comprehensiveness. The self, liberated to a considerable degree from its own need to repulse attacks, is free to unite with the other in a new way. Again, this is not a glorification of indeterminateness or a loss of self by melding with reality beyond one's personal confines. On the contrary, the self more fully recognizes its own finite limits and knows the need for restraint and critique in dealing with freedom. Liberation without restraints and without criticism, whether on the personal or social level, soon devolves into confusion and formlessness. These conditions lead to the demise of identity on an individual plane and invite fascistic control in the body politic. But the self, as it becomes liberated from its need to defend itself at all costs, and as it opens to comprehensiveness in an empathetic way, operates in a religious mode.[30] Moreover, this religious style is especially appropriate to middle age, when the defensive compulsions of youthful self-definition can give way to a freer, more flexible life in mind and emotion.

We have already discussed the sense of loss that the middle-aged person experiences in reference to diminishing time. Confrontation with one's finitude accentuates the shortness of one's remaining years, and it highlights fears of senescence. There is no denying the linear movement of time in our lives; this commonsensical dimension of aging needs no proof, only observation of the world around us, where people exist at different stages of the life span. But this ordinary appreciation of temporal sequence from childhood to old age, the horizontal or historical understanding, needs to be balanced by a more vertical and timeless perspective on the aging self. Without the latter dimension, the potentials of midlife and elderhood are diminished; the full reality of living in time is truncated.

For there is within each of us at every reflective period of life a coexisting presence of the *puer* and the *senex,* the archetypal images of youth and age. In the depths of our psyches live an assortment of child-images: the pouting, demanding, spoiled, or hurt child; the spontaneous, resilient youth who is ever leaping beyond the confines of linear history to probe the transcendent and eternal. We also carry within ourselves the *senex,* the wise old man, awakened in us by our experience of other elders, as well as by our own immersion in the historical process of aging. This inner *senex* can be the experienced guide offering us wisdom, or it can be the frightened, autocratic oldster who holds us back from adventure of mind and body. Both the *senex* and the *puer,* in their various forms, coexist in the present, in every now. In this light we are at once young and old.

The crucial issue is our ability to hold these opposite images of the soul in a balanced tension at any particular time. As James Hillman states, "the healing for which we long will combine puer and senex in one."[31] This is not a collapsing of the archetypes into one, for that would produce only the sad child who was born old or the frivolous elder who childishly avoids the message of finitude. Rather, the healing comes from holding the opposites in a "balanced tension," as "two faces turn toward each other in dialogue."[32] The *puer* voice, at its best, invites one to experiment, aspire, venture, play; the *senex* responds from history with warnings about similar projects and their consequences. Icarus needs Daedalus, lest the soaring youth come to disaster from the ever-present sun. But Daedalus also requires Icarus for there to be any soaring at all.

Mythical imagery reminds us of the paradoxical opposites in polar tension within the psyche, and myth also draws meaning from these oppositions. The dynamism of the *puer* challenges the historical order of the *senex,* as though eternity breaks into the calculations of linear time. Although there is a progressive mediation of the opposing archetypes for the benefit of the whole person, they remain discontinuous. Yet it is a "meaningful discontinuity . . . or call it living from the principle which Jung circumscribed as synchronicity."[33] Synchronicity implies an event that is paradoxical in that it is not the result of temporal causality, or ordinary before and after sequencing; thus it has the character of a chance, serendipitous happening, mysteriously related to other events in one's life. Synchronicity also describes an event in time that is all at once, *syn-chronous,* or with-the-present-moment, an occasion not extended in time. These are all ways of indicating the atemporal, paradoxical dynamic of *puer* and *senex* within us at any moment of life. This neglected dimension of aging is particularly worth dwelling on in middle age, when the sands seem to slip faster through the hourglass.

Moreover, the self in midlife is generally more capable of allowing the nonlinear experience of *puer-senex* to emerge. This emergence requires breaking through the ego-controlled psyche of youth to permit the archetypes of the unconscious to surface. Youthful ego writes its script almost entirely within the space of historical, extended time. When I grow up, I will become. . . . When I achieve this goal, I will move on to such and such. . . . The slackening of this ego control in the midlife crisis of finitude allows images to pour into consciousness from the deep psyche through dreams, fantasies, and other inspirations, loosening the ego's tight hold and nourishing it with new vision. As the ego listens to these novel promptings, in a spirit akin to that of receptive religious faith, the middle-aged person realizes that he or she is not only growing older, but is simultaneously young and aged, new and old. This insight is mirrored beautifully in the following passage of Augustine:

> New we indeed ought to be, because the old man ought to creep up on us, but we must also grow and progress. Of this same progress the Apostle saith, "Though our outward man is corrupted, yet the inward man is renewed day by day" (II Cor. 10:16). Let us not grow so as to become old after being new, but let the newness itself grow.[34]

Although he was mainly referring to the newness of Christian conversion, Augustine presupposes a break in the ordinary way of viewing temporal progression. Time not only drags on as "tomorrow and tomorrow and tomorrow, creeps in this petty pace from day to day,"[35] but within the context of faith, the kingdom is also now, the old and the new stand transfigured together in each moment. It is remarkable how strongly the following lines of Augustine resemble the *puer-senex* dynamic: "Let your old age be childlike, and your childhood like old age; that is, so that neither may your wisdom be with pride, nor your humility without wisdom."[36]

This potential richness of every moment, from a nontemporal perspective, does not deny, but rather complements the temporal view of aging. These moments of *puer-senex* presence in the now are not atomistically separated from one another, as though clock time were so many distinct, isolated points leading to a meaningless end or midnight. Our culture of technological rationality tends to divide up time in this naive way, making it hard for us to conceive of it otherwise. Rather, time flows continuously for us, always allowing a double interpretation: the atemporal understanding of *puer-senex* archetypes in the dialectic between consciousness and the unconscious, and a grasp of temporal flow as continuous, but recapitulating at each moment our personal and collective past, present, and future.

David Tracy addresses this question in the context of aging.[37] He discusses three modes of human temporality from a Christian viewpoint: the traditionalist, based on the past, especially the scriptures; the prophetic, which underscores present action for personal and social conversion; and the apocalyptic, or future-oriented understanding of temporality. Tracy's point is well-taken; no one or two of these aspects of time can be understood as sole arbiter of meaning. Rather, all three perspectives contribute to a fuller interpretation of temporality in any given moment. "Whether 'young' or 'middle-aged' or 'old,' we can learn to revere all three models of meaning [the traditional, the prophetic, and the apocalyptic] as each is an authentic expression of our experience of time. . . ."[38] Since in midlife we stand closest to all three general phases of the life span, with youth and elderhood on each end, this vision of the value of past, present, and future appears most appropriate. Furthermore, this tripartite blending, in any moment, of the continuous sweep of time, affirms the significance of the entire aging process.

In this section on potentials for the developing self, we have called for a new inwardness in middle age. The special encounter with personal finitude in midlife causes a crisis of value and meaning. The ensuing turmoil or disquiet in the soul prepares a person for creative *metanoia*, or changes of heart and attitude. In this struggle, the self in midlife is summoned to a more contemplative mode of being amid the continuing responsibilities of worldly involvements. Contemplation fosters alternate ways of viewing and experiencing the meaning of one's life. Thus aging, with its threats of decline and even despair, can be transformed into a temporal and a timeless opportunity to enhance the basic worth of the self.

World and Work

The potential for transformation of the self in middle age is closely intertwined with one's stance in and toward the world. The aspects of freedom and comprehensiveness discussed above suggest that a self that has begun to come to grips with its own finitude in a spirit of prayerful reflection may be increasingly outgoing. When we refer to the world in this context, we mean both the immediate world of work and the wider zone of public involvement. By the middle years, one is usually immersed in a career or occupation, with its particular limitations and promise. Because of age and other obligations, the options for career change have narrowed for the middle-aged person. This remains generally true despite an increase in midcareer job shifts, referred to by R. J. Lifton as the phenomenon of "protean man."[39] This increased ability in recent times to change occupations in midcareer may leave a person with only temporary satisfactions. When the novelty of the second or third career has faded, an individual may realize that old dissatisfactions and unmet longings have merely been transferred to a new terrain. Meaningful midlife spirituality demands a deeper transformation of attitude and rationale for worldly engagements. This kind of change is similar to religious conversion in that it demands a new way of understanding oneself in the world. While one's situation in life may remain unchanged externally, a profound shift can occur in one's inner purposes and outward stance.

In theological parlance, one opens the self to the grace of becoming a pilgrim-seeker, a *viator,* or wayfarer in the world. Such a religious pilgrim has abandoned the illusion of constructing a permanently stable place of safety and satisfaction. W. Bouwsma emphasizes the Christian ideal of growth through the paradoxical experiences of the cross.[40] These experiences may be understood as repeated conversions, which are paradoxical because of the simultaneous experience of pain and joy. There is a death to something and a rebirth to something else. The greatest tragedy for a religious person is not being a sinner, but the embracing of stagnation, the refusal to grow. Middle-aged persons can be brought to the threshold of the spiritual pilgrimage through the experience of the transience of all things. This is the insight of Ecclesiastes: "Vanity of vanities; all is vanity. . . . One generation passeth away and another generation cometh. . . ." (Eccles. 1:2,4).

Younger people can understand in an intellectual way the transient nature of earthly life. But for the most part, unless illness or tragedy strikes, youth does not grasp in a personal, existential way the pilgrim aspect of life. The future seems relatively endless, and personal energies are almost entirely expended in creating a safe place for the self in that future. In other words, the seeker in midlife moves away from being a taker and self-preserver toward being a giver and risk-taker. In contrast to the attitudes of youth, this movement is based on a personal realization of finitude, of *my* death. Yet as Jaques points out in his discussion of death, the middle-aged artist arrives at "sculpted creativity," not by fleeing from the world of dying, but by living in it with a new perspective.[41] Living in this new way requires one to replace anxiety about death with faith. Whether this faith is explicitly religious, that is, formulated in the traditional idiom of religions, or not, it is required by the recognition of one's helplessness before death and other adversities. Without faith in some goodness beyond and superior to the self, the fear of one's own death may lead to active and passive forms of denial. The result is an inability to embrace the world in a life-giving way because the self is too preoccupied with its own survival.

When the affections and understanding begin to be healed by this midlife conversion, one can turn to the world with a spirit of caring and commitment. H. Nouwen cites two important aspects of caring that particularly apply to those who have entered middle age. He names these qualities poverty and compassion. Poverty in this sense is to be stripped of the illusion of ownership, that is, of permanent possession of things. Such poverty instills a quality of heart that appreciates life "not as property to be defended but as a gift to be shared."[42] Compassion is the ability to suffer with or to enter into the pain or struggle of another. It is difficult for one to do this unless he or she has suffered and concretely encountered the humbling limits of finiteness. Yet it is precisely this compassion that helps one "see beauty in the midst of misery, hope in the center of pain."[43]

Caring, as a mixture of poverty and compassion, leads to commitment. In midlife, commitment includes, but transcends, a mere need to be needed. One wants to contribute in the remaining span of life according to the new realizations and resources of middle age.[44] This frequently entails taking on the role of mentor to younger persons. On the one hand, the middle-aged person takes on the demanding task of guiding his or her children toward adulthood. In the area of work, persons over forty, once protégés of a mentor, become guides for younger members of their occupation. Levinson underlines the need for mentors, who at their best combine the optimal qualities of parent and friend.[45] These guides represent the skill, knowledge, and achievement that younger persons hope to attain or surpass. The problems of relating as mentor are similar to those found in any close friendship that calls for substantial readjustments at a particular stage of life. Domination, resentment, and jealousy can poison the relationship, just as gratitude, devotion, and candor can enhance it, especially in midlife, when the apprentice must separate from the guide. Levinson notes the poor quality of mentoring in many schools and workplaces. In a highly individualistic and competitive culture, the benefits of mentoring are hard to experience. This is particularly unfortunate for middle-aged individuals, who tend to be cut off from the younger generation and unable to exercise this satisfying form of commitment.

If mentor-protégé relationships must be altered in midlife, such change should also be applied to religious life in the explicit sense. Yet in this area mature patterns seem to be even harder to realize. Many persons either reject their earlier religious mentoring and give up on the development of a spiritual life or they protract a childhood relationship to religion well into later maturity. Few become their own gurus in middle age where religion is concerned. This is partially understandable, given the mysterious dimensions of the religious life and the close associations of religious injunctions with parental mandates. It is nevertheless unfortunate when middle-aged and older persons are stunted in their ability to move beyond institutional rules to formulate their own religious perspectives.

To become one's own mentor in religious matters does not necessarily mean rejection of older ways and earlier guides. Rather, becoming one's own guide suggests growth in which one preserves
what is valuable from the past and moves on confidently to a self-
directed religious life. This kind of midlife commitment is what R.
Howe describes as the movement from dependence on others to responsibility for one's own choices and actions, or the shift from security to maturity.[46] To make this change successfully involves a
reassessment of one's attitude to authority. This implies a willingness to accept authority figures as they are, that is, as a mixture of
good and bad, of wisdom, fallibility, and other limitations. Such acceptance requires embracing the same pros and cons in oneself.
The result is an acceptance of authority without needless rebellion
or sulking withdrawal, together with an acceptance of self as an
authority without guilt or bravado.[47]

Considerable potential for growth in middle age resides in a person's attitudes toward work. Whether manual or intellectual, work
is the mode by which people express and define themselves in the
world. In midlife a person is called to revise the structure of meaning surrounding his or her work world. R. Gould lists various reasons for work in the younger years. Beyond the more obvious motives of necessity, the exercise of talents, and being part of an
organization with extrinsic meaning, Gould centers on a motivation
that particularly lends itself to spiritual reflection. We work to "get
bigger," that is, we use work to establish an immunity pact with
death, and to stave off the annihilating threats and hurts of childhood.[48] The key to this insight stems in part from a distinction between external and internal reasons for working.

In younger years external rank and status are extremely important to help secure a personal identity; in this process internal
needs are often sacrificed. We perform according to the expectations of teachers, family, and employers. Working affords us a sense
of security, identity, and social acceptance. But these largely external motivations, satisfactory for the younger years, are no longer
sufficient for the midlife transition. The middle-aged person's inner
clock reminds him or her of personal finitude and, therefore, of the
illusory nature of external success. Regardless of whether work has
brought success or failure by midlife, the central issue is the experience of disparity between what has been gained from living in a

particular work structure and what personal goals would truly fulfill an individual.[49] In midlife transitions most people experience dissatisfaction with the continued pursuit of what others expect them to attain; they are ready to investigate and search their souls for their true aspirations. Inner voices call for a reassessment of motivations regarding career involvements.

Gould identifies the new rationale for work in midlife: "We must do work that confirms our talents and expresses a psychodynamic theme close to the core of us."[50] The key element is "the expression of a psychodynamic theme at the core of us." This is admittedly hard to realize in many jobs, but to whatever degree that our work can be motivated by these inner needs in midlife, it will foster spiritual development, an integration of the personality, an overcoming of one-sidedness. From this perspective, Gould's "psychodynamic theme at the core of us" must be understood in the plural: neglected themes calling for greater completion. The Jungian notion of compensation helps us to understand these inner "work themes" in midlife. For the great majority in an externally oriented, technological society, the summons toward integration necessitates styles of work that foster a measure of inwardness and attention to the voices of the deep psyche. How this occurs depends largely on one's education and sensitivity to inner needs.

Yet it would constitute an unwarranted elitism to exclude the working classes from a need to transform the meaning of work in midlife. For those involved in physical or technical labor the whys and hows of work may also need to be reexamined; a number of industries today have begun to grapple with these changing requirements in the workplace.

Jung's idea of compensation suggests several alternatives for the transformation of work in middle age. For example, those long engaged in intellectual or academic pursuits may be inclined to link these involvements to more active and worldly functions. Those long involved in practical, mundane affairs may need to reduce such activities, or to invest them with a new contemplative spirit. The main point of these examples of compensation is that the deepening of one's reflective spirituality in midlife can be attained through a variety of approaches, physical or mental, mundane or spiritual. The important need is to strike the right balance, usually over a period of years of trial and error, that will permit us to cultivate those "psychodynamic themes at the core of us."[51] The goal of this process is to turn one's working life into a religious experience, rather than merely an ambitious career.[52]

Yet to turn one's work into a spiritual experience is not an invitation to passivity and disdain for all ambition. Religion has often preached an excessive otherworldliness, as though involvement in worldly tasks were sinful. Such preaching loses sight of the theological truth that honest work is an earthly participation in divine energies. The middle-aged are put into an unnecessary double bind when they are told that a main task of this period of life is to provide for the economic security of their families, yet they are not to be ambitious for the attainment of these goals. In educated circles today, there is an attitude that regards ambition as antisocial, insatiable, driven, corrupting, and equivalent to a vain will to power.[53] Ambition, bent chiefly on money, prestige, and power, can lead to destructive ends for individuals and society, as history abundantly demonstrates. But ambition, as a combination of self-discipline and drive to succeed, can also contribute to the public good, the alleviation of suffering, and the enlightenment of the human spirit. Between these opposite objects of ambition falls a whole range of desires for and enjoyments of material things or personal attainments that are legitimate and valuable. The optimal balance lies somewhere between the vulgar, calculated, and opportunistic advice of Michael Korda (*Power! How To Get It, How to Use It*) and the languid jeremiads of Christopher Lasch, condemning our culture as motivated by grossly selfish ambitions (*The Culture of Narcissism*).

In the context of these reflections on middle age, it is very important not to place introspection and inwardness in an intrinsic opposition to wordly interests and ambitions. The spiritual transformation of work in midlife must not be interpreted as a condemnation of the desire for pleasure, possessions, fame, or accomplishments. It is a question, rather, of how and why we pursue these things. In part, these ends can be sought for themselves; our motivations are usually a complex mixing of the self-centered with the altruistic. As long as they are not sought with dishonesty or callous disregard for others, these pursuits may enhance the individual and even be useful to the public. The spiritualizing of work in midlife is not meant to remove, but rather to deepen its satisfaction. The development of inwardness helps us to pull back from heedless racing after goals that are foreign to the true needs and wants of our deepest selves.

A contemplative approach to work can also aid us in placing these endeavors into a wider scheme, seeing our efforts as a modest but responsible contribution to the general welfare. The inward route should not be understood as a diminution of our dreams, courage, and resolve to do important things in the world. Rather, learning to ponder in the heart leads us to choose our work, not according to outer compulsions or conventions alone, but according to the inner determinations of what we ourselves choose as congruous with self-enrichment and public service. In this sense, the spiritual transformation of work fosters both a greater appreciation of worldly matters and the ability to take hold of our own destinies through more authentic choices.

The introspective approach does not mean a rejection of joy and zest in one's work, as though a world-denying somberness were synonymous with making one's career a religious experience. What counts is why and how we embrace our work. Is it simply a means for escaping deeper questionings, or for immortalizing ourselves through dominance over persons and nature? Or has work become a flexible means for spiritual exploration and for the service of a wider community? These two aspects, moreover, are closely joined, and they combine to promote the mentor-function of midlife. Indeed, as we develop a more comprehensive and personal understanding of life, we can be of greater help to others.

The making of work into a spiritual experience has long been a cherished goal in religious traditions, East and West. The Ignatian ideal of the "contemplative in action" portrays a person for whom worldly service has value in itself and is also an occasion for inward maturing in union with God. Moreover, the contemplative in action is most likely to be an older person, who has experienced the inner struggles and gradually learned to shift from an ambitiously dominant stance to one of prayerful empathy. In a somewhat similar way, the highest ideal of Hinduism's life stages, the *sanyasin*, describes an individual who, through a long process of purgation and enlightenment, is able to be fully in and united to the world, yet not of it; the *sanyasin* does not seek to possess the world for purely personal ends.

A middle-aged person's potential for spiritual growth in the world depends, to a significant degree, on the understanding and use of power. Despite contemporary complaints about feelings of impotence in a world of bureaucracy, everyone exercises some form of power, either as influence on or control over those about one. The employment of power may be mental, emotional, physical, or a combination of these. Before midlife, especially for men in our culture, power is sought mainly to protect and to enhance the ego, to secure a stable identity. To a large extent, the quest for power is self-serving; parents, teachers, even friends are used for self-centered purposes. This is not something to be condemned as unworthy of younger people. It is in keeping with the needs of youth; such power-seeking helps to separate the developing ego from family influences and allows it to fashion a distinct identity. The problem for individuals and for society arises when the youthful use of power for mastery and dominance becomes the sole way of exercising power for the whole span of life.

Such an understanding of dominant power pervades modern culture, especially in technologically advanced areas. This is not to deny that power, as external control, also reveals itself in more tribal and agrarian societies. In such environments power as dominance stems from forms of patriarchy in which male authority exercises hierarchical control over society. But when technological mastery is added to a heritage of patriarchy, as in industrially developed nations, dominative power is further championed, without opposition, from childhood to old age. Indeed, the manipulation, ordering, and controlling of external reality is of the very nature of technological society. This point is emphasized, not to encourage a Luddite attack on the machine age, but rather to suggest the special difficulties for a middle-aged person in our culture who would embrace a transformed notion of power and personal significance.

Passage over this arduous terrain in midlife begins with an internal revolution of the psyche that results in a kind of religious conversion. The first step toward this new way of understanding and exercising power is a deepened awareness of the destructive potential both in nature and in the self. Levinson refers to this midlife perspective as a truer grasp of the destruction/creation polarity.[54] The seasonal cycles of destruction and rebirth impress us with the essential rhythms of nature. A heightened sensitivity to these cycles can inspire us to respect and protect many life-death rituals in nature. Moreover, we learn a certain humility by contemplating and cherishing ecological systems as we begin to see that our own power is limited; for we grow and die as part of a much larger natural environment. This insight itself initiates the possibility for nature mysticism in our spiritual lives. But beyond this recognition of the destructive/creative rhythms of nature and our own place within them is the more crucial awareness of how we are implicated in peculiarly human destructiveness. Humans, as creatures of vast reflective abilities and sweeping gifts of memory and anticipation, also bring to earth the moral evils stemming from hatred, malice, and selfishness.

The crucial first phase in a renewed attitude toward power is the acceptance of one's own role in fostering these particularly human forms of evil. Since middle-aged persons have a longer history of the exercise of personal power, they are more often aware of the ways in which others have damaged them and they have harmed others. For all their apparent rebelliousness, young people frequently suppress deep wounds stemming from childhood abuse. The overwhelming need of youths to establish independent identities often leads them to bury or disguise angers and resentments of earlier hurts. Excessive concern over such grievances might impede the more immediate task of securing some measure of identity in the world. In midlife, with a greater sense of personal identity and more distance in time from earlier injuries, they can face these injustices and emotional hurts. Sometimes middle-aged persons must face unexpected traumas or losses. In addition to understanding how they have been damaged by others' use of power, those in midlife are in a particularly good position to acknowledge their own abusive exercise of power and to confront the resultant guilt. Levinson aptly summarizes this universal condition, noting that a person must come to terms with grievances and guilts that produce a view of oneself as both victim and villain.[55]

Levinson does not, however, sufficiently pursue ways of dealing with destructive uses of power in middle age. It is not enough merely to acknowledge and assume responsibility for the damage we have incurred or caused. Working through our history of complicity with evil, on both conscious and unconscious levels, calls for additional stages of healing forgiveness. Forgiveness implies more than confrontation with grievances, more than admitting hurts against ourselves and taking responsibility for injuring others. Laudable as these moments in the growth process may be, they can result in merely excusing others or ourselves. To forgive is more than to excuse. We can excuse another and still remain embittered toward that person. We can excuse ourselves while we continue to carry oppressive guilt for our deeds.

Forgiveness, however, requires an empathic healing of memory. Sufficiently removed in time from earlier hurts, the forgiving person in midlife reconstructs and enters into the context of earlier injuries. Damage done by parents, lovers, or peers is understood in a fuller sense. The perpetrators of injury are recognized as victims themselves of other persons and of limiting environments. We can forgive hurts without harboring resentments, and we can be freed from the emotional chains of bitterness in order to move on in life. The central Christian story, describing Jesus suffering empathically with those who wronged him, is a clear religious model of such forgiveness. Similarly, forgiving ourselves involves more than ignoring, or even excusing our misdeeds through various rationalizations. To experience the healing effect of forgiveness in the depths of the psyche we must enter vicariously into the pain that we have caused others through a misuse of power. Through such empathy, a spiritual cleansing takes place, a resensitizing of ourselves to the meaning and the uses of power. In and through this human process of forgiveness we are caught up into the forgiveness of God, which enables us to forgive.

A second phase in the midlife shift from dominative power to serving or enabling power follows from the empathic experience of forgiveness. Once forgiving and forgiven, we can pursue nonviolent forms of power. We learn to use a kind of eliciting or enabling energy that allows others to respond authentically and humanely. This is the opposite of coercion, be it physical or mental. The basis of nonviolent power is charity or love. In its finest manifestations, it does not seek to use the other for personal advantage, but strives for a union with that which is loved, allowing others freedom to exercise their own authentic energies. Thus nonviolence represents a significant change in our attitude toward the world. We no longer seek to use self-serving force, but exercise power as a serving, enabling energy.[56]

Moreover, such exercising of nonviolent power allows us to love ourselves. Perhaps this is one of the great exchanges to which persons in midlife especially are invited: to substitute, for the power that promises to preserve the ego against adversity and death, a new power that, by releasing us from the all-consuming lust for survival and enhancement of the self, allows us joyful love of our deepest self and others. This reversal of our basic attitude toward the world is one of the highest ideals to which humankind can aspire. It will always remain a partially achieved goal, for the yen for dominative power is forever slipping back into the psyche. From a theological perspective, this transformation of power cannot be attained by human effort alone; it demands an openness in faith to the influence of divine grace in the soul. More subtle theological questions arise at this point; they can be sketched here without leading us too far away from our inquiry into the potentials of midlife.

First, we must ask how fully a person can effect this inner transformation of stance toward the world? In the Christian tradition, there exists a spectrum of responses, from the Catholic understanding of cooperation with grace to the Calvinist insistence that such a conversion of spirit is totally the work of God. The former tradition is based on a doctrine of creation that more completely espouses the presence of the divine energies in the natural order of things. The Reformed tradition is understandable, in its historical context, as a prophetic demand for respect of the gratuity and sovereignty of God's grace. Nevertheless, it also runs the risk of an exaggerated distancing of divine from human activity, thus lessening the intrinsic worth of human responsibility, choice, and action. Within Protestantism, however, there are also traditions, such as the Wesleyan, that strongly emphasize the importance of human activity.

A second, closely related, issue concerns the mode of divine presence or activity in this transformation of power. On the Catholic side of the spectrum, God's engagement in the human tends to be more implicit and intrinsic. God, whether explicitly named or not, operates quietly at the core of an evolving natural and human history. Wherever the reversal of power occurs in the world, whether among explicitly religious believers or among those who ignore or reject traditional religious idioms and confessions, the divine enabling of grace is at work. Liberal Protestant theological positions

draw close to this understanding. We do not outline these theological differences in order to prove that only those on one side of the
spectrum can adequately account for the activity of grace in the
movement from dominative to nonviolent power among individuals
and groups. Rather, the reason for this brief sketch is twofold: to
underline the further dimension (apart from a psychological explanation of the transformation of attitude toward power) of inquiry
that theologians bring to the topic; and secondly, to clarify our approach to the subject.

This inner conversion or transformation of power points to the
outward goal of seeking a new balance of power and love within the
world, not in flight from it. Levinson affirms this point, arguing that
Shakespeare's Lear (and, indeed, Shakespeare himself) too drastically separated the life of love from the exercise of power in the
world.[57] Yet the excellently appropriate passage from *Lear* cited by
Levinson need not be interpreted in such a separatist manner. The
"prison" that Lear and Cordelia move toward at the end of the play
can be understood symbolically as that inner place of the psyche,
that "hidden garden" of the psalmist, whence important influence
can be exercised on the world. The following passage need not represent a flight from the world, but rather a journey toward our center, a "confined" and special space where destructive power-lust
can be transformed through the grace of forgiveness and the integration of Lear's feminine side into his psyche:

> Come, let us away to prison;
> We two alone will sing like birds i'the cage.
> When thou dost ask me blessing, I'll kneel down
> And ask of thee forgiveness. So we'll live,
> And pray, and sing, and tell old tales, and laugh
> at gilded butterflies. . . .
> And take upon's the mystery of things,
> As if we were God's spies: and we'll wear out
> In a wall'd prison, pacts and sects of great ones
> That ebb and flow by th' moon.[58]

If, in midlife, we can begin to enter the "wall'd prison" of psychic
depths with the traits of forgiveness, prayerfulness, song, and play,
we will be in a special position to exercise nonviolent power, influencing the "pacts and sects of great ones" in the world.

A new balance or interpenetration of love and power within the
world becomes the special goal of the middle-aged seeker. Because

by midlife we have been forced, through personal crisis, to pull back from earlier patterns of using power, we can see the destructive consequences of such power, both in terms of its dehumanizing impact on ourselves and its devastating effects on the social order. At a still deeper level, the dangerousness of this power stems from its heedless use for personal aggrandizement. Such dominative power cuts us off from the wider community and from our own deeper needs. Against this tendency, the inward journey of midlife allows us to see the fallacy of pursuing dominative power in order to protect our precarious finitude, convicts us of our own destructive participation in such exercises of power, and finally, opens our eyes to the reality that dominative power can only be transformed into serving, enabling power by letting ourselves be rejoined to the source of love and unity. Tillich sharply asserted this interlinking of power and love, individual separateness and communal bonding:

> Life is being in actuality and love is the moving power of life. . . . Love manifests its greatest power there where it overcomes the greatest separation. And the greatest separation is the separation of self from self. Every self is self-related and a complete self is completely self-related. It is an independent *center*, indivisible and impenetrable and therefore is rightly called an individual. . . . Love reunites that which is self-centered and individual. The power of love is not something which is added to an otherwise finished process, but life has love in itself as one of its constitutive elements.[59]

But Tillich also knew that the ultimate cross-fertilization of power and love calls for an act of faith, a trust in the force of divine love, in and beyond the self, that can give the grace to let go of walled-off individuality and surrender, in hope, to the still-dim vision of universal love. Tillich describes this movement in terms of self-acceptance:

> Man can love himself in terms of self-acceptance only if he is certain that he is accepted. Otherwise his self-acceptance is self-complacency and arbitrariness. Only in the light and in the power of "love from above" can he love himself.[60]

The midlife crisis of the self, by starkly presenting to us our finiteness in the face of death, opens up the personally experienced possibility of, and need for a unifying love. When we have undergone this inward voyage, we will engage in the world and our own occupations with a vision, at once humbler and yet more potent, of the unification of the human community.

This movement from within ourselves results in efforts for a nonviolent revolution toward greater justice and fellowship. In their middle years, several major modern proponents of nonviolent social change, including Gandhi and Martin Luther King Jr., manifested the need for inwardness in order to effect enduring improvement in society. Each of these men discovered, in the meditative solitude of their souls, two important negative convictions and the possibility of a positive outcome. Inwardness taught them not only that evil was widespread in social institutions, but more important, that all persons harbor evil within and participate to some measure in it. Just as we must come to see ourselves bonded to others in the potentials of love, so we need to realize that we are part of structures of oppression. Midlife can become a privileged time for encountering our Shadow, allowing it to convict us of our complicity and thus curtail our tendency to project evil solely onto others. The Shadow archetype also enables us to creatively rechannel the hidden energies within the seemingly dark force.

The second, but kindred, conviction concerns the radical inability of our own humanness to accomplish significant improvements in the world. Yet, paradoxically, this grasp of our weakness is not debilitating, but strengthening. For it is only by breaking down our illusions of power that we encounter in solitude the mystery at the heart of the world that permits us to resist "the executioners of the world."[61] The positive result of these movements downward and inward is the beneficial revolution of truth-force (*satyagraha*). In the words of James Douglass:

> In a revolution through solitude the people are one at the same time as each satyagrahi continues to stand utterly alone in the presence of the One, who grants a revolutionary power of community through the radical poverty and interior silence of each satyagrahi, each man poor in spirit. In a revolution of truth-force, of the power of being, there is no way up except down, no way to power except through renunciation, no way to union in community except through self-surrender in solitude, no way to being except through nothingness.[62]

Again, this movement downward and inward, this reflective prayerful style in midlife allows us to serve the community with more wisdom and altruism. Knowing our own complicity in evil and our inability to transform others at a deep level makes us question our motivations for wanting to reform the social order. Are our positions dictated mainly by self-serving needs to enhance our egos through making others think or act as we would have them to do? Are we using others, under the aegis of reform, to further our desire for dominative power? In brief, are we acting out our unresolved psychological needs, using others in the process, rather than working through these inner problems? Without contemplation in solitude, we may be exercising on others and on ourselves a subtle but destructive violence. The point of reflectiveness in midlife is not to immobilize us through torturous soul-searching. Rather, it can free us for a less self-contaminated involvement in the problems of others and in issues of social reform.

A dual transformation is thus possible for the middle-aged person facing the world. A new inwardness, a search for depths in the face of personal finitude and the brokenness of human society, leads to nonviolent commitment toward nature and humankind. W. Dennis's study of creativity in middle-aged persons indicates a high potential for peak achievement during this period.[63] Yet this creativity is usually measured in terms of external accomplishments in science, the arts, and other professions. While such sociological measurements are useful, they can be misleading. The middle-aged person who has become open to an inner journey of transformation experiences inward and outward forms of creativity that are especially difficult to measure. Researchers have few precise ways of measuring basic changes in attitude and consequent shifts in the way people deal with the world. The potential for transformation in midlife has been likened to setting out on a journey into uncharted waters. J. McLeish calls such a person a "Ulyssean Adult," recalling the Greek hero who in midcareer leaves the haven of Ithaca "to sail beyond the sunset, and the baths of all the western stars, until I die."[64] McLeish underscores Ulysses' spirit of search and adventure, of courage and resourcefulness.[65] But like the nineteenth-century Tennyson, McLeish presents the Ulyssean quest mainly as an external venture; this approach to midlife too easily becomes an extension of the muscular, dare-devil pattern of youth.

Caught in the heroic vision of a warrior leader, one can miss the direction of Ulysses' new voyage. He sails "beyond the sunset," to "the baths of all the western stars," a remarkable symbol for the inward journey to those darker realms of the psyche not explored during his great exploits in Troy. Dante, as opposed to Tennyson, characterizes Ulysses' second journey as a spiritual quest when he has the Greek hero exhort his aging crew on the westward trip: "Consider your origin: you were not made to live as brutes, but to pursue virtue and knowledge" (*Inferno,* Canto 26). Later verses use symbol to describe Ulysses' new vision of a journey into depths, into mysterious places not subject to rational, measurable calculations: "And turning our stern to the morning, we made of our oars wings for the mad flight, always gaining on the left" (*Inferno,* Canto 26). They set their course toward darker realms, away from the morning light of life, and they made progress on "the left," *la sinistra.* The left in medieval symbology represents Lear's "mysteries of things," as opposed to the right, which symbolizes Apollonian clarity of rational thought.

The inward journey, the pursuit of virtue and knowledge, helps the middle-aged person to relate to the world through an ethical posture of empathetic service. In an important conference on the national quality of life, M. Marty stressed the ethical contribution that middle-aged persons can make in society.[66] Yet a question arises about the type of ethical stance that can most enhance the quality of life. In our American milieu, we usually think of forms of service to the needy or social programs for a more just society. Such programs call for pragmatic planning and vigorous execution on the concrete level of goods and services. There is undeniable worth in and need for the peculiarly American genius of problem-solving, motivated by sentiments of responsibility and justice. These imperfect efforts at social betterment represent one of the brighter pages of our ethical history. But in many ways these strenuous programs for social welfare are based on a one-sided and possibly self-defeating ethic.

Our common social ethic is founded unreflectively on certain pragmatic, quantitative premises: more is better; possessions solve human problems; material growth and productivity will insure the future. To ignore the value of such a pragmatic ethic could be interpreted as a flight from social responsibility. It is hard for Americans to heed the scriptural injunction, "not by bread alone . . ." in formulating a social morality. An ethic devised by middle-aged persons who have engaged seriously in an inner quest criticizes the limitations of these ruling presuppositions. Empathetic service entails more than giving people things or programs; it also requires listening for spiritual needs and yearnings, which cannot be satisfied by our usual welfare plans. The pragmatic, materialistic approach may even hamper the development of quality in life. A new ethic, stemming from inward reflections in midlife, can make us empathetic to spiritual needs for beauty, human communication, contemplation, and enjoyment.

As the middle-aged person develops an ethic from within, one rooted in issues of quality, as well as quantity, a gradual process of "detribalization" takes place.[67] We learn to listen to inner voices of conscience and intuition, as well as to the external dictates of the given social milieu. It is paradoxical that when we become more individuated, authentic selves, the possibilities for a universal perspective unfold. Tribal or national customs and values can be criticized from a broader perspective because the individuated person is less dependent upon these values for identity and is more aware of the injurious dimensions of the tribal creed. Simultaneously, movement away from a particular context creates wider bonds with humankind. If we, as individuals, feel especially hurt or betrayed by earlier dedication to tribal ideals, we may break sharply with those ideals. Outward polemic diminishes when the inner person finds his or her own foundations of meaning. According to Levinson, such a one "forms a more universal view of good and evil, and a more tragic sense of their coexistence in himself and in all humanity."[68]

Although he mentions a new type of rapprochement with the tribe for the individuated person, Levinson does not stress the importance of this renewed particularity. We can understand that, in a world threatened by the destructive forces of nationalistic, regional, racial, and religious hatred, a call for universalism is paramount. However, without negating the significance of the ecumenical outlook, a strong case needs to be made for the preservation and enhancement of healthy particularity and diversity. More pernicious even than the diluting influence of homogenizing cultures is the self-deception of fancying oneself a *homo universalis*, without the limitations of historical particularity. This self-delusion leads in two directions: toward avoidance of responsibility for our own complicity in the evils of our tribe and toward superficiality in assessing the beliefs, intentions, and actions of other groups. There is a soundness in rooting ourselves in the positive aspects of a particular history. On a history, both in a group and a personal sense, we build and modify our identity. The ecumenical movement among religions has in recent decades come increasingly to recognize the valuable polarity between the universal and the particular. These two poles can be mutually correcting and enriching.

Play is another way of fulfilling some of the potentials of middle age. The ability to delight in nature and other persons can be especially fostered in midlife. In midcareer many people begin to recognize the strains and limitations of youthful strivings to gain stature, approval, and other rewards. Moreover, a heightened appreciation of the irony, tragedy, and paradoxical complexity of the human scene can instill a certain tolerance and even humor. This spirit is not to be confused with apathy or lack of care. Rather, it is an attitude that relieves somberness and staleness. Under the best circumstances work can become a form of play, which involves curiosity, risk-taking, and zest. There is something eminently religious in the ability to laugh at and enjoy one's own foibles, and to realize that, given enough time, all things human (and perhaps even divine), go badly. Those who understand and accept this possibility with a touch of humor are more likely to renew and rebuild the broken pieces of life than the overly earnest.

Our suggestion that even divine things sometimes go badly is not without theological underpinnings. The world is the *lila,* or play, of divine energies. Can we imagine God playing without occasionally dropping the ball or missing the target? It is unfortunate that we have erected, for our own security, such a stern and infallible image of God. Some aspects of process theology allow us to mitigate our severe and perfectionistic projection onto God, whose very limitations summon our devoted involvement in building the world. In the same vein, many presentations of the Christ-figure as a clown evoke at once humor and deeper sympathy with suffering humanity. This element of play appears to reflect the Pauline sense of the foolishness of God that is wiser than the wisdom of men. The person of genuine faith, as Bouwsma points out, should be able to relax somewhat in the face of life's adversities, since they are so often beyond human resolution: "Play is a natural expression of the joy of faith, which makes it possible to engage in life, even the hard work of life, as a game that has its own seriousness."[69] Liturgy and sacraments, with their dramatic enactments, staging, color, and song, strongly manifest this dimension of play amid serious themes of life and death. The link between creative discoveries and a playful attitude is important to grasp. When the mind is less pressured to perform according to the expected canons, it is free to allow unusual combinations to occur within the imagination.

While persons in midlife should be able to be playful toward the world, this playfulness is qualitatively different from the playfulness of childhood. The child may remind adults of the value of play, but the intrinsic quality of playfulness in a child and a middle-aged adult is considerably different. To the extent that the adult has come to terms with death and his or her own complicity in the brokenness of the world, the meaning of play is significantly altered. It is no longer merely the spontaneous or designed glee of childhood imagination. For the middle-aged adult who has emerged from various transitional crises, play is pervaded with the pathos of its own special transitory beauty. Play is strangely able to evoke our sympathy with the tragic dimensions of life. In a sense, the mature adult plays on the verge of tears. The French Catholic writer Charles Péguy could be seen with tears rolling down his face as he stood on train platforms watching fellow Parisians pass. Péguy's playful seriousness led him to tears at the sight of human beauty and tragedy mixed together.

Friendship and Intimacy

A third area of special potential for growth in midlife is that of friendship and intimacy (the realm of the other). We have already discussed relations to others with regard to the stance of the middle-aged toward the world. Here we are primarily concerned with unique personal relationships with family and close friends. It is in such encounters that we meet the other, not in some abstract orientation to humanity, but in concrete situations that draw out genuine positive and negative feelings. Our facile self-deceptions about love for and service to humankind are tested by the quality of special relationships. We have already considered the destructive threats to personal relations in middle age. A new awareness of finitude, of being cheated or trapped by time, of need for a new identity, leads many individuals in midlife into a disruptive search for new intimacies and friendships. Others respond to middle-age intimations of dissatisfaction in relationships by immersing themselves in familiar routines and pleasant distractions. This latter course may be more harmful to spiritual growth in midlife than the former, where disruptive events stimulate the potential for relationships based on new assumptions and motives.

Midlife transitions provide the opportunity to move intimate relationships and friendships to deeper levels. This movement toward depth in human encounters is often enhanced in middle age for two principal reasons. If growth toward personal maturity has not been arrested in younger years, a more individuated identity emerges by midlife. When our own identities are firm, there is less tendency to project our needs onto others, that is, we can more clearly distinguish between ourselves and others as unique personalities. The danger of a weak sense of our own identities is that we begin to see the other as a mere distillation of our own self-projections. But, of even greater importance, midlife confrontation with our own limitations, including our mortality, makes it possible to view self and intimate other with new eyes. Although Jaques misdefines mysticism as a flight from the world, he correctly notes the potential for fuller relationships realized by working through the personal encounter with death. Jaques notes that Dante, as he reached midlife, avoided both a world-denying mysticism and a manic defense against death, with "consequent strengthening of character and resolve, under the domination of love."[70]

When we become conscious of our unhealthy defenses against extinction and release our fearfulness in faith, our attitude toward the intimate other changes. As we accept our finitude in midlife, we are willing to lower our masks and allow more of our true selves to appear to the other. We recognize the deficiencies in our own ability to love by acknowledging the illusions, and even hatred, that enters our relationships with intimates. When we embrace our fundamental precariousness as humans, we become more willing to expose our vulnerabilities to the other.[71] When an ambience of trust exists, middle-aged adults are better able to reveal their authentic selves to another. The need for dissimulation fades when we realize that time is not on our side. We must risk mutual revelation, overcoming our fear that the other cannot support the truth about ourselves. It requires faith to give the self to another when it does not feel safe to do so. We long to reach beyond appearances, to touch and be touched by the other at the centers of our beings. In marriage, this development helps us to relate to a spouse as a distinctly other person. As our youthful inhibitions subside and we develop expressive skills in midlife, verbal and nonverbal methods of communication can improve.

Noted sex therapists Masters and Johnson describe the marriage crisis of the middle years as the result of emotional poverty, a condition created by lack of verbal and nonverbal means of communication.[72] R. Howe describes this lack of communication as the "tragic situation of two persons behind their respective masks, trying to find each other . . . each will remain lost, alone, and—though married—unmarried."[73] Such partners may not have developed enough affective autonomy to be able to distinguish and express their true feelings to each other. Moreover, they may have failed to build an environment of truthful interchange between one another. When trust and honest communication are linked, sexuality itself takes on a new perspective. Sexual acts transcend the attainments of self-gratification and performance that may have been important during younger years. Sexual pleasure is heightened through a new sense of mutual devotion. In caring for one another's vulnerabilities and differences, we are promoting the genuine individuation of each person.

In this way, sexuality can become "sociality."[74] This term does not signify a diminishment of the physical enjoyment of sexuality, as some erroneously believe is inevitable in older persons. Rather, sociality means that, more than being a narrowly sexual function, focused mainly on self-gratification, sexuality includes a caring for, and expression of, the whole social context of the lovers. Where mutual love and respect obtain between spouses, sexual responsiveness increases with time.[75] But this wider context of life includes children, friends, and associates; love extends from sexuality to embrace a larger community. As couples age, they enjoy the opportunity of reaching beyond the limitations of a nuclear family closed in on itself.

Middle-aged spouses, as the in-between family, can reach out across generations to the young families of their children, as well as to the elderly families of their own parents. In their relations with the younger couples, the middle-aged relatives need to respect youthful independence while acting as guides and helpers when necessary. In their relations with elderly parents, love moves them to responsible care and devotion. This integrational dialogue within a three-tiered family can be mutually enriching for all. But moving beyond the restrictions of the immediate family, midlife demands also an opening up to the wider community in civic and social responsibility.

Anne Lindbergh described a couple as two sea shells no longer facing each other, but rather linked together facing outward toward the world.[76] This imagery offers an ideal for a Christian family. The nuclear family is called to mirror the whole household of God, the *oikoumene,* to reach out to the whole human family. The experiences of the middle-aged couple, if their values and goals are deepening, particularly suits them for such a wider mission of family. Indeed, this spiritual mission of the married needs to be exercised also toward those whose intimate lives have taken socially "deviant" paths, such as single, divorced, or gay people. Too often the nuclear family is hostile or indifferent to the sensitivities and needs of such persons.

But this outreach into the community, the building of caring networks of families and commitment to important causes, calls for an enriching of relations within the family. Otherwise, exterior activity becomes a poor substitute for the intimacy lacking within the home. A home environment of respect and care has special obstacles in the middle years. Difficulties with teenage children, finances, and health may be compounded by disenchantment between spouses. This disillusionment can stem from the spouses having grown apart over the years in interests and purposes, as well as from the challenges to intimacy in midlife already discussed. Couples who begin early enough, and are basically compatible, can resist this debilitating disillusionment. They can identify their personal assets and update values and priorities in the marriage. Spouses may need to rethink their vocational and avocational lives together as they review the meaning of their marriage in terms of desires and expectations.[77] They can also help by reserving quiet times for togetherness, for sharing and learning about feelings and needs. Place must be made for leisure and playfulness in sex, family life, and other situations.

Yet this process of expanding and deepening emotional life in middle age requires us to face considerable pain. It is painful to become aware of our own weaknesses, hostilities, and self-deceptions. Moreover, opening ourselves empathetically to the feelings of anger and disappointment from the intimate other toward us entails significant suffering. Yet the endurance of hostility, even when motivated by friendship, must always be a part of a love relationship. The fundamental Christian paradigm of the cross portrays the loving acceptance of suffering and hostility. This endurance is not a masochistic form of self-victimizing, which seeks to gain control over others by becoming their victim. Rather, the bearing of whatever suffering is required to deepen a relationship stems from a prior willingness to embrace one's finitude, one's own death. Such a person realizes that all defenses against the ultimate foe must crumble; in light of this, the sufferings necessary to experience a quality relationship in the remaining span of life are worthwhile.

In an almost paradoxical way, a renewed ability to play in middle age also depends on a personal acceptance of death. In earlier periods of life, when a person is striving to shore up his or her own identity and carve out a niche in the world, play generally tends to be seen as the reward won by hard work. The main stuff of life is work itself, which seems to assure personal and familial survival. The "cure of work," as Gould referred to it, serves as an antidote to threatening illness or death. But when a middle-aged individual has successfully faced finitude, the alleged medicine of work is revealed as a placebo, unable to cure death. Work, when not invested with false expectations, can become a form of play, especially if it is harmonious with the needs for growth of the individual. Other forms of play, whether routine-altering diversions or artistic involvements, are permeated by a new spirit. Intimate relationships, and life in general, call us to let go of deadly seriousness and replace it with the joy of living in our sometimes painful finitude. With this new point of view the variety and frequency of play can be increased.

Contemporary literature on middle age, probably influenced by the modern women's movement, underscores the importance of gender-role reversals.[78] This aspect of midlife change especially affects the development of intimacy and friendship. Men, who have been culturally educated toward aggressive styles, begin to sense the inadequacies of these learned responses. They feel the incompleteness of not being able to experience and to express the "softer" emotions. They want to be able to share empathically their deeper longings, and even vulnerabilities, in a nonthreatening atmosphere. Nevertheless, while this movement to challenge the one-sided stress on toughness for men has grown, it is by no means a universal phenomenon in our culture. Fears of effeminacy and weakness keep many men from unlocking the "feminine" traits of their personalities. An excessive militance in sports and politics, coupled with disdain for gay people and for nonviolent methods, continues to characterize a large portion of the male population. Gould, focusing on a significant aspect of this problem, argues that only those who have achieved sufficient confidence in their own maleness in midlife can risk opening up to their feminine sides.[79] (We are using "masculine" and "feminine" symbolically, referring to traits so described in the culture, not to biologically fixed characteristics among men and women.) Women, who in their younger years have been culturally trained to cultivate their nurturing, affective, other-directed roles as childbearers, become more tolerant of egocentric, aggressive, and worldly strivings in themselves. Again, such a generality must be qualified in a variety of ways in relation to the actual lives of middle-aged women. Moreover, it is hard to predict the patterns for midlife among women in the next century because so many young women today are entering worldly careers that traditionally require the tougher "male" traits.

The potential for acute problems or for new growth in intimate relationships depends on how the masculine-feminine polarity is resolved. Positive development in marriage can be stymied if a wife clings to stereotypical expectations concerning masculinity when her husband is ready to embrace his own "feminine" side. Similarly, a man will harm the relationship if he stifles his wife's midlife efforts to foster her career. Beyond the level of worldly occupations and public styles, the partners can cut off or open up an inner road to spiritual development by their way of dealing with these role-reversals, or better, complementary roles.

In this respect, both Freud and Jung can serve as guides to the psychology of the adult turning in midlife onto paths that lead to religious depths. From a Freudian perspective, the middle-aged person can have a sufficiently established sexual identity to let down the earlier fearful barriers to (psychologically) wanting the parent of the opposite sex. In the Jungian idiom, the individual who has already stabilized a culturally acceptable ego as male or female is ready for a new venture toward inner depths by encountering within the psyche the neglected archetypes of the opposite sex. One result of this journey toward the unconscious in myth and image is that we are less inclined to project expectations and demands on the intimate partner. Such projections are very common among younger men and women, and they often lead to great misunderstandings and animosity between partners. When we are, however, able to make peace with the unprojected masculine or feminine opposite within ourselves, we are more willing to respect the partner as truly other, untrammeled by our own needs and demands. The chief bane of friendship, whether in marriage or elsewhere, is lack of respect for otherness, with its consequent possessive abuse of the friendship.

This pursuit of the masculine-feminine polarity manifests intrinsically religious aspects. It can offer us the healing of memories that leads to forgiveness and reconciliation. Hurts received from parents, intimates, or other friends are no longer lumped together in the psyche and projected outward as accusations. The injuring mother, father, lover, or friend is distinguished from our own inner archetypes of the opposite gender. This clarifying of images doesn't minimize real injuries, but it allows us to recognize the harming parties as distinct, as other. This very distancing offers perspective: There is more to the other than our internalized image. We see the other as an independent person, with a distinct individual history and with his or her own injuries from the past that may have been transmuted into hurtful conduct. From this recognition and insight flows the grace of forgiveness and new reconciliation with "enemies."

Such an event is religious because it leads to greater honesty or truth about self and other; it is religious because it makes possible a new level of love. Again, whatever leads to an increase of forgiveness, truth, charity, and reconciliation among people is intrinsically religious.[80] The particular idiom of a given religious tradition may express these human realities in its own way. The differences between religious systems are important; since this diversity itself is valuable, we should resist reductionistic attempts at homogenizing them. Nevertheless, this variety of traditionally religious approaches points to certain common human realities (variously understood and practiced), including the forgiveness and reconciliation discussed above in reference to midlife sex-role shifts.

In explicitly religious terminology, the quest for a more adequate balancing of masculine and feminine dimensions in middle age can foster a renewed understanding of God and of salvation. In the West, our most basic image of God is that of father. Millennia of patriarchal inheritance have fashioned a culture that imbues us with a fundamentally masculine and paternal image of the divine. This image is more than a mere abstract concept; it is positively or negatively rooted in a whole complex of inner feelings and outward emotions. Modern psychology has underscored the formation of this God image in reaction to parental figures, especially the father. Various aspects of this Father-God image, the loving and solicitous father, for example, have proven to be very beneficial in spiritual development. But contemporary feminist theology has stressed the constricting and abusive aspects of Father-God images as motivating factors in both personal and institutional religion. Since the feminist arguments against masculine theological language have been thoroughly broadcast in recent years, they need no repetition.

Our main point here is the influential link between ruling symbols in our life-style and the prospects for developing a more adequate image of God. Since the divine has universally been regarded as combining and transcending the highest attributes of the world, it follows that the reality of God must surpass both masculine and feminine imagery. But for our personal knowledge and religious experience to better encompass that vision of God, we must concretely realize a closer melding of the masculine and feminine in our own psyches. This requires more than rational knowing about God; for it is the inward attuning of our deepest images, those symbols fraught with emotional intensity, that can produce a more adequate vision of God's reality. This reordering of images can be especially vibrant in midlife, when one-sided patterns of the past are challenged. Thus our youthful conceptions of God, whether they spring from the masculine hero figure on a strenuous quest or from paternal sources of power, can be revised more adequately by masculine-feminine role reversals in middle age.[81]

This theological perspective implies a view of religious fulfillment, or salvation, that stresses gradual growth toward a more excellent union of opposites in the soul. It is an immanent vision of salvation that avoids reductionism. Moreover, it is personal without neglecting the vitally important matter of ethical responsibility. The word *salvation* is related to healing, which in turn is a derivative of wholeness. But we misunderstand the theology of wholeness if we envision it in a Pelagian or romantic way. The Pelagian understanding, a constant temptation in an age of technology, reduces religious salvation to human growth through therapeutic techniques. Religious wholeness, in our sense, requires the operation of surprising and challenging grace within and beyond human developmental processes. This definition of salvation as a limited process of making whole is intrinsically religious and this-worldly at once. Grace not only builds on nature, in the traditional phraseology, but it also compenetrates the natural order of things. Furthermore, to insist on the graceful presence of God in the natural order does not implicate us in reductionism, in the denying of transcendent possibilities. Some form of life after death, or continuance with God, can remain a deeply religious hope.

A romantic view of wholeness allows us to envision the possibility of achieving genuine personal and social integration of opposites within the span of our lives. Although scripture seems to corroborate such visions, with allusions to lambs and lions lying down together, for example, such images are eschatological ideals, only partially attainable in the broken realm of this world. Therefore, the hope of salvation or wholeness through a compensatory balancing of polar tendencies during the aging process must include a realistic grasp of the ineluctable presence of evil, suffering, and imperfection. These negative dimensions, as we have seen, may even play an indirect role in furthering development, both personal and social. Middle age offers the most fertile potential for reconciling opposites inwardly and in reference to others. Yet even in the finest examples of such transitions, the process remains imperfect and unfinished.

One thing remains to be said about the term *unfinished*. The growth metaphor, as an image of the aging process, can easily be misleading. There is a tendency, when thinking in terms of organic development, to imagine an end point, which represents the culmination or apex of wholeness. The plant reaches the fullness of its growth, of its organic balance between inner and outer elements, then decline begins. It is as though the full extent of growth is already "known" and programmed into the plant's seed. While this analogy holds with regard to *physical* human growth and decline, it distorts and hides the truth about aging in its mental and spiritual dimensions.

P. Pruyser calls this view of the aging process "the peak-slope illusion."[82] This image can be found in literary renditions of the "ages of man," as well as in economic models, which depict the productive years with an upward slope and retirement with a downward one. In reference to aging, "this powerful iconic illusion thwarts us from seeing, or making, alternative patterns."[83] Rather than as upward or downward movement, aging can be conceived as a venture forward, toward new discoveries. As symbolic creatures, we remain ever unfinished; this is our glory. The human spirit, through its conscious and unconscious life, is forever open to the unexpected, to shaping a new story.

New potential for openness to the other, as inwardly appropriated and outwardly encountered, can enliven friendship in midlife. In addition to intimate friendships, the middle-aged person needs other friends and support communities. The literature on aging stresses the importance of keeping old friendships and of cultivating new ones in midlife. Such friendships are valuable both in themselves and as a bulwark against excessive loneliness in old age.[84] Vaillant, in his summary statement about the men in the Grant Study, insists on the overarching significance of the quality of sustained relationships.[85] This longitudinal study indicates that healthy development in midlife depends less on the absence of traumatic events in childhood than on continuing, nurturing friendships. Vaillant explains that by developing mature defense mechanisms a person can adequately cope with childhood hurts and fashion a lively, happy personality by midlife. The subjects of the study who were not able to establish vital friendships in midlife manifested negative personality traits including isolation fantasy and loss of zest or creativity. This emphasis on midlife friendships does not negate the importance of an environment of trust and love in childhood; indeed, much of the potential for future friendships is shaped by a child's earliest relationships. But later relationships may be equally significant in personality development.

Thus, middle-aged persons are in a unique position to contribute to and benefit from support communities. We have already discussed the potential for those in midlife to involve themselves creatively in the world. But commitments to causes in the public realm need to be reinforced by support communities in which closer friendships are cultivated.[86] Without these networks of friendship, contemporary nuclear couples and single individuals are often isolated and overburdened in their efforts to meet emotional and intellectual demands. People often feel cut off from deeper social interaction in our vast, impersonal, bureaucratized society. Although we have stressed the cultivation of the inner person in middle age, inward development itself is enhanced by deeper friendships. Communities of support may be formally organized groups that meet at fixed times to explore personal issues or social questions. They may also be informal networks of friends.

But the important elements of a support community, as distinguished from typical occupational or social groups, are personal caring and sharing. The middle-aged person who has made some headway on the inner journey can enrich such communities by sharing personal experiences and insights. Moreover, the middle-aged, partially freed from earlier illusions about themselves and from the need to control others, can exercise a finer quality of caring for friends. In the middle years, therefore, support communities can become the environment, according to Paul Tournier, for moving beyond "the superficial relationships of working life and of sexual attraction . . . [toward] a deeper personal commitment."[87] Yet this kind of commitment in friendship cannot succeed unless it also takes on a transcendent dimension, to become spiritual love.

In ordinary usage, the word *spiritual* is regarded as the antithesis of the real, material realm. Spiritual love, however, is most deeply immersed in and tempered by real encounters in the world. Only through this type of love can the recalcitrant stuff of human relations finally be transformed into caring communities. Such groups are a form of gospel *agape* by which we are able to transcend the possessive, oedipal aspects of *eros* to arrive at a benevolent caring about others for their own sake. This friendship does not imply that we know what is best for others or can save them from themselves in some messianic way. In the end, this can serve only to inflate our egos. Rather, this kind of love expresses an intrinsic respect for the friend, enhanced by a heightened empathy and acceptance that stems from our own experience of finitude in midlife.

Throughout this chapter we have sought to explore the unique and intrinsically spiritual dimensions of human development in midlife. The aging process can also be understood through reference to central themes of the Judeo-Christian tradition concerning self and community. Be it *hesed* (steadfast love) or *agape,* these faiths help develop a self-reconciled and self-loving individual within fellowships that foster love and justice. One purpose of community, whether in churches or synagogues, is to be a milieu of conditioning wherein a person can seek fuller life. "Milieu of conditioning" should not be regarded as an externally manipulated Skinner box. Rather, church or community as a conditioning environment can be understood as an ambience that invites the self away from destructive toward creative choices. Of course, this is to speak of church or community in the ideal, but the deficiencies of concrete fellowships do not negate the motivational reality of the ideal.

Moreover, these communities or churches exist wherever we find the spiritualizing process of growth, either within the psyche or in interpersonal relations. This does not negate the significance of particular religious traditions and specific religious language, symbol, and ritual. Rather, it emphasizes the universality of the religious dimension as intrinsic to human becoming. Midlife challenges and potentials offer special opportunities for human and religious development because they mark a watershed in the life cycle. To grasp this in brief compass we must return to basics.

From early childhood we are insecure, feeling threats to both physical survival and to the expansion of our potential. As finite beings, confronting death, we are anxious and fearful about realizing our selfhood. As a result, we are inclined to decide and to act on whatever appears to give us meaning, security, or pleasure. In a society of people all similarly insecure and anxious, we grasp at available means for self-realization, however destructive and enslaving for self or others. Patterns of inward and outward violence are chosen because these seem to be the only viable means to allay our primordial insecurity and anxiety. Many of these negative developments result from ignoring the special call of middle age.

We fear the call to embark on the inward journey towards a revision of self and community. Instead, we plunge ahead with the death-denying aggressiveness of youth, intent on establishing and defending our egos. Yet the invitation to reverse these tendencies is heard in the transitional challenges of middle age, affording us, if we hear this summons with responsiveness, unique opportunities for personal growth and community service. Through the negativities of this period, we learn to accept our limits, and even to transform them into occasions for spiritual growth. We come to accept a world both evil and good without losing our commitment to make it a more humane place. We begin to discover within ourselves a new center for integrating the light and the dark, consciousness and unconsciousness, the inner and the outer, past, present, and future. In brief, we are enlivened with a sense of balance, fresh purposes, and new dreams.[88] Therefore, the summons inward, to revise one's priorities and to alter one's way of being in the world, is a religious call to new levels of human-spiritual transcendence in midlife.

III

REFLECTIONS ON EARLIER YEARS AND MIDLIFE: INTERVIEWS

After examining the challenges and potentials of middle age from a conceptual viewpoint, we turn to concrete expressions. No one is born directly into midlife; we all enter this phase of the life cycle sustained, burdened, and otherwise influenced by an extensive life history. The way in which we confront and cope with the dilemmas of midlife will be in part determined by the values developed since childhood. As we have seen, this development of personal values is not a linear or cumulative process for most people. An important dimension of middle-age transitions consists in questioning earlier convictions and life scripts. Yet this same earlier formation supplies the scaffolding on which the transforming personality can be erected.

To incorporate such personal, historical aspects into this study, I interviewed twenty-two men and women during the spring and summer of 1980. These individuals, representing various religious traditions, were mostly over sixty years of age. It is important to remember, therefore, that their memories of earlier years will be marked by the feelings and insights of elderhood. They will not be as close to the experiences related as they might have been in their middle years. Yet what is lost to memory by temporal distance may be more than compensated for by the perspective gained. Moreover, the memories that last into elderhood may have been particularly significant in shaping emotional and intellectual commitments.

The persons interviewed have devoted a major part of their lives to religious reflection in their various professions. The population of interviewees was purposely limited to such persons. I hoped thereby to draw from them richer reflections on issues of religious and ethical values, since these people had done a great deal of thinking about these topics. Thus, not only is the population of interviewees intentionally narrowed, but the questions asked were also focused on value formation and development.

This chapter examines such value development under three categories: influences of youth, choices of life direction, and transitions of middle age. These life reviews illustrate a movement inward in religious growth as individuals progress toward middle age. Some of the spiritual moorings of childhood remain in all cases, even though they may be abandoned for certain periods. But the earlier religion and ethics is transformed into less moralistic and more personalized spirituality by midlife. Personal crises, as well as historical events, acting like catalytic elements, shape this process. A legitimate objection to generalizing about these cases as illustrative of a contemplative direction in midlife would be the strong, traditional religious formation in the early years of most of the interviewees. Yet, while this caution is valid, two other significant conclusions could be drawn from these life reviews. First, a similar pattern might hold true for many persons whose childhood was not as explicitly immersed in religion; for them the idioms might be different, but the outcome quite similar. Second, it is meaningful that for this group of interviewees the interiorizing of their religious life through various crises appears to have helped them cope creatively with elderhood, as will be seen in chapter six.

Childhood and Family Influences

Freud, the master of suspicion, taught us to be skeptical about memories of childhood. He pointed to the censoring activity in our unconscious processes, which manages to repress and disguise unpleasant memories. While Jung did not disagree with the partially repressive function of childhood memories, he was more favorably disposed to positive symbolism from our earliest years. Concerning the psychological value of these memories, it would be well to distinguish in general between those repressed or suppressed recollections that relate to neuroses and the memories sustained by conscious ego over many years. The latter memories may be skewed by unconscious factors, but there is no reason to discount their basic worth as indicators of past influences. Moreover, the memories that perdure into elderhood would seem to carry a special weight as formative elements in the personality.

For nearly all those interviewed, the primary matrix of religious and cultural values was their family of origin. Although these values will change in important ways by midlife and elderhood, the basic memories of religious education and moral formation are rooted in the earliest years of home environment. I use "religion" and "morals" in the broadest sense, to refer to that climate of beliefs and practices concerning God as well as the ethical expectations that flow from religious tenets and cultural mores. Dr. Jack Boozer, a professor of religion at Emory University, explicitly underscores the complexity of cultural and religious factors as they affected his childhood in a small Alabama town:[1]

> I think that in my situation I am not aware of any distinctiveness between the mores of the school, the mores of the church, the mores of the community, and the mores of the family. So religion was integrated into all of these in such a way that we were not only encouraged, we were required to attend Sunday school and church.
>
> We never had a meal without a blessing. Although we didn't stick to it rigorously, there were often evening prayers. At certain celebrations, Christmas for example, we would always read a scripture passage and have a prayer.

The same theme is echoed by Rev. Clarice Bowman, who grew up in the North Carolina mountains.[2] She was to become one of the first women to be ordained in the Methodist Church, as well as a professor of theology in various schools. Her earliest recollections of religious formation indicate immersion in a familial milieu before she rationally reflected on it:

> My parents were the most important influences on me in religious education. They had little formal education, but they were widely read and deeply involved in the little Methodist church in our town. One of the most secure, comforting kind of memories that I have is of going to church, not only in the daytime, but occasionally to evening services, with my father holding my hand. We walked together, and perhaps not one single word was said the whole time. There was a fellowship and a sense of importance about it all. I think that feeling of

importance, of being somehow of high significance to my parents caught hold of me before I could rationally interpret what was happening. And the same with my mother. One of the finest of my memories is of her singing as she washed the clothes by hand with an old washboard, and cooked, and did a million other things. We had very little in the economic realm and yet we didn't realize we had very little.

Dr. Albert Outler, outstanding emeritus professor of theology at Southern Methodist University, recalls a natural "rhythm of . . . lifestyle" as the son of an itinerant preacher in the southern states:[3]

I was born in a Methodist parsonage in Thomasville, Georgia. It was the year 1908; the atmosphere was of the eighteenth century: very warm, secure sort of Methodist pietism with a very stable home life. It included a daily discipline of prayer and Bible, and an unembarrassed discussion of the spiritual dimensions of life. There were the usual religious crises that came along in childhood and early adolescence, with the usual responses. My father was a minister, but I wasn't aiming for the ministry, not in any conscious avoidance of it, but because I was very interested at an early age in letters and had aimed at a life in literature. I suppose the most formative influence besides my parents would have been my older sister, who was very precocious and who took me on as a kind of charge. She taught me to read when I was three and a half. Then she decided that I was to be a preacher, so she would be the congregation and I would be the preacher.

Then in Sunday school, some of the congregation took a particular interest in me. I had an actual black mammy, who loved to take me to the services in the black churches. Black culture, black religious music, and black religion seems perfectly natural to me. I feel as much at home in a black church as I do in a white church. From my earliest memories all of those were important influences. We were pretty well secure in the home. We moved on a regular itinerant basis, which was the custom in the Methodist Church at that time . . . I would think that family prayer, grace at meals, and the yearly revival were highlights of my religious experience. They came within the rhythm of a lifestyle to which we were all accustomed.

Religious education is also remembered as strongly moralistic, emphasizing norms of conduct approved by one's social and ecclesiastical ambience. Dr. Earl Brewer, professor of society and religion at Emory University, notes this moral dimension stressed in rural southern culture:[4]

My father was a hard-working farmer. He had very little education. My mother was the one that I was closer to in the very early days, partly because she was at home more and she was also having additional children. So that my early memories were her taking care of me and taking care of the other children. These relationships during those very early times were ones of dependence upon them and following their rules and regulations. And I remember getting spanked when I disobeyed them, which was not infrequent, but it was not, I guess, excessive. We had no relationship to the church in these early years. I can remember only one minister visiting our home, and this was before I started to school. And I remember how excited my mother was and how concerned she was about this visit and the visit apparently didn't make any difference to anybody. It certainly didn't make any difference to me. And my memory of it is not of the minister so much as it is of my mother's embarrassment over the minister's dropping in without any notice and embarrassment over the shape of the house and things like that. And she took some of that embarrassment out on us after he left.

At home there was no instruction regarding the Bible or religious matters as such. We never had prayer that I recall at all. Of course there were moral precepts, and we participated in a fairly rigorous program of behavioral rules and expectations: being responsible, not cheating or lying, being obedient to parents; there was a good deal of stress from the whole rural culture on this.

This theme of moralism, from which he would depart in midlife, is also stressed in Boozer's early education:

The home was a place of security, and it was a place of real love. My mother's understanding of religion, and she was the main one who was religious, was predominantly moralistic. Nevertheless, she was capable of and did love and express grace; but it may well be that people who have difficulty or people who have to struggle acutely to make it or people who are involved in upward mobility tend to emphasize morality more than grace and forgiveness. We were trained to work, to study, to strive, to be honest, to be just, to be truthful. I guess that kind of morality is pretty much included in the Boy Scout laws. I was a scout. I think a lot of people would have entrusted things to me because they knew I wouldn't have thought of telling a lie. I'm not saying I never did anything deceptive. Telling the truth was an absolute value for me. I couldn't have imagined withholding the truth from somebody who asked, because that would have been a violation of my own moral integrity. The moral thing did come through in those years in terms of what kind of morality was possible for a Christian. And that tended to center, not on race relations or the use of violence, but it tended to center of what kind of words you use. You don't use bad or profane words. And in a sense I got the impression all sexuality was evil. Therefore, for me, ballroom dancing was evil because it stimulates one sexually. So the religious side of that moral education was that I could not dance.

The importance of family influence in religious formation remains constant, even though it takes on different colorations in the Protestant culture of small midwestern towns. The notes of simplicity of life and endurance of the hardships on the Nebraska prairies sound through the reflections of Anne McGrew Bennett, a leader among church women for issues concerning women and world peace:[5]

> I was born in the sandhill country of Nebraska. I suppose my earliest memories are those of a family being very much contained and sufficient of itself. We made everything. In those early years there was not even a telephone. We couldn't see any near neighbors, although there were some about two miles away. I have early memories of terrible winds through that area of western Nebraska, prairie fires that burned everything, hail storms that knocked everything out and left the ground bare. All sorts of calamities. But somehow my family always, as we used to say, made do. We survived. And along with these particular memories I have others of a very warm family, of the community coming together.
>
> The fact that my parents organized religious services in the community is one way I was introduced to moral values and religious values. I grew up taking religious services for granted, going to church several times on Sunday and several times during the week. The church was just the center of our lives. And it continued to be. When I think of those services I see my father teaching one class and my mother teaching another class. My parents were very aware of the feelings of other people too. I remember on one occasion there was a Christmas celebration for the people in the community. And before we went my mother said to us, now there will be a Santa Claus and there will be gifts, but you're not going to get gifts there. You're going to get gifts at home some time later. Well, we went to the celebration and we found that some of the families had taken very expensive gifts for their children and many other families had nothing at all. My family was aware of this and they didn't want to do anything that would set one part of a group against another.

Dr. Carroll Lemon, who served as a minister in various midwestern churches, and also as a leader in the ecumenical movement, talks about the matrix of the church and the small religious college where his father and mother were on the staff.[6] We note the balancing of maternal and paternal influences on the child: his mother supplying an ambience of love and kindness, while a stern father provided him with the best translation of the Bible. Lemon would later break with the dogmatic rigidities of his father, but he recalls how deeply rooted he was in the church when he muses on the habit of sitting in the "family pew":

> I was born in a little community around a church college, Cotner College, a college of the Disciples of Christ, which was in a suburb of Lincoln, Nebraska. So it was predominantly a religious community. My father had been business manager of the college; my mother came there to teach English. So my memories of childhood are mostly of a church and college community. One of the things that seems important is the family pew in the church, which not all families maintained, even at that time. But we did. And I always now find myself sitting in relatively the same part of the church as we sat in when I was a boy. My father was a very strong personality, and pretty dogmatic and narrow. He was an evangelist for a time before we came to this college, and he was very strong in his religious convictions. I have always said that I had a lot to be grateful for. My father, for example, was a very careful student of the scriptures, and he insisted that I should have the best translation available. I remember those were the first days of the American Standard Version. He was a strong Campbellite, and trained me in the Campbellite spirit of the Disciples of Christ. Two emphases particularly, the Disciple heritage and concern for Christian unity, were implanted in me.
>
> My mother was a very sweet spirited person, and I'd say that the emphasis in her life was love, tolerance, kindness, and forgiveness. So when people wonder why I turned out the way I did, they get started with the aggressive character of my father and forget the sweet spirit of my mother. The fact that I became a liberal and a humanist traces back to the influence of my mother.

In the reflections of Dr. Lavinia Scott, who devoted a major part of her life to the African missions as a teacher and school principal, one hears the chords of familial influence on children in a small-town setting in the midwest early in this century.[7] The themes recur: parents dedicated to each other and to the church, simplicity and frugality of life, strict disciplining of children coupled with a basic love of them, clear moral rules, and immersion in the activities of the church from early childhood:

I was born in Yankton, South Dakota, in 1907 and had a very happy childhood. I was the youngest of four children. My father was teaching at Yankton College and we were very much tied in with the life of the college as well as the life of the Congregational Church in Yankton. My father was very definitely head of the family. I think mother usually got her own way, but she did it in the traditional feminine style as well, you know, just her own winning way. She adored my father, and it was mutual. I think I got my earliest ideas of God from him really, because he was strict and yet very loving and had very stern ideas about honesty. The one almost unforgivable sin was lying. And the only punishment I really remember was for telling lies when I was a small child. We got over it fairly soon because that was, as I say, the one very strongly disapproved thing. But we had a great deal of freedom, as I look back to it. Perhaps it wasn't as much freedom as young people have in these days, but it seemed so then. I didn't feel restricted. And we were poor. My father's salary for years was $1400 a year, and out of that he tithed. So there wasn't much for frills. But we had a comfortable home; we had plenty of good food.

If we had to be disciplined, when my father would think we needed a switching with the cherry switch for having told a lie, I remember mother stood by with the tears streaming down her face, but she didn't interfere. And I guess she knew it had to be done, but it made her sad.

They were just both very much devoted to the church. We had family prayers, and there was Bible reading. I remember my father kneeling on one knee, with his other knee up; we were very small and knelt against his knee when we were having family prayers. And I think we all took part, and we always had grace at the meals. Mother was deeply religious; she was always active in the church and women's organizations at Sunday school. She loved young people and was interested in drama. Often when she had the Sunday school class, she would have them put on a play or something of that kind.

Although Dr. John C. Bennett, well-known theologian/ethicist and former President of Union Theological Seminary in New York, thought of his childhood as different from that of his wife, Anne, he expresses important similarities.[8] He misses the warmth of her family, but his grandmother seems to have provided him with motherly caring. A liberal, well-to-do eastern parish would, no doubt, have been a different environment from that of the Nebraska plains. But John Bennett's early years were also surrounded by church routines and the theological library of his father:

Well, my background was entirely different from Anne's. It was much less warm for one thing. My mother died when I was born and during the first five years of my life her mother lived with my father. There was also an aunt with us part of the time. But at any rate, my grandmother brought me up to quite an extent in those five years. And she was very warm. My mother was really her favorite and I sort of represented my mother to her. It was very obvious that was the case. My father was very reserved, but he was very loving and concerned. But it wasn't a warm atmosphere such as the atmosphere that Anne had. In other respects it was very different. I lived in a suburb of New York. My father was a minister there in Morristown, New Jersey, for twenty-three years. I always went to the church both morning and evening. I did love to hear my father preach. He influenced me more that way than other ways, I would think. Also, going into his study when he wasn't around and reading his books was very important. I don't know exactly when that began to be important. But it was very important reading the theological literature. He was a graduate of Union Seminary in New York and I never knew anything but Protestant liberalism.

The memories of Dr. Benjamin Mays, former President of Morehouse College, church leader, and long-time Chairman of the Atlanta Board of Education, recalls his early years as a black child in rural South Carolina.[9] The thoughts of this highly respected octogenarian reflect his life-long rebellion against all forms of slavery and his search for human dignity in a religious environment. The listener senses the influence of a loving mother and the importance of the black church for Mays's formative years:

I think that my life in a way was born in religion. I say that because my mother was extremely religious. She was unlettered. She never had gone to school for a day in her life. She could neither read nor write. She was born in 1863, so in a way she was born on the edge of freedom, in the year that Abraham Lincoln issued his Emancipation Proclamation. Of course, slaves were not free until the Civil War had been fought. Mother was a child of slavery. My father was born in 1856, so he was about nine years old at Emancipation time. My mother and father were religious, my mother more so than my father. We lived miles from the church, the Mt. Zion Baptist Church. We walked to church—at least I did. We had preaching once a month. The minister had four churches and he came to us on the second Sunday in the month. The school I attended was named after a white farmer, and it was located near his house. You can tell what race relations were like. They named a black school for a white man. I walked four miles to school, eight miles round trip.

My mother had morning and evening prayers. She was always

praying, particularly in the evening, and in the morning if we did not get out to farm too early. She would get down and pray, and she would pray for all of us. Mother did not have a very happy life. My father was not a heavy drinker, but, as I look back at it, he couldn't take it. When he got some whiskey in him, his eyes would sparkle and he would want to fight my mother. That meant that all of the kids just went to mother's side. Father was not too religious. He went to church on the second Sunday, but sometimes he would get with the wrong group and they would go down into the woods and drink a little liquor and come in the church after the preaching started. So when it would frighten mother, we would all protect her. I would read to mother because I felt that she was lonely in that situation. I would read the passages of scripture that I thought would console her. That is one reason why I said that I was born in religion. She believed very much that God answered prayer.

The seeds of his long career championing interracial justice can be seen in the following conversation with his mother; his aversion to inequality between the races was already pitched in a theological idiom:

I remember saying to my mother once that I did not believe that God made black people and white people different. I did not believe that he brought black people into the world to hew wood and plow with a mule. "We are the same as a white man," I said. That disturbed my mother a great deal, particularly when I said that if I thought God did that to me, I would never pray another prayer.

Dr. Lawrence Jones, Dean of the Howard University Divinity School, stressed the importance of a warm and encouraging family environment in the formation of his values as a black youngster in a West Virginia town.[10] He expressed great admiration for the integrity of his father, whose honesty as an accountant was respected by people of both races. But an overriding factor in his spiritual formation was the integral role that religion played in all the events of family life:

Religion was an integrated part of our life. It wasn't a matter of your being religious when you go to church. If something good happened in my father's store, he'd say that God did it. I remember that my sister got sick. She had double pneumonia, and mother was putting on medications. She got us all in the front room and said, "Now we are going to pray for your sister." We prayed for my sister. Some-time her fever broke and she got better. The family's understanding was that the Lord did that . . . God did that. When I was going to college, they said that the Lord would take care of that. So there was nothing in our life that God was not agent in. We would do our part, but God was a living reality in our lives. In algebraic terms, he was the known quantity. Life provided the unknown quantity; God was the known quantity.

Among older Catholics whose lives as religious professionals or as lay persons were immersed in spiritual concerns, the family is also cited as the principal source of values. However, there is often a greater stress placed on the influence of the parish church and school than among Protestant interviewees. Perhaps it would be more accurate to focus on Catholic schooling as the main point of difference. The following three reflections on childhood bring out the importance of the Catholic school. Sister Anita Caspary remembers the total environment of a Franciscan parish and school that surrounded her childhood.[11] Dr. Caspary, who taught English at Immaculate Heart College, went on to become the Mother Superior of her order and led a large contingent of her nuns into new styles of Christian living after a long controversy with the Cardinal of Los Angeles. She notes the close intermixing of family, priests, and nuns; she also underplays moralism in her early formation:

Our whole background was intensely religious. The sisters were Franciscan Sisters and the fathers were of course Franciscan Fathers. The Franciscan Sisters couldn't, but the priests dropped in for dinner regularly, and we were good friends with them. We just lived that kind of life. The church had statues all over the place, and a great number of devotions to various saints: St. Anthony and other Franciscan saints. We could identify all the statues. Feasts Days were immensely celebrative. Moralistic education was not emphasized. There was a great atmosphere of love. I can remember sermons on the mystical body and the love that we should have for each other, on the brother-and-sister relationship that we should have within the church itself. There was a feeling that if you were outside, you were outside. There was a kind of protective wall out there against that world which was not Catholic. I think that in the whole religious way that I looked at life there was a constant feeling of presence of God. I lived and moved in that atmosphere. I suspect that my brothers and sisters did too. We didn't discuss it, as we were a private family in respect to religion.

Fr. William Monihan, S.J., formerly director of the library, and now a development officer at the University of San Francisco, recalls a typical background for Catholic youths who entered the priesthood.[12] Various traits of this environment would be a stable, caring, and religiously observant (by at least one parent) family, involvement in parochial school and/or Catholic high school, and participation in the life of the parish church. To this traditional matrix, Monihan adds the importance of scouting in his upbringing:

> I was born in a very average family in this very average economic bracket, perhaps on the lower side of middle class. The major influence was home. I guess that is true of most people. My mother was, I think, the greatest influence on me. My mother's time to pursue other things than the family and the house was very limited. But she did always have the curiosity to learn. I began to read as a youngster, but not as much in retrospect as I would have liked to. But I was inclined towards books and reading from the very beginning. However, my mother, since I was a little boy, encouraged me to go out and be with boys my same age, play games, and all of that. The Boy Scouts was a major influence in my life. It was a very considerable influence on me in terms of the finer things in life. I am not speaking of cultural things, but the finer things of civic, moral life. I received all my basic training in religion from the Holy Family Sisters at Holy Cross Church in San Francisco. We did not have an active parish life at all. But my mother and father were very strict as far as going to Mass and going to confession at certain intervals and going to communion.

While the following two persons did not attend Catholic grammar schools exclusively, the overall influence of family and church strongly affected their religious formation. Fr. Daniel O'Hanlon, S.J., a widely published theologian and professor at the Jesuit School of Theology in Berkeley, California, notes an incident of strict observance so characteristic of many Catholics in the pre-Vatican II era:[13]

> My main source of values was certainly the home. Perhaps my parents were a little bit overstrict in a legalistic way, but that was not unusual at that time, especially for English and Irish Catholic parents. I can remember, for instance, the time of my first communion. I accidentally scooped up a handful of crumbs on my way out of the kitchen and put them into my mouth on the way to church. There was no question about the fact that there was no possibility about my making my first communion with the group because I had broken the fast.

Along with this went a very strong observance of church laws: Sunday mass, confession once a week, all those sorts of things.

Sister Mary Luke Tobin, a national leader among American nuns and a well-respected person in the ecumenical movement, remembers a loving family situation in a Catholic atmosphere.[14] Her father was not a practicing Catholic, but she emphasizes the early impact of kindly women who taught her catechism. The experience of a loving home seems to have made possible her positive outlook toward a benevolent God:

> We were brought up in the Catholic faith. My father was not very practicing, as we used to say, but he was a Catholic from birth. Their parents had come from Ireland on both sides. They kept the faith, and I, therefore, grew up in a Catholic atmosphere . . . I was thinking of my mother's faith pattern and remembered that one of her favorite scripture quotations was "Lord, I believe, help thou my unbelief." That showed the two aspects of her faith, doubt and assurance; this was a very real inheritance for me and something very good.
>
> I remember catechism classes. And I remember some sisters and some laywomen because we were a new parish in a new part of town, and therefore we didn't have sisters at first. So my earliest instructions were from kindly women. So I went through the regular first communion and confirmation classes and all. We did not have a Catholic school in that area, and therefore all the Catholics had to be excused from public school to go to instructions.
>
> If I have any kind of healthy self-image or self-concept, it is certainly because both parents gave it to me. I came at a time in their marriage that was very good, too. They had had a son, and they surely wanted a daughter. I knew that I was loved. I pushed that sometimes as far as I could. Without ever explicitly voicing it, I knew it.

The author of important books in church history and the dean of American Catholic historians, Msgr. John Tracy Ellis recalls growing up Catholic in a family of mixed church traditions.[15] Tensions between Catholics and Protestants were evident both within his wider family and in the careful avoidance of the worship of other churches. His mother's Irish Catholicism manifested both strict observance of church rules and a quaint sense of the immediacy of God's protecting presence:

> I was born of a father of English Protestant tradition and a mother of Irish Catholic tradition. My father was a Republican and my

mother was a Democrat, so the house was divided on these matters, although it was a basically happy home. Although my father was baptized a Methodist, he did not practice as such, but my grandmother Ellis was a devout Methodist. After my grandfather's death in 1914, she used to live part of the year with us. During those months one of the things I had to do was to drive her to church. I can remember my mother saying one Sunday morning, "It is time now to drive your grandmother to church, but do not go beyond the door." There was no ecumenism at that time as far as we were concerned. My mother was very correct in her religious life, although I would not call her deeply devout. I say she was "correct" in the sense that she would not dream of missing Mass on Sundays and holy days, nor would she let my brother and me miss Mass. In a word, mother showed all the characteristics of traditional Irish Catholicism, which was her inheritance. Thinking of mother's traditional Catholicism, there comes to mind an incident that happened years and years ago. It was a summer night that brought a sudden thunderstorm. I was awakened by the thunder and lightning, and I remember my mother going about in the dark with the holy water bottle, sprinkling it on us, and hearing my father call out to her—Ida was her name but he always called her "Ide"— "Ide, what in the name of God are you doing?" It was only one of the many strange happenings that the good Protestant had to put up with from his Catholic wife!

Mother's faith was altogether real, as I have said. When I think of her having told me of grandfather Murphy on occasion walking into town from their farm on a winter Sunday morning, five miles through the snow, it helped to impress on my mind the depth of faith to which my mother and her brothers and sisters—there were twelve of them—were heirs, an inheritance which she passed on to me, thank God.

It is particularly interesting to note how a convert to Catholicism in midlife carries with her a mystic sensibility that has its roots in the Christian Science movement of her childhood memories. Louisa Jenkins, a highly esteemed artist of Carmel, California, came to her conversion through many sufferings, and after exploring various spiritual routes.[16] Her beautiful scroll works, while portraying eastern and western unitive influences, are also in continuity with her childhood recollections of the close interlinking of matter and spirit according to the teaching of Mrs. Eddy and the intuition of her own mother. In the following excerpt, we detect the direction of her whole life as an artistic vocation to heal destructive splitting within and outside of ourselves:

My mother became a Christian Scientist, and I was brought up in Christian Science. Now, this is more like our present attitude in the scientific world. We're always talking about the transformation of consciousness from matter into spirit. If you go back and read some of the things that Mrs. Eddy said, they're very much like Capra, the physicist, today. So this was more of a pattern—not seeing it so much in a linear way as seeing it in a pattern. I went to Sunday school. My father just sneered at it. He didn't even believe in an afterlife. He was an atheist. So, you see, religion to me is your glue that holds you together underneath. And with this confusion of the very religious, intuitive mother and the opposite in my father, you can see how this made a split in the family.

Perhaps the clearest examples of preconceptual religious formation come from Jewish respondents. Rabbi Aaron Blumenthal denies any "beginning" to his religious education. Blumenthal, whose long career in the rabbinate culminated in the presidency of a national association of rabbis, portrays a kind of total immersion from childhood in Jewishness in both a religious and an ethnic sense:[17]

The only thing wrong with the question as you put it is the assumption that my religiousness had a beginning. Now, both of my grandparents came from Europe approximately at the beginning of the twentieth century. My father came from Russia; my mother came from Romania. My parents kept a Jewish home. That meant that the home was kosher, that my father arose in the morning to recite his prayers, and to do so he put on something called *tefellin*. And if by any chance he tried not to recite his prayers, not to wear his *tefellin*, my mother just wouldn't give him his breakfast. It was a strictly observant Jewish home. All the ritual that one can imagine was observed in the home. So was I doing anything religious? Yes, of course! I was observing Jewish ritual. Did I identify it as religious? No, I was just doing what a Jewish boy ought to do. That's all. There was no "beginning." My mother's father was a very pious Jew and a very learned Jew, of whom I think my mother stood in some awe. He set certain patterns for her.

The home continued with every Jewish custom and ceremony observed. I got up in the morning, and before I could read I was expected to recite. For a Jewish child in the morning there are two or three lines of prayer that you recite. You sit down to eat, you're expected to cover your head and you're expected to recite the blessing. You don't know what it means, but your mother teaches it to you and you say it. You go to the bathroom, you come out, you wash your hands, you recite a benediction. And we lived in a neighborhood that was practically a ghetto. There were only a few non-Jews around, but basically we lived in a strictly Jewish neighborhood. Some of the people were beginning to change, but, in my case, most of the people around us were observant Jews like my parents. It would have been unthinkable, for instance, for anybody in the neighborhood to go out and buy some pork. Just unthinkable. I went to Hebrew school and I loved it. As I think back I imagine that my teacher, who we called the "rebbe," was a sloppy old guy who had a stick, and he used to bang us up a little bit every once in a while. But we spent . . . three hours a day there. When I reached the age of ten, I began spending four hours a day after public school studying this whole vast treasure house of Jewish learning: the Bible, rabbinic literature, and, of course, I believed implicitly that this came directly from God. And if I were to do my homework on Saturday afternoon, it would be an awful sin.

Some who grow up in an orthodox religious context do not continue to observe the practices or hold the tenets of their religion. Many variables of personality and circumstance conspire to incline persons away from an intense religious upbringing. Some rebel for a period and then return, often to a revised form of religiousness, while others reject traditional religions for the rest of their lives. The first type of rebellion will be seen in the lives of some of these interviewees. The second form of rejection can indirectly affect an observant parent who is saddened by the religious apathy of a son or daughter. Rabbi Simon Greenberg, professor of education and homiletics at Jewish Theological Seminary in New York City, will reflect on the latter situation in his own life.[18] Greenberg's childhood was deeply involved in Jewish practices and thought from his earliest days in a Ukrainian village:

My memory goes back hazily, but with sufficient clarity, to the town, the little village in which our family lived in the Ukraine under the Czar in Russia. My father had served in the Russian army for four years, but when the Russian-Japanese War broke, he did not feel like fighting for the Czar. He had a wife and three children at the time, so he therefore made his way to the States. It took him about a year or a year and a half to save up the money required to bring my mother, her sister, and three children to the States. We came here and lived in a small village in the Catskill Mountains called Woodridge. There were two books that I became acquainted with very early in my life. The first was the Hebrew prayerbook, the daily prayerbook. The second was the five books of Moses. My father and mother were Sabbath observers. Our home was kosher. My father was not a theologian in any sense; he was not a religious professional in any sense. He was a hard working man, a laborer who had some special ability in wine-making . . . we lived a very, very modest life.

By the age of thirteen, I got into the habit of praying every morning. My parents never had to ask me to do it. I loved the prayerbook. My father was active in arranging for a Hebrew teacher to come into town and the building of a Hebrew school. I studied every afternoon. I attended the synagogue's services in town every Saturday. I liked to come and join the people with their prayers in the morning. Saturday afternoons were particularly impressive, because in those days there was no electricity, so there were no lights burning during the day on Saturday in the synagogue. We would come to the afternoon service, and between the afternoon service and the evening service, as the day was setting, it was always a romantic period. On occasion, the youngsters would play hide-and-go-seek in the dark, among the benches. But on many occasions one could sit and just feel the day setting, or we would have one of the vegetable dealers in town who would get up on the platform, and we would recite certain specific Psalms. He would recite a verse, and we would answer responsively. By the time that I was thirteen, I knew my prayerbook almost by heart. I knew fully the content of the five books of Moses in Hebrew. I could read them; I understood my prayers. I had come very much to forming a habit of observing the Sabbath without feeling that it was a burden, and without having any friends that were Sabbath observers—even in that small town.

Mrs. Sylvia Heschel, pianist, teacher of piano, and widow of the famous Jewish thinker Abraham Heschel, speaks of a home environment in which the spiritual radiance of her mother would make the meaning of the Sabbath come alive:[19] "In my childhood I was undoubtedly affected by my parents' religious beliefs. These were manifest in their thinking and their actions. I recall my mother's joy when she returned from synagogue services; it seemed to light up our home."

Crisis, Conversion, and Life Direction

In the following section we look closer at concrete events that helped to shape the life paths of the interviewees. Crises of faith may have included family problems or intellectual challenges; conversions could be sudden or gradual, but they typically involve an intensely emotional religious memory. All of these happenings play a role in the choice of life directions. Although the formation of religious convictions has intellectual content, the actual moments of high dedication involve the whole person in an emotional and voluntary way. With most of the interviewees such occurrences were "episodic," in the words of John Bennett, but their importance in fashioning a vocational direction can be seen in the lasting impact they leave in memory:

> At Williams College I was quite active in the Christian Association. I remember going at least twice to a Buchman (later Oxford groups) house party. And you asked Anne about conversion. I don't know whether you would be quite correct to call it conversion, but I had several episodes approaching that. Especially these weekend house parties, but also going to conferences, sometimes at Silver Bay, of the Student Christian movement. . . . They were very important for me. People like Henry Sloane Coffin and Harry Emerson Fosdick and Sherwood Eddy and, yes, John R. Mott were there sometimes. Those were very great experiences for me, those student conferences. And I don't think liberals have anything like that now. They were important, yes they were. Episodic conversions that were very important.

In a remembered scene of marvelous intensity, Rabbi Blumenthal delineates the experience of a young Jewish boy who is swept up in the tears, feeling, and meaning of three generations in his observant family. It is as though the whole religious experience of Judaism is caught up for him in the chanting voices of his grandfather, father, and uncles. After fifty years in the rabbinate, no event quite matched its intensity:

> I remember a story which is very characteristic. My grandfather was an amateur cantor; he would chant the services. He died at the age of ninety-four, which was the year of my Bar Mitzvah, so of course I did not know him very well. But I have some very vivid recollections of my grandfather. He used to conduct services on the High Holy Days. He had three sons. The three sons served as his choir. They never rehearsed. They simply went up to the pulpit and they sang the service. And by coincidence one of them was a baritone, one of them was a tenor, and the other one was a bass. And as the grandchildren grew older, we used to sing with them. It might begin, say, at eight o'clock in the morning, and it did not end until after sunset. It is divided into three parts . . . my grandfather would begin, say, at about eight-thirty or nine o'clock, and he would conduct the service until about three or four o'clock. The last time he did it, as I say, he was ninety-four years old. And in the course of that prayer there comes a

moment when he spreads his hands and says, "Almighty and powerful God, grant me success in my prayer," and he would burst into tears. My father seeing his father in tears would break into tears himself, and so would his brothers. And what would happen to me? I saw my grandfather, my uncles, and my father. And I as a little child, maybe of eleven or twelve, would also weep with my grandfather and with my father. It's very difficult to describe the impact of that experience, but let me tell you, there's been nothing like it in my life ever since and I've conducted this service myself for fifty years in the rabbinate.

In a significant contrast to Blumenthal's experience, Clarice Bowman vividly recalls a classic Protestant revival that marked a turning point in her youth. In its holistic intensity the event is similar to the Jewish experience, but it is different in two important ways. The most marked difference concerns the need to feel sinful as a prerequisite to conversion. Secondly, she is initiated into the community of the converted as an individual, rather than as a member of a multigenerational family:

There were revivals going on. And I had a cousin way up in the mountains where my father grew up, but she was two years older than I. Still, we both adored music and played hymns and had a wonderful time. We would go to revivals and take turns pumping the old organs because when you pumped through one verse you were really winded. So she'd take over, and we would help each other back and forth. Sometimes there'd be three or four invitation hymns. And then there came a time when I was around twelve and I thought "my goodness, this invitation means me." Suddenly the thought came that the minister was talking to me. Was I ready to make any sort of decision? And I kept on for a while wondering what in the world people meant by conversion and salvation and all that. It was as if it were something I had to go through. But it was not at all clear. But I was under some sort of cloud. I felt I was wicked. And for four days I couldn't see color. Everything was black and white. I mean there was just no color. I was just so far down in my pit of wickedness. I needed so much. While I was feeling so badly I said to my cousin very timidly if she had been converted. In her two years seniority over me she said, "good night, haven't you been converted yet?" On a Sunday morning it was bright and beautiful, and when the choir sang, I went forward and gave the minister my hand. It was kind of an ecstasy experience in a sense. But I didn't have an understanding of what was going on really, seriously. But I felt, now I'm over the line, into this group who are saved for eternity. Just like that. I've had many, many backslidings since then! That's part of the Methodist doctrine. But it was difficult to talk to my parents about it. In some ways they were deeper. They didn't need words for understanding. I think they knew how I felt.

You know, the revivals were a great social occasion for the mountain people. Some of the dear sisters would get to shouting. Pretty soon I felt the contagion and it dawned on me, too, that I could shout. And, oh boy, I could outshine the others. I didn't know what it was all about, but it was part of a group contagion. And later I realized, when I was going at it theologically, that such things are cultural in a sense. Now, those people didn't roll in the aisles. The women just shouted and threw their arms in the air. But then a sober thought came afterwards that some of those who shouted most in those meetings, I knew were not such saints in their daily living.

Doubts becloud faith at various stages of the life cycle. Bowman's crisis of belief came in a Bible class at Duke University, where the simpler tenets of her mountain upbringing "went out the window" by which she was sitting. More important than the two-year stretch of doubt, however, is the reflection on what kept her in the church. It was not intellectual reasoning primarily, but rather her singing with the choir in a local church. This seems to underline again the holistic and communal basis of religious conviction:

The first day I sat in a class on Bible at Duke. I had so much anticipation for the time when I would get to that point, and the Bible seemed the most imporant course. And the professor began by saying, "You probably think that the world was made in six days. Well, I'm here to tell you that it wasn't." He had a twisted mouth; he spoke out of the corner. I'm sitting by a window. And my religion went out the window. At that moment I experienced all the doubts, the questions, even rebellions that had been, maybe, gathering a head of steam. But I thought, well, this professor must know. Therefore, I must trust what he says. Not anything like that ever happened before. And for two years I walked around like a zombie, with no faith whatever. It was that sudden. I guess for many it isn't. I tried to pass the course, but it was agony. Actually, he was not the kind of professor who explained things or what led up to his making that statement. Later he tried to fill in, but I was already gone. I knew that if I couldn't believe the Bible, I couldn't believe . . . I had to believe what he said, therefore, I couldn't believe the Bible. But I didn't dare tell my father and mother that I'd lost all my religion.

I stayed in the choir at Trinity Church in Durham. I mean, I just had to be in that choir; I just had to sing. And by going to the worship services there and being in the choir, regardless of whether I believed a word of it or not, I would sing and enjoy it. After a time some of the meaning of the worship service there began to coalesce with my earlier, more wholesome experience. So that without rationally figuring it all out and telling my emotions what to feel, I was brought back into the tide. And after two years I began to realize that I hadn't lost it all. I still could pray. It was the choir that held me.

Sylvia Heschel also speaks of religious inspiration through music. Revelation as a teaching became understandable to her because of her prior experience of being inspired at the piano. Heschel's reflection emphasizes an experiential readiness for the content of religion achieved through the holistic event of music:

> The experience of both playing and listening to music deepened my religious beliefs. There was the experience of inspiration in playing, and there were the exalted moments of listening to inspired playing. There is more within a human being than one can sustain or conceptualize. One can believe because of these moments.

In the following conversion experience, we find typical elements that lead to an altar call in the evangelical tradition. But Earl Brewer's resistance to further induction into a particular church brings out the needed interplay between the holistic emotionality stressed above and the role of critical intellect in religious matters. Only in such a dialogue between mind and heart can thoughtless adherence be avoided and a more refined, personal conviction be built:

> I started attending the Methodist church in that community when I was in the eleventh grade, but in that same community I had a conversion experience in the Baptist church. They were having a revival meeting and this was the standard expectation in the community. And I attended the services there with some of the young people who attended our services. I think as I recall the experience it was a fairly typical emotional revivalistic setting. The minister was very persuasive in his preaching, and painted a fairly vivid picture of hell and how small a disobedience could lead you there. And I was aware of the fact that I told a few lies and I had disobeyed my parents and I had engaged in activities with young people that he was talking about. And I was emotionally upset and became rather tensed up over my reflection on myself and my situation in relation to his preaching. So it was after I'd heard him about twice, I think, that I responded to an altar call along with some other friends. And following that I felt a good

deal better. It was a catharsis and a real emotional release to have gone through this experience.

In the discussions with him that same week, the pressure then moved from getting me down to the altar to getting me to join the church. And in the discussions with him I began to sense a sort of single-mindedness, or as I really thought of it, a narrow-mindedness, and an excessive urging me to join the church. And I resisted there. My educational background had not included any religious instruction in a formal way, but I'd done a good deal of reading. So I was not ready to close off certain areas of my experience, and I felt that if I followed his single-minded intensity about joining the church and becoming one of them, that might happen. I remember I was very much emotionally upset over this because he had been the person whose call I had answered to go down to the altar. And, therefore, I felt strongly inclined to do what he wanted me to do. But I did resist it and I did talk to the Methodist pastor when he came around on the circuit to preach for us, and I decided to join the Methodist Church.

Family crises also provoke religious insight and decision. For Clarice Bowman, the death of a sister presented the problem of the justice of God. What kind of God would allow such a lovely child to die? Theodicy questions of this type cause some to reject traditional beliefs, but Bowman found herself strengthened through the trial after the experience of her father's scripture reading. She was able to place the loss in a wider context of God's purposes:

> When I was twelve years old, one of my sisters died. And at the time of her death I was trying to figure out what kind of a God would allow such a beautiful little girl to go. I tried to pray, but couldn't quite. The kind of prayers I'd heard ministers use at church and the kind of prayers that occasionally the Sunday school teachers used and the prayer that was surging in my own heart—it was hard to get them together. Hard to make a real prayer. But I think I was not resenting God, not saying "why" in anger, but rather there was something so much bigger than I could understand going on in her death, which was the first death I had ever encountered close up. And my father at that morning when she had died during the night brought us all together and opened the Bible to the Book of Revelation, chapter 22. And how he had the background or knew or somehow sensed to use that particular place, I don't know. But it meant something shining and wonderful, almost carrying me beyond the sense of just loss, which, of course, is poignant. But to something greater. A sense of a greater plan, somehow. When my father read this, even though I couldn't understand the words, it was the picture, it was the sense of a greater ongoing being.

Rabbi Greenberg reflects on a similar family trauma, when his wife faced death shortly after the birth of their first child. In such situations the usual consolations fall away and one is reduced to bedrock resources. For Greenberg, the Psalms became the only instrument by which he could cling to meaning in religion. He enters into a major theme of the psalmists: the prayer of faith in adversity. He goes on to discuss religious doubt as indispensable in the rhythm of faith and unbelief; Job and Ecclesiastes instruct him on crises of faith:

> When our first son was born, Mrs. Greenberg developed septicemia, which in those days made her chances of coming through very slight. I remember clearly that the only place that I could find any kind of strength . . . for weeks she was unconscious . . . was by reading the Psalms. It was the only literature that I could read that in any way served me. I have been a lover of Psalms ever since. That has been for me a kind of paradigmatic experience. I have had serious times later, but during those weeks when her life was hanging in the balance, the only thing that I could do and the only place that I could find any strength in addition to my regular prayers, was in the Psalms. I happen to believe that God hears prayer. I don't pray to "whomever it may concern." I think that prayer makes no sense without believing . . . I use the word believing because we don't know.
>
> The other thing that ought to be mentioned is that very early I became acquainted with Job and with Ecclesiastes. There is really nothing that anybody has ever said since in attacking the religious point of view that hasn't been said in those two books. To me, it was always a marvel that the rabbis included those two books in scripture. I think they showed as great a genius for religion by including them as the prophets did in what they said. I think that it is the only religious tradition where all the arguments that could be mustered against God are right there. What could you say that Job did not say? What could you say that Ecclesiastes did not say? So, I did not have to go to the philosophers for doubt. It is there. It doesn't take a great deal of philosophy to recognize that the human mind is so constructed that you can't possibly think white without thinking black. If you do, you are on your way either to insanity or to fanaticism. The ability to doubt is indispensable to one who wants to remain a believer without going insane or becoming a fanatic.

Family crises that impinge on religious belief are stimulated not only by illness and death, but also by psychological conflicts between parents and children. Dr. Helen Hole, a retired teacher of literature and provost at Earlham College, remembers a classic confrontation with her powerful father that helped to eliminate for some time her adherence to Quakerism and to institutional religion in general:[20]

> I went to Vassar College. Now the picture begins to change because this is when my rebellion began. My father was a very powerful personality, really very powerful. And I have a fairly strong personality myself. I began slowly and very gradually to realize that I was going to have to disentangle myself from my father if I was ever going to become a person of my own.
>
> At the same time I became rebellious about religion. I decided that religion, institutionalized religion, was not for me. I was through with it. No more interest in it . . . Vassar in the 1920s prided itself on not accepting any ideas of anybody else. You had to do all your own thinking. I never rejected the idea of God. I always thought there was a God. But I didn't think he had any connection with this game of institutionalized religion. So I didn't really reject religion exactly. I disassociated myself from the expression of it, including my Quaker forebears.

There seems to have been a twofold movement in her return to deeper religious convictions. On the one hand, she met her future husband, who probably aided in her process of separating from psychic entanglements with her father. And on the other hand, an unusual encounter with the writings of Catholic mystics inclined her to find again the roots of mysticism in her own Quaker tradition. The mystic dimension also seemed to counterbalance the critical rationalism of her Vassar experience:

> My husband was very important in my development. He was a very religious man and he'd grown up in a very religious family . . . much more so than mine. He was much more interested in the institution of religion. He wanted to work within the church. And this didn't fit with my preconceived ideas. So we had this adjustment to make before we got married. One of the chief reasons we made it was that, before I fell in love with him, I'd begun to get tremendously interested in the mystics. This was after college was all over, and I thought I didn't believe in religion, institutional religion at least. I came across a book, the autobiography of Mme. Gruyon, which, as I learned afterwards, is a rather inferior manifestation of mysticism. I read everything by St. Teresa that I could find; and John of the Cross, St. Francis, Brother Lawrence, all sorts of books by mystics.
>
> And then a very strange thing happened. I had to go to meeting because I was teaching in a Quaker school. They didn't tell us we had to

go, but we all knew that we really should go. So I always went to meeting. I was sitting in meeting and it suddenly came to me, this is the same thing! I'd never made any connection before. The idea of the mystics was that you can come into contact with the spirit of God. That's what we were doing in Friends meeting, or trying to. Well, that was the moment in which the thing began to move. That had happened before I fell in love with this man. And so we were able to proceed from there.

Louisa Jenkins recounts her youthful break with a dominating father that was also connected with the abandonment of her Christian Science religion. The rebellion against her past during the turmoil of American involvement in World War I propelled her into a personal image that she characterizes as "hard" and "selfish":

> Before going to school I remember going to a Saturday art class. My father said, you can't make a living at it, you can't be an artist. At that time it was a fear, I suppose, on his part that I wouldn't be able to support myself. It wasn't a thing that women did, you see. Society was still sexist. So he said you can either marry or become a school teacher. Well, I rebelled and ran away from home. That was the end of that. This was during the second year of college, at the time of the First World War. Then, my Christian Science religion disappeared, too. I had no formal religion then until I was baptized a Catholic later in life.
>
> My sweetheart went off to war, and that was the end of that, you see. It was grief, it was separation, it was this war to end wars. He returned after the war, but then I was too different. There were those years of separation and I'd gone through all sorts of things. And so had he. I had to go through a very immoral sort of a period. And he came back and he saw this lovely virgin was no longer a lovely virgin. I was a hard, selfish person who was going to succeed, who was going to make money, to make a success, with a terrific *animus* drive.

The choice of a life direction or career is undoubtedly the result of many influencing factors. But when the interviewees are asked to underscore the most significant elements or persons that drew them on a particular vocational path, some cite social issues, others focus on interpersonal influences, while others remember very personal moments or convictions. John Bennett, who teaches and writes extensively on Christian social ethics, recalls the impact of World War I, as it was filtered through the preaching and writing of liberal Protestant leaders:

I became more interested in social issues on my own. And I date that pretty much from about 1912, the time of the election. I was in favor of Roosevelt, as my father was. But in 1916 my father was very much opposed to Wilson and I was in favor of Wilson. I remember that was one difference. I had read a good deal way back in those days of the things that were said by the kinds of preachers I admired. Henry Sloane Coffin (later president of Union Seminary) was one of them. Dr. Charles E. Jefferson was another. He wrote a book on international peace. I read lots of these things about war written by our leaders in Protestantism. This was before the First World War began. And I can remember being very hostile to the preparedness movements, very much like the kind of thing going on now. My father, during the First World War, spent quite a long time working in the military YMCA in Camp Upton. He was very much for the war. I don't think I was very much against it at that time. I can't remember that I was. But I do remember now the horrifying effects of the headlines in those days, headlines about casualties. A headline would speak of one hundred thousand casualties. This would be true day after day.

In a similar vein, the Depression of the 1930s and the lot of the poor in the South were formative in shaping the social-justice orientation of Earl Brewer. His antiwar feelings also began as a child during the First World War:

The Depression influenced my values. I did then and I still do identify my interests primarily with the powerless. For example, when we were in Atlanta in the thirties there was a developing Communist movement in the South, among blacks and farmers, poor farmers, sharecropper-type farmers such as we were. There was a group like that on the campus. I identified with that group, not in a leadership way, but in a fellowship way. My opposition to the racial barriers at college was a part of that. I can remember my antiwar feeling developing back in the First World War, when I was just a preschooler. I became a conscientious objector while I was in college and joined the Fellowship of Reconciliation. I was very much interested in social problems. I remember, for example, that during that period Emory University owned a lot of property in the downtown area. Some of this was commercial property that had been given by the Candlers at one stage or another. But a lot of it was housing, and a lot of this housing was just slum housing. We went down and visited some of these slums. Some of the stories that developed out of that concerned the really pathetic conditions that people, mostly blacks and poor whites, were living under in Emory housing. It was just inconceivable.

One of the most dramatic memories of events that marked a life direction came from Benjamin Mays, whose long career as a black churchman, educator, and civil rights leader began in rural South Carolina in the last century. He discusses the necessarily muted, but very real movement among slaves for freedom. In this context, he recalls the humiliation of his father before the guns of a mob:

> Most of the ministers that I heard had to preach something to enable the Negroes to endure. So they would go to the field and sing, "You got shoes / I got shoes / All of God's children got shoes / One of these days gonna put on the shoes / And I gonna shout over God's heaven," or "Swing low sweet chariot / Coming for to carry me home." The masters interpreted that to mean that the Negroes were happy. But they were fooling the masters. They were looking forward to the time when God was going to free them. Whether you call it God or not, it did bring on a great Civil War and the Negroes were freed. They might have done as the Indians and fought back. They would have been annihilated. Most slaves that tried to pull off an uprising and fight their way were destroyed. In other words, Negroes never did accept slavery. They were fighting in the only way that they could fight.
>
> At the age of four I saw my first mob, where a group of white men were riding on horseback, their guns on their shoulders, on their way to the Phoenix riot. Everybody in the county was going up to Phoenix, about four miles from Greenwood, to lynch Negroes, because there was a Republican man named Tolbert there who was trying to get Negroes to vote. He would take a Negro to the balloting with him, and they were being refused. What happened was that they shot this man, and they blamed it on the black people. So that started the riot. They came from everywhere because these Negroes were uprising against white people. Our house was by the side of the road and white and black people would pass by. I saw the mob make father get down and bow before them with their guns drawn; they made him do it two or three times. I remember that as if it were yesterday . . . that was in 1898. I was born in 1894 and I was four years old when I was a witness to it. I prayed. I would hitch my mule to a tree and go down in the woods and pray. The essence of that prayer was asking God to help me to get an education. At night I would go out under the moonlight and I would pray the same prayer.

Other interviewees highlight interpersonal factors in molding their decisions to pursue life in the ministry. Mary Luke Tobin remembers an English teacher and a parish priest who were influential in her choice to enter the sisterhood. She also notes the rightness in retrospect of such a vocation for her:

> I made the decision for a religious life, to enter the convent, in my senior year in high school. Since I had decided that rather suddenly, my mother very wisely said to me, "You have just now made your mind up on this. It would be foolish for you to do this now. Give college a chance." So I did . . . that is why I went to college for two years. I really went the first year because she asked me to. Then she said, "stay another year." And I did. But I never changed my mind because I knew that was what I was going to do. I think it's good that I had those two years afterwards. What happened was that, as I always remember, my mother went to Mass during Lent. When I was a senior, I remember that that became important to me. I began to go to Mass. The decision was only after that kind of regular attendance. Also, I think that I had a very outstanding English teacher in high school who was Catholic and who introduced me to literature of an absolutely unbelievable range. There was a kind of coming together for me of those values, an appreciation for Catholic writers that I had not had before. Then I had this outstanding pastor that I was telling you about, who was certainly an influence in my life. I remember a sermon that he gave in which he said . . . it was Good Friday and I remember him saying, "There is the Redeemer, both arms extended, everything given. How reluctant we are to give even a little." That was a clear influence in my decision. When I look back on my life, and I think about my decision, it was a very right one, I believe. I haven't regretted it. I have had a full and a rich life. Suppose the circumstances were other, I might have married. I was just as attracted to boys as the other people in my class were. The oldest memory I have about that is saying to myself, "Okay, I know what this means to be a nun. I know that I won't have somebody's arms around me. I am going to do it." I don't know what that says, but I have a clear memory of that.

Anita Caspary, who was to follow her most influential mentor as Mother General of the order, remembers the nun who most deeply influenced her decision to become a sister. Sister Eucharia seems to have typified the spirit of other women in that order:

> I went to a Catholic college because of the family tradition of having Catholic education as far as possible. But when I went to the days sponsored for recruitment, I met this most unusual woman, Sister Eucharia, who was perhaps the strongest single influence in my life outside family. She was Dean of Women at that point. She was so out-

going, so warm, and so friendly. The other thing I noticed about Immaculate Heart College was that the nuns were different. They were all very individual; they were all personalities. There weren't many sisters because not very many had been sent to graduate studies during the Depression. Those who were sent on appeared on a day like that and got acquainted with us. It was an all-day program. They were very free.

Sister Eucharia was always trying to bring me out of myself, so to speak. Any talent that I had she was for developing to the fullest. She was for all of the girls going to all of the dances, that kind of thing. She was always pushing us out into public events. I felt that if I could be a nun like Sister Eucharia, who later was the Mother General, I would be very happy in that kind of life. I also loved to teach, and I knew that from having taught her classes when she was ill. I knew that part of it was good. Also, I think that even though I set it aside for a couple of years of college and went out a great deal and tried to forget the whole thing, I always knew intuitively that was what I wanted to do.

It is interesting to recognize that such important choices are less the result of some rational calculation than the outcome of following an inner, intuitive vector. In addition to the influential women, Caspary says that she "always knew intuitively that was what I wanted to do." So also, William Monihan, who attributes his vocation largely to the influence of Jesuit teachers, claims that "God directs us without our knowing it":

The Jesuit scholastics at St. Ignatius High School had the greatest influence on the direction of my life. Scholastics are seminarians, young men in the middle twenties, who teach the high school boys. They are very young fellows, and they did everything with us: played ball, went on picnics with us, and did everything that we did. So these men who are still in their training as Jesuits were of tremendous influence on me. One time when I attended St. Ignatius Church with my mother, she said that she would like me to join the Sanctuary Society, which is an altar boy society. So in my sophomore year I joined the Sanctuary Society. In this way, I got to know better the scholastics, the young seminarians. That was of tremendous value to me . . . in my junior and senior years of high school, I decided to join the Jesuits. It might be helpful to know that at my present age, nearly sixty-six, I think that God directs us without our knowing it. So one arrives at a certain spot and looks back and says, "Oh, how did that happen?" I do not feel that God taps you on the shoulder and says, "This way rather than that way." One goes almost blindly. How otherwise can a seventeen-year-old boy proceed, except blindly or emotionally driven by a certain interest? Obviously, I was surrounded by influential young Jesuits. I was a very young seventeen and a half. I was just a little boy. I did not shave for four years in the Order. I would say that I made a decision to enter the Society of Jesus, but it was not that much of a decision. It was a seventeen-year-old boy's decision. I knew in the context that I was giving up married life; I was giving up comforts and home. But when I was that age, I was generous, ready to do everything, because that to me was the perfect life, the happy life, as Aristotle would say.

Other respondents focus on more personal convictions and events characterizing vocational directions. For Daniel O'Hanlon, the chief motivation to enter the Jesuits was a sense of security in saving his soul:

> As I look back on it and try to figure out what the major motivation was to enter the Jesuits, I think that it was some kind of eternal security in the sense of saving my soul. I was very conscious at quite an early age of death, though not in a pessimistic way, because I was a very light-hearted person . . . I think that people thought of me as that sort of person. But I was very conscious of the transitory nature of everything that passes away. I was very much caught by the idea of things that last. In a sense it was a kind of a motivation you might call spiritual. It just seemed that if you weighed the values, this was the sensible thing to do. My motivation shifted later to something that was a little less crude. My vocation was primarily a vocation of a religious life and not the vocation of becoming a priest.

Lawrence Jones remembers a particular place, the University of Chicago, where his decision to enter the ministry was made. Both the choice and the surrounding motivations are joined in a local event:

> The business of religion and Christianity was always important for me. I always had an interest in God and in questions that related to God and all that. I would go to church regularly, and could remember some sermons that I heard. I always had the vision that I could do that; I really could do that. One day, I remember well . . . it was hot . . . I was at the University of Chicago and had left my cubicle and was walking out across the midway. I made a conscious decision that I would be a minister and I would try to live a Christian life. I have a little speech I give sometimes of the liberating moments of my life, and that was one of them. What I did at that point was to say, "What-

ever the cost of this decision in social terms, I'll take that." It was 1943.

In a delightful way, John Tracy Ellis recalls the little boy who was already playing at being a priest:

> There was no instruction that I can recall in the home, except perhaps for mother to hear our catechism lessons now and then. But she was watchful that we said our night prayers, and she was likewise alert that we attended St. Patrick's School. In regard to my early memories on the score of the priesthood, I do recall something that may have suggested that it was on my mind. My parents had very close friends, Charles and Loretta Talty, with whom they frequently played bridge. The Taltys had no children of their own, but they raised Mrs. Talty's niece, Nellie Fay, who was just my age. When they came for a bridge game I would get a tablecloth and drape it around me as a vestment, mount the stairs, and then have Nellie kneel behind me and answer the prayers while I played being a priest. I was nine or ten at the time. What the psychiatrists would make of that, I do not know!

Midlife Transitions

As Rabbi Blumenthal remarks in the following excerpt, many persons like himself do not encounter a significant midlife crisis. Such persons, usually enjoying good health, find enough stimulation in their careers and satisfaction in family life to avoid traumatic experiences in middle age. It may be, however, that some of those who sail through the middle years without crises will be even more intensely affected by the diminishments of older age. Problems of health, career loss, and family difficulties are sometimes delayed to elderhood for those who transit smoothly through middle age. The rabbi, however, is certainly aware of important crises that befell his congregants in the middle years. His two examples serve to underscore different ways of coping with crises of marriage and occupation; they also point out the changing, permissive social climate that fosters confusion, as well as hope:

> Values were changing and it was painful, but it had nothing to do with my age. Personally I was fortunate. My family life was very good and I was rising in the national leadership of our movement. There must be millions of people like me, busy and devoted to their work, in good health, and not anticipating the problems of aging.

A few weeks ago a member of my congregation died at sixty-five. He had been a successful businessman, an intelligent man, with married children. Fifteen years ago he divorced his wife and married his mistress. His wife was dull, and he must have been unhappy, watching himself growing older and life becoming less and less attractive. The point of time in which we live gave him the courage to divorce his wife and try to improve the quality of his life.

Assuming that my father thought some of these things, he didn't dare utter them, and he would not have implemented them regardless of the depth of his misery. Our world is very much different. It is a much, much more open world. I don't blame people for saying at the age of forty-five, "What have I achieved?" or "Where am I going?" Why not? I knew a man who lived all of his life in a business which he hated. This was during the Depression, and he stayed there because he had very little choice. He came home feeling miserable every day. You will not be surprised to learn that I buried him when he was comparatively young.

Other interviewees discuss important changes in their spiritual lives during the middle years. For Jack Boozer, the movement was from the moralistic faith of his youth toward a faith "marked by grace and unconditional love." Although he cites intellectual theories congruent with his new awareness, it is the concrete experience with his own wife and children that gradually worked a change in his religious outlook:

In all probability, the years 1950 to 1960 were crucial for a transition from a moralistic faith to a kind of faith marked by grace and unconditional love . . . I can't remember that there were one or two main turning points. But gradually it happened and the times at which I was shaken as to the stability and rightness of my own position were when I would discipline the children. And I have physically disciplined them. I spanked them hard and they cried, and sometimes they would come back later and just tell me that's all right. I just was melted by that kind of response of the child coming back. Finally, I began to get some insight in terms of what was happening to me during these episodes. And the punishment as they got older, of course, ceased to be physical. It was in other ways. We would talk things through and I would just say, well, we have to do something about this breach to show that this is a serious breach. And you have to pay for that in some way.

But I think that through the children and also through the graciousness of my wife, I came to understand something of the genuineness and the joy of mutual existence, what Buber calls the interhuman, what George Herbert Meade and others call the social self. I guess I came to the realization that we are all social selves, that we are intertwined in the lives of one another. And that the quality of that intertwining is more important than the correctness of any position either party takes on any specific issue. So a quality of relationship is what acquainted me with dimensions of love and dimensions of affect and dimensions of grace which I had not known before. I'm not suggesting that all moralism was eliminated, but I think I came to understand the unconditional dimension of the grace of God, which is tendered to us in the unconditional nature of genuine human friendship or genuine human relationship.

Mary Luke Tobin emphasizes a similar change in her religious perspective through a retreat-seminar with a priest-psychologist. Before becoming Superior General of an order of nuns, she saw herself expecting too much from the nuns, without sufficient regard for their own needs, fears, and abilities. These expectations could be understood as a kind of moralism: Such and such rules have been promulgated; they must be observed in an objective way. By contrast, she learned a new openness to others that allowed them to present themselves with their authentic needs and desires:

> Contact with a Dominican priest, Noel Mailloux, was a turning point for me. It couldn't have happened to me at a better time. It was right before I became Superior General, and the whole twelve years were made infinitely easier. I told you that earlier in my life as a superior my expectations of people were such that nobody could fulfill them, because that was the way the life was supposed to be. Those two classes with Mailloux in 1958 and 1959 were a complete revolution for me. Revolution and a revelation. He had been trained in theology. His superiors decided to send him to Europe and asked him to go into psychology. He just opened a new world for me. He emphasized a more human side of life. He was well integrated. He had a kind of openness to persons and to the fears that make people what they are. I can hear his accent, "What is producing this anxiety?" This is one thing that I remember from him: that one's whole set of fears influences one's character . . . so there was a sense of conversion. My way of dealing with people was totally different after my experience with Noel Mailloux. It was an opening, a great opening . . . and so I would say that it made my relationships with people better. I was not expecting of them what couldn't be expected of them. It is silly to expect that you can bring about a change in other people's attitudes. So I considered it invaluable.

In the following three examples, deep religious changes in midlife were accompanied by intense psychological struggles and inner sufferings. Daniel O'Hanlon speaks about a compulsive drivenness to perform in his career as theologian and teacher which led to ulcers and an extended period of depression. A one-year journey to Asian monasteries with participation in meditative practices brought about a midlife transformation affecting him in body and spirit. This form of contemplative conversion allowed him to make peace with the demon of exaggerated expectations that pursued him in younger years. Moreover, the movement toward a contemplative spirituality did not isolate him, but rather made him more sociable and spontaneous:

> That brings us to the depression that hit me. But let me go behind that first, because there is something else connected with it. When I was working in the third session of Vatican Council II, it was very difficult work; simultaneous translation is extremely exhausting. This whole health thing that I have been talking about had been with me since my teens. I must have consumed mountains of antacid pills over the years. Anyway, it caught up with me then because the grueling work of simultaneous translation was coming at me day by day. It came to the point that there was a rupture of an ulcer and I had to be hospitalized and have surgery. That would have been in 1964. For six or seven years after that things were not really right. Then in 1969 this depression hit me hard. It took me about three years to gradually work my way out of it. The first few years in Berkeley were such years. Then in 1973 I had a sabbatical year and decided as an expansion of my ecumenical enterprise to move out into the Hindu and Buddhist worlds. I spent thirteen months in Asia. I visited a number of meditation centers and got into a totally different world. When I came back my health was better than it had been since I was sixteen, and in general I was better emotionally and spiritually.
>
> I had been working all my life, learning languages, reading books, getting classes ready, and never being satisfied with the class. Somehow or the other, what happened in this process of spending a whole year in this totally different, low-keyed, slow-paced world of Asia was a freeing of my spirit from compulsions. I was forced to adapt to a different style of life. I learned certain meditation techniques. I ended up changing my eating habits, becoming a vegetarian . . . but somehow that year slowed up something that seemed to be chasing me. I do not entirely understand the process, but I do know that a very significant shifting point in my life occurred, and its effects remain with me to this time. It also made me more social, more spontaneous, more affectionate. It was not an entrance into some sort of antisocial asceticism that was severe and isolated.

The experience of a benevolent presence of God within the soul dramatically altered the spiritual life of Dr. Ewert Cousins, professor of theology at Fordham University.[21] Cousins, then a member of the Jesuit Order, had been grappling since his novitiate training with a spirituality that was largely ascetical and moral in orientation. A crisis, partly provoked by delaying his ordination to the priesthood, led him into psychotherapy and toward a new awareness of a mystical spirituality more natural to him. Again, the catalysts for change are not theoretical or abstract; rather, they are concrete: strong psychological suffering, the environment of a chapel during a eucharistic devotion, and the hug of a small Indian girl.

> The Rector sent me to a man in Kansas City and they had me take a Rorschach test. The Rorschach test showed I was very upset. The doctor wanted to send me to a place like a hospital to get immediate therapy. And then I had the biggest religious experience of my life. I had gone to see this therapist once and it was catalytic. I said, this is what I've been looking for. This man was asking the right questions and all the right things happened. That Sunday I was kneeling in chapel for the Benediction service and something happened. I was teaching Catechism to little kids on the Indian reservation and a little girl came up and hugged me. It was the first feeling of affection I felt in myself in months. Then that afternoon in the chapel I was kneeling and looking at the monstrance exposed holding the Eucharistic bread. And I had a tremendous, overwhelming experience that I could love God. I just never had anything like that in my life. And it came up in my body, pouring out into consciousness. Then I had a feeling that Christ was not an obstacle. I could love God. And this continued intensely for about forty-five minutes. I could still feel the effects for hours later. All over my body there was tingling and tremendous illumination and great energy, a feeling of energy and liberation. It was that love was the ultimate reality and I could love. I could love God. I felt that this was so deep an experience that it was a major life experience. My whole life is contained in this one experience from here on out.

Whereas for Cousins a psychiatrist acted as an indirect spiritual guru, a Guatemalan shaman with psychic powers helped to provoke a psychospiritual crisis for Louisa Jenkins in midlife. Her life as an artist had led her by circuitous routes to professional successes and relational disappointments. In the process her spiritual life faltered. The death of her adopted son became the final catalyst that linked a shamanic seance with a life-altering conversion experience in a Catholic mission church:

> While I was in Guatemala with my friend Maud Oakes, we went into the high mountains on horseback to visit a shaman. And the shaman was very important. He goes into a seance and he moves into another world, returning to give advice and help all the people that are in this little dark hut where we were for a night seance. Now it couldn't have happened except that Maud lived there and got into that world. She took me into the unconscious world, into the world of seances with a shaman. This is a mysterious place. He told Maud what was going to happen to her and what was going to happen in my life. He talked through an interpreter, so Maud was translating from the Indian into the Spanish into English. He said I was going to go back to my home to experience a sudden death near me. My whole life would be washed away. I would lose everything and I would have to start a new life.
>
> I went back to Pebble Beach, with which I had become very dissatisfied. There was a lot of searching for something. And things were starting to happen in my interior life. I felt that I was being pulled or pushed into some other kind of life. Ten years before this, I had adopted two boys from the cradle in Chicago. One died very suddenly by an accident. This threw me into a complete nervous breakdown. I just didn't know anything. I should have been put into an institution and taken care of, but I was allowed to wander around. Absolute agony. And at that time I had no religion. So, one day in my travels, I stopped the car in front of the Carmel Mission and I went into the little chapel. I didn't know anything about the Catholic religion. And I went in and I knelt down in front of the altar. And it was like a waterfall of peace coming down. And I knew that I was taken care of, I was immersed in this love, and I walked out of there a different person. I didn't have any theology, I didn't have any dogma, I didn't know what was there. All I knew was that I was different.

The problems of midlife frequently cluster around one's work. When the hopes of earlier years go unrealized, disappointment sets in. Even a successful teacher and recognized scholar like Albert Outler had to deal with a sense of incompleteness in the projects he desired to accomplish. Yet the very realization that he probably would not be able to "put a roof over" all three circus rings of religion, psychology, and ecumenism made him reevaluate the purpose of his enterprise. He was looking for a permanent tent, whereas the nature of a circus calls for a tent that can be dismantled and erected again:

I got caught in the middle-aged trap like everyone else does when I realized that this three-ring circus of religion, psychology, and ecumenism that I was trying to run was getting out of hand. The effort to see it steadily and whole wasn't ever going to come off. So that I've got all sorts of programmatic essays and articles, enough to be academically respectable, but never the overview for which I've been struggling. The acceptance of the prospect of not ever getting that done was pretty devastating, and still is—a lot of wasted effort and some wasted talent. I may never harvest the fruit of some of these things. For the only kind of harvest that I would want would be all of them under one roof. I am not able to see myself doing that right now. This was compensated for, however, by the accident of the Second Vatican Council, because, while I was facing the fact that I was never going to get the big vision put down on paper, I could be a spectator at a landmark in modern history. That was not therefore just a distraction but a genuine alternative, because it set up another agenda that I have been working at ever since. I am still working, you see, with Roman Catholics in consultation and study.

This reminds one that there may be no time at which one is ready to put a roof over all of these circus rings. It may be right that a circus is pitched like a tent, dismantled, set up again, dismantled, and set up again. My original vision probably needed to be revised in this way. Or at least I have become content with it being so revised.

As a dean at Union Theological Seminary in New York, Lawrence Jones encountered job-related difficulties during the turbulent period of the late sixties. Schools were in turmoil over the Vietnam War, and the Seminary sought to revise its curriculum and its mode of governance. Jones speaks about potentially disillusioning matters, but the very impasses in bringing about the reconciliation he wanted caused him to fall back "on the things in which . . . life is rooted":

My major problems at Union derived not from student relationships, but from some of my relationships with faculty. I have not to this day understood how some members of theological faculties can split what they teach and write about from what they do. I guess that is the great enigma of the church to me: how spirits don't get transformed. It's the transformation of the spirit that means conversion or liberation. It is being free from the necessity to win. If somebody insults you, that is okay. If somebody says a harsh thing, that is okay. If they disagree with you, that is okay. You do not have to stoop to low and mean things.

Richard Niebuhr saw God as being the valuer, the One in light of whom other people assume value. That is the linchpin of all that I think, and leads me to three basic conclusions. I often tell my students here that if they were ever to ask me, "Are there certain things in which your life is rooted?" I would tell them these three things. One is that God does not require you to be successful. He requires you to be faithful, to be true to the truth as He has given you to understand it. The second tenet upon which my theological thinking rests is that God's grace is sufficient. His forgiveness, which issues in responsibility, is sufficient. There is no dimension of your life which is beyond his loving grace and forgiveness. The third part is that you can trust in the trustworthiness of God. It is not confidence in propositions. It is confidence in a power and a spirit.

Middle-age crisis becomes much more acute when one's career is abruptly changed by outside forces. William Monihan faced the crisis of his life as a Jesuit when he was removed from his post as librarian without consultation with him. He vividly recalls the anger, the hurt, and the oscillations between spiritual acceptance and explosions of righteous indignation. The resolution of this traumatic experience blends psychological and religious insight:

In 1964 I went to Europe to buy ten thousand volumes for the library, on the average cost of five dollars a book, including the transport home. Prices today would be three or four times that amount. I felt that I had made a contribution. Even for my travel, my living expenses, and for the books, it cost the University nothing, because I had raised the money. I arrived home in July 1964 and found out that I was no longer head librarian. I had been moved out of my office without even knowing about it. That hurt me very much. One gets thoughts of self-pity. "Here I did all this, and they do this to me." I was very angry. I was appointed to be a development official, meaning a fund raiser. I resisted that. I wanted to do the fund raising as I had done it in the job of head librarian. I was very angry about that. I did not go to the office to take up my job in the development office for at least a month. I walked the streets. I walked to the ocean. I walked and walked trying to get my anger out.

I had both high spiritual motivations and explosions of anger. I was so angry between, say, July and Christmas of 1964 that I thought of leaving the Order. It was not for any specific reason. I guess that I felt pushed out, and I wanted to push back. One of my ways of pushing back psychologically was to say, "Well, I don't like you either." I did not take any steps to leave the Jesuits, but it was such a crisis in my life that the thought of leaving the Order did come to me very strongly. Also, perhaps I survived the incident because I released my anger. I feel that one has to resolve anger, to get it out of one's system, to expel it, to get back to ordinary psychic life. It is something inside of one that one must discharge, because otherwise you cannot live a normal life. But there are some who hang on to it and cling to it for years, and they are bitter people. I would say that somehow, vaguely, my religious faith has been growing as a participation in divine guidance. Looking back on this crisis, I see it as great classroom instruction by the Lord. "Do you understand?" "Yes, I understand." Like a little child. So this classroom instruction by the Lord in the life of the spirit is so important. In retrospect, it was the best thing that happened to me. I am now so attached to my work in development that I would yell, kick, and scream if I were to be taken out of it.

Anita Caspary was at the center of a widely publicized controversy between Cardinal McIntyre of Los Angeles and her Immaculate Heart of Mary congregation. As the Superior General of her group, she attempted to lead the nuns in the progressive directions of the Second Vatican Council. The Cardinal insisted to the point of ultimatum that these nuns adhere to older observances and ministries. The resulting schism in the order forced Caspary and a large number of her colleagues to abandon the traditional ties of the sisterhood with the Catholic hierarchy. She reflects on both the personal impact of these events and their meaning in the broader and mysterious plan of God:

I suppose that during those years it was just hanging on, just surviving from day to day. I suppose that in a way I was developing, but it is not the way that one usually thinks of developing. Since then, I think that I have had to come to terms with a lot of things—that maybe the community was meant to die. If that were so, it was still going to be all right. We had done what we were supposed to do. That was difficult to come to terms with. I think that I am at peace with that whole notion now. Also, while I have been away for these past five years, it has been good to think about the fact that in reality we do not do a lot. It is pretty much in God's hands. It is not human effort that will bring about changes in attitudes. It is not human argument, although that is helpful, human instruction, and all of the rest. We were very privileged to have a great deal of background and instruction before we went into this. We are meant to do something more than we are doing now. That I know.

I think that the strongest sustaining thing in all this was a very strong personal love for Christ himself. This has been a thread that has carried through pretty well, even though a lot of other things have come into the picture. What might have been a very anthropomorphic view has changed a great deal. A pervading sense of God's sustaining love, you know, is something. "The absurdity of the redemption," as one of my girls put it, talking about Flannery O'Connor, you know . . . the terrible mercy of God is an idea that I can't get away from. I don't want to get away from it.

For some the crises of midlife stem not from career issues, but from family problems. Simon Greenberg reflects on the sadness he experienced when one of his sons ceased being an observant Jew and abandoned a coveted academic appointment. Yet the rabbi knows that one's children cannot be minted like coins; he submits in faith to possible divine purposes beyond his present understanding. He strongly affirms his son's ethical sensitivity as a heritage of Judaism, but he also believes that the ritual dimension of religion is important to sustain the ethical:

Of the two boys, one of them remained pious and became a professor of Bible at the University of Pennsylvania . . . the other got himself a doctorate in physics and remained a very observant and pious Jew until he passed his thirty-third birthday. I do not know what happened. He left academia and organized his own school because he did not want his children to attend public school. Now he has gone into a business venture. But one of the children is becoming interested again in Judaism. I certainly was saddened by this. On the other hand, I believe that one of the blessings is that we cannot turn out human beings like the mint turns out coins. I say that God moves us and He must have his own purposes. I do not yet know what purpose may be involved. But I accept it, saddened by it without any doubt. Of course, I am saddened by the fact that he took his whole career—he was teaching physics at Columbia—and threw it into the wastebasket. He turned profoundly against academia. He did not like the atmosphere on the campus. He is a highly sensitive, morally sensitive, individual, and he couldn't stand the bickerings, the jealousies, and all of that on the campus. He wanted to go to a place where he could be on his own and do what he wanted to do. But I have no doubt that my son's ethical sensitivity was determined by his Jewish background. In fact, he knows his Bible well, and he was a pretty good student of the Jewish tradition. You know, there is a famous rabbinic statement based on a passage of scripture that says, "God said, 'Would that they would forget Me and observe my Torah.'" There is no doubt in my mind that between the ethical and the ritual, the ethical takes precedence in the Jewish tradition. However, I am of the opinion that the ethical, which over a period of time is not nourished by ritual, will deteriorate.

A similar episode had an impact on the midlife of Earl Brewer; both children became "radicalized" in the culture of the sixties, departing from the expectations and life-style of their parents. The experience was profoundly agonizing for the Brewers. A certain ambivalence was felt; in one way, the children's questioning of middle-class ways helped Brewer to liberate himself from some aspects of these values. Yet a sense of disappointment lurks in the background; no doubt, their hopes for their children had positive dimensions that may never be attained:

> Crisis experiences in midlife had to do with our children. They were growing up in the sixties. They got themselves involved in the activities of the sixties. Our son was at Emory College while we were away in New York on leave. He became fully radicalized and involved in the radical activities on the campus. I remember he called me one time and he said I better get the bail money ready because he was being arrested by a sheriff of DeKalb County because of his activities here on the campus. Our married daughter later became radicalized and was divorced. During this period our relationships to both the children had a profound impact on us. There were some agonizing moments. There is a sense in which both our children are still radicalized, being involved in various kinds of movements. Their attitude toward money is not the Depression attitude; nor is their attitude toward work the work ethic. Their attitude toward the church and their involvement in the church has been completely reversed from what it was when they were growing up. This is something with which we've had to accommodate.
>
> Now there are two sides in that. One side is sort of a negative side, that you see your children not living out the dreams that you had for them and thought earlier they had for themselves. And this lies in the background of your consciousness. The positive side of this has a liberating aspect. Because I've been greatly benefited by the liberation of the children from the sort of standard-brand middle-class values which our family held, I've broken away from these along with them in a variety of directions. And I consider this to be liberating, although there lurks in the background a kind of a disappointment.

The death of her famous and much-loved husband, Abraham, was the most profound suffering of Sylvia Heschel's life. Years after his death, she still found it hard to talk about the event. The context in which she addressed the happening provides a fitting conclusion to this chapter. For it emphasizes two qualities outstanding in the religiousness of all the interviewed persons: a sense of communication with and continuance with God. In and through the stages of life portrayed here, even in the times of rebellion and loss of faith, the respondents manage to keep open channels of communication with the transcendent dimension of existence. Like Sylvia Heschel, they anchor their religiousness in an experience of God's presence in the world, giving continuance to all that is of value:

> My husband's unexpected death was terrible for me. Five years before, he had survived a massive heart attack; the doctors were surprised at his recovery. I believed it was the combination of a bright young resident doctor who worked on him through the night, and mostly the heartfelt prayers of so many friends and admirers. This time, there was no time for prayer. He died in his sleep.
>
> It is customary in Judaism that on each tombstone there be these following words: "May his soul be bound in the bundle of life with the Lord." (Samuel 1 25:29) So it was, it seemed to me . . . his spirit had disengaged itself from his body.

IV
ELDERHOOD:
THE CHALLENGES

An aged man is but a paltry thing.
A tattered coat upon a stick, unless
Soul clap its hands and sing, and louder sing
For every tatter in its mortal dress . . .
    W. B. Yeats, "Sailing to Byzantium"

Nobody wants to grow old. Attaining old age may, as W. C. Fields observed in another context, be preferable to the alternatives. As a state of life, however, elderhood, especially in its later stages, is not a condition desired by young or midddle-aged individuals. We may be encouraged that many old people have lived with dignity and creativity, but we are not anxious to arrive at that point in our own lives. As we shift our reflections from midlife to elderhood, it is important to dwell on the peculiar bias that we bring to the later years. It might be objected that many cultures, throughout history, have honored old age; this has been true in the Orient, in some primitive and tribal groups, and in earlier agrarian western civilizations. Old age may have been easier in such cultures, but it is doubtful that elderhood was a desired state. The physical drawbacks alone, the prospects of illness, decline, and death would seem to argue against the desirability of old age.

The point is that we are not neutral about becoming aged. In fact, we consciously or unconsciously abhor it. Middle age, as we have seen, presents serious challenges to the developing personality. Yet, despite the crises and perplexities of the midperiod, we do not approach it with the dread that accompanies thoughts of old age. This negative attitude is more than the sentiment of a middle-aged author who feels closer to the ending time. It can also be observed in the way some young people avoid the very elderly or are embarrassed in their presence. Most of those who watched Lord Snowdon's widely broadcasted television portrayal of the old, "Don't Count the Candles," experienced some depression.

Again, it is vital, at the beginning of our exploration, to face our own abhorrence of elderhood. Unless we confront this sentiment, almost taste it, our attempts to cope with old age risk superficiality. We will be too easily inclined to seek solutions in social programs or leisure-time activities, as though programs might disguise the true challenges of old age. Spirituality for aging will remain shallow unless we dwell in some depth on the special and threatening problems of old age. This means grappling seriously with the psalmist's injunction: "So teach us to number our days that we may get a heart of wisdom." The numbering of our days means more than counting them; it implies a pondering of the time ahead in its personal and social perplexities, as well as its promise.

As we approach old age we must confront the "overwhelming question" of T. S. Eliot's Prufrock, whose life leads him down many "Streets that follow like a tedious argument / Of insidious intent / To lead you to an overwhelming question . . . ."[1] Yet, with a hundred distractions Prufrock repeatedly dodges the great questions of meaning and love in life. Old age and the spectre of his own death, however, keep the question relentlessly before him: "I grow old . . . I grow old . . . / I shall wear the bottoms of my trousers rolled." And again, death lifts up the question: "I have seen the moment of my greatness flicker, / And I have seen the eternal footman hold my coat, and snicker, / And in short, I was afraid." We are all Prufrocks, skirting the overwhelming questions of life. By confronting the challenges of elderhood, we shall look hard at questions attached to being old, the "ultimate stigma" in our society.[2]

Simone de Beauvoir echoes an ancient chorus of negative attitudes toward old age in western literature. She describes the aged years as a calamity.[3] Just as we cannot concretely imagine our own dying process, so we can never see ourselves as truly old because the changes are so frightening.[4] She points to certain primitive tribes that are repelled by old age, which they regard as a degeneration from the ideal of the human condition and, in the person of the aged king, a threat to the welfare of society. Among the American Indians, examples can be found of the abandonment of the sickly aged, who are left to die far from the tribal center. The ancient Greeks also practiced such removal of the old. The law of Chios prevented "him who was unable to live well from living ill"; hemlock was used to poison those over sixty.[5] Herodotus, characteristic of many classical Greek sages, expressed the vicissitudes of growing old:

> . . . there is no man . . . who is so happy, as not to have felt the wish—I will not say once, but full many a time—that he were dead rather than alive. Calamities fall upon us; sicknesses vex and harass us . . . so death, through the wretchedness of our life, is a most sweet refuge to our race.[6]

Sophocles depicts the old Oedipus as one claimed by age: "dispraised, infirm, unsociable, unfriended, with whom all woe of woe abides."[7] Again, in the *Rhetoric,* Aristotle expressed the Greek horror toward old age as that "demon" that enfeebles the powers of enjoyment and the sense of beauty and poisons the springs of social intercourse.

This image of dire old age extends into the Christian tradition. A dual sense of physical decrepitude and moral decline marks many references to the later years in the earliest patristic writings. For the Pastor of Hermas, old age is a metaphor for spiritual and moral shortcomings:

> Because your spirit is now old and withered up and has lost its power in consequence of your infirmities and doubts. For, like elderly men who have no hope of renewing their strength, and expect nothing but their last sleep, so you, weakened by worldly occupations, have given yourselves up to sloth, and have not cast your cares upon the Lord. Your spirit therefore is broken, and you have grown old in your sorrows.[8]

Augustine, perhaps the most influential theologian on successive generations of Christianity, repeats this dim view of old age: "For when life draws toward its close, the old man is full of complaint, and with no joys . . . groans abound even unto the decrepitude of old age."[9] This negative attitude toward the aged is not the whole story in the Christian tradition, as we shall see. Nevertheless, it represents a strong current of deprecation running unabated through the centuries. Negative images regarding the old abound in religious writings. Such imagery is important because of its contribution to what today is called "ageism." In the present century we have come to see more clearly the impact of mental metaphors and spoken words on the formation of racism and sexism. Our manner of speech betrays our feelings about other races, about women, and about the old. The cumulative effect of these images and utterances shapes stereotypes of certain groups, with destructive consequences for the individuals within them.

Although we rightly criticize the exaggerated youth cult of today, its roots can be found, at least indirectly, throughout western literature. The theme is ever the same: the ugliness of physical decline as compared with the beauty of youth. Milton sounds this note clearly in *Paradise Lost:*

> This is old age; but then thou must outlive Thy
> youth, thy strength, thy beauty, which will change
> To withered weak and gray; thy Senses then
> Obtuse, all taste of pleasure must forgoe,
> To what thou hast, and for the Aire of youth
> Hopeful and cheerful, in thy blood will reigne
> a Melancholy damp of cold and dry
> To waigh thy spirits down, and last consume
> The Balme of Life[10]

When Boswell attempted to present a few optimistic ideas on aging, Dr. Johnson cut him short: "What, Sir, would you know what it is to feel the evils of old age? Would you have the gout? Would you have decrepitude?"[11] However much we restrain the process by nutrition, exercise, and hygiene, or by the gift of good genes, Milton's "beauty which will change to withered, weak and gray" remains an important loss for each of us. Whether on the conscious or unconscious level, the loss of youthful vigor and attractiveness upsets us at a profound emotional level. It is not enough to criticize the modern divinization of youth, with all its shallow pretensions. For deeper spiritual development, the aging need to confront their true feelings about physical decline. From a Buddhist perspective, the beginning of wisdom for Gotama the Prince was a direct exposure to the infirmities of age. Only then could the Buddha-to-be realize with concrete emotional impact the transitoriness of life and the futility of craving permanence.

Beyond the image of physical decay associated with old age is a litany of supposed vices repeated endlessly through history. Repulsive moral traits are attributed to old persons throughout literature. In "The Reeve's Prologue," Chaucer interlinked bodily and moral decline:

> Yet in our ashes is there fire to reek.
> Four embers have we, which I shall confess:
> Boasting and lying, anger, covetousness;
> These four remaining sparks belong to the old. . . .
> Our ancient limbs may well be hard to wield,
> But lust will never fail us, that is truth . . .
> The stream of life now drips on the chime;
> The silly tongue may well ring out the time
> Of wretchedness that passed so long before;
> For oldsters, save for dotage, there's no more.[12]

In the same vein, Montaigne perceived more wrinkles on the souls of the old than on their faces. Envy, greed, injustice, and malice appeared to be the special promise of old age:

> But, methinks, our souls, in old age, are subject to more troublesome maladies and imperfections than in youth. . . . We call the difficulty of our humours and the disrelish of present things wisdom; but, in truth, we do not so much forsake vices as we change them, and, in my opinion, for worse. Besides a foolish and feeble pride, an impertinent prating, forward and insociable humours, superstition, and a ridiculous desire of riches when we have lost the use of them, I find there more envy, injustice, and malice. Age imprints more wrinkles in the mind than it does on the face; and souls are never, or even rarely seen, that in growing old do not smell sour and musty.[13]

These depictions of elderhood mold collective, inherited attitudes that manifest the curious interplay of psychological projection and ageism. Surely some old people display many of the traits cited by Chaucer and Montaigne. But the common, almost socially acceptable, ways of attributing reprehensible qualities to the old awaken the suspicion that mental projection is at work. The obvious physical decline of aging persons becomes an occasion for projecting onto them moral flaws. The observed physical infirmities of the old become convenient excuses for ascribing moral weakness to them.

This mental projection is at the roots of "ageism," that cluster of attitudes and practices that leads us to discriminate against old people. A twofold confrontation with such projection can help us begin to deal creatively with ageism. First, youthful and middle-aged persons might inquire into the fears within themselves that make it so easy to project harshly on the elderly. This kind of soul-searching means encountering the inner, usually unconscious, Shadow archetype. By recognizing and appropriating many of these rejected and projected qualities within our own souls, we can understand how we came to associate them with the old. We must recognize how we pillory those whose physical disabilities remind us of our own future. With imaginative ease, we blend these physical handicaps into moral vices. Secondly, the old must ask themselves not only how much they have become the unwitting victims and perpetrators of ageism, but also how much they live out, as a kind of self-fulfilling prophecy, the very stereotypes that society has imposed on them. This process of liberation from destructive projections offers an indispensable threshold to a genuine spirituality of aging.

Our reflections on negative images of old age impel us to a more specific investigation of the problems of the elderly. These problems can be seen as challenges for creative coping on the three general levels of self, world, and other. But before launching upon these issues, we must address a few preliminary questions: What is "old age" or "elderhood," as we use these terms here? Some persons seem to be old at forty, in that they resist personal growth and adventure. Others are youthful at seventy, filled with zest for life and involved in various activities. Who then is old and who is young? Chronological age offers some guidelines; we know that the forty-year-old and the seventy-year-old are at different phases of the biological life cycle. We must avoid the restrictive characterization of life stages, attributing certain traits without qualification to this or that decade. Nevertheless, from a biological viewpoint, it seems reasonable to speak of persons over sixty as elders. Social scientists employ still other distinctions, referring to the young-old and the old-old as those younger and older than seventy-five. Many persons in their seventies experience health problems that limit activities that might otherwise be possible. Yet these limitations are offset, as several studies indicate, because older people are capable of optimal mental functioning despite health problems.[14]

In addition to biological criteria for old age, there are social factors that influence age categorizations. Compulsory retirement at sixty-five or earlier, for example, tends to cast an aura of oldness around those no longer in the labor force or removed from their principal career roles. Again, the heightened pace of the contemporary technological and business workplace leaves little room for slower "senior citizens," who are stereotyped as less productive. They are seen as not only old, but relatively useless. Eligibility for Social Security and Medicare marks a person as old in the eyes of society. These are only a few of the forces of social change that constantly stigmatize the aging process.[15] Moreover, when the elderly congregate in distinct communities, they further the appearance of an aged cohort segregated from other age groups.

Therefore, both physical and social variables must be kept in mind when we talk about the meaning of old age. This nuanced assessment of what constitutes elderhood can be described as a multidimensional understanding of the aging process.[16] Such an approach enables us to avoid single-theory solutions to the problems of the elderly. Sociologists teach us that any theory is inadequate if it fails to incorporate features that explain and predict different outcomes for different groups of individuals.[17] This point takes on special relevance for a spirituality of aging. No single type of religiousness will satisfy every individual confronting the challenges of old age. Some will find more help in mysticism, others in liturgical involvements, still others in social gospel activities or combinations of these and other forms of spirituality.

Do people become more religious as they age? A number of studies have attempted to determine the correlation between religious interest and elderhood. Most of these inquiries focus on frequency of attendance at and involvement in church or synagogue.[18] Other interviewers ask the elderly about the importance of religion in their lives. While there does appear to be a heightened interest in religion among older persons, the conclusions of these studies remain ambiguous and somewhat external to our themes.[19] The word "religion" is popularly associated with attendance at church or syn-agogue, or with the degree of participation in such institutions. While these involvements may indicate something of the degree of one's inner spirituality, such external activity may also have little or no relation to spiritual depths. The role of the churches in the lives of the elderly is an important topic, and certainly pertains, at least indirectly, to our concerns. A number of works, including the seminal book by Maves and Cedarleaf, concentrate on the weaknesses in pastoral care of the old and suggest ways to improve ministry of and to the elderly.[20] But our principal interest is the attempt to discover and elaborate a religiousness or spirituality *intrinsic to* the aging process.

The sometimes unique problems of elderhood are also fraught with potential for growth in spiritual life. Life itself, in its daily struggles, is the primary locus of holiness. Yet, to tap this rich source of religious becoming, we need to "have faced and dealt directly with the fact of loss in older years. If we avoid the one [loss], we shall be ambiguous about the other [religious growth]."[21] It is in facing and coping with the challenges of old age that we establish continuity with our past lives. In this era of rapid change, old people encounter serious discontinuities with what has gone before. Yet the very coping with these dislocations becomes the new growth of "continuity on which we can now draw."[22]

Challenges to Self

For many persons, old age is a time for experiencing losses and diminishments that deeply affect basic self-image. This is especially true of a "throw-away" culture, in which we discard whatever is old as no longer stylish or useful. The losses may be mainly external, but they are internalized so as to diminish self-image. Deaths of friends or family members and loss of a place in the work world through retirement frequently remove a sense of worth or usefulness. Of course, this experience is accentuated in a technological economy that demands rapid production. Buying power tends to decline drastically in an inflated economy. In a more internal way, other diminishments are felt. Health may deteriorate, or a gradual decline of strength may become noticeable. It is paradoxical that at a time in life when we are less able to change because of social and personal diminishments we are required to make severe changes in job, housing, and status.[23]

This combination of real and perceived losses diminishes self-esteem and causes the old to be "wounded in their narcissism."[24] When psychologists use "narcissism" in this context, they do not mean the exaggerated self-love associated with the legend of Narcissus, who fell in love with his own image. Rather, narcissism refers to a person's basic self-concept, that central ego-unifying image of self. Rochlin sees narcissistic injury as the basic problem of an aging person:

> The greatest test of narcissism is aging or old age. All that has come to represent value and with which narcissism has long been associated is jeopardized by growing old. The skills, mastery, and powers, all painfully acquired, which provided gratification as they functioned to effect adaptation wane in the last phase of life. One's resources, energies, adaptability, and functions, the intimacies of relationship upon which one depended, family and friends, are continually being depleted and lost.[25]

Those who argue the importance of narcissistic hurt admit that social attitudes and practices toward the old can further intensify this injury. But they maintain that merely altering societal treatment of the aged will not suffice to relieve the problem. Feelings of inferiority and lack of self-esteem are indeed major causes of depression among older persons.[26] Discarded, rejected by a culture of material success, the old experience a loss of self.[27] Although social betterment programs for the elderly are essential, it is important to remember that some of the most profound traumas of aging are beyond social remedies.

Afflicted by these hurts, many of the old tend to retreat to thoughts of earlier life stages.[28] It is crucial for developing a spirituality of aging that the elderly themselves be willing to enter empathetically into their own narcissistic injuries, instead of distracting themselves with conventional diversions. Again, the road to spiritual depth does not skirt major problems, but enters into them with full recognition. The way out is not around, but through the pain of loss. Theological reflections on redemptive suffering, inspired by faith and hope, seem appropriate as spiritual supports for the old in this context. But those who would aid the elderly, whether through counseling or in other ways, should themselves seek to experience, insofar as possible, these narcissistic injuries and the consequent sense of self-loss. Without such vicarious entering into the plight of the old, these helpers will be of only superficial assistance to the elderly; moreover, they will fail to learn from their seniors both the pain that they too will face and the courageous wisdom to endure it.

Beneath the various diminishments and losses experienced by the self lurks the major threat of death. Meissner notes, "Perhaps the greatest loss of all is the encroaching deprivation and ultimate narcissistic trauma of death."[29] The sense of one's own mortality caused an underlying anxiety in middle age, but in elderhood death becomes a surer proximate reality. It is not that the old fear death more than those in midlife. Evidence indicates that many elderly persons have worked through the fear of their own deaths.[30] This may be particularly true for those who have derived a sense of wholeness from interpersonal and career engagements. Moreover, those for whom religious faith is an intrinsic and vital force in life seem to approach death with more serenity. Yet, despite the admirable attitude of some older people in confronting their own deaths, this final diminishment presents a profound challenge to the elderly. Even if death itself is not feared, the dying process, with its sufferings and indignities, offers a frightening prospect.

The middle-aged may observe occasional peers who are stricken down early in life by terminal disease or accidents. For the elderly, the loss of friends and other contemporaries after difficult illnesses becomes all too frequent. Whether conciously considered or as a subliminal influence, the elderly become intensely aware of the hastening approach of the long night: "To feel how swift how secretly / The shadow of the night comes on. . . ."[31] "Swift," "secretly," and "shadow" in Archibald MacLeish's poem connote special meaning in old age. The swiftness of approaching death threatens the self's sense of the time remaining to conclude unfinished business. The secret approach of the end further confirms the elderly self's inability to control personal reality; death, the final event, cannot be commanded or manipulated by human reason and will. While there may be some value in raging against the dying of the light, as Dylan Thomas would have it, a more receptive-contemplative stance is a wiser attitude for enriching the last years. The "shadow" represents the ominous or fearful dimensions of death. However well one has prepared for death, frightening and depressing aspects of the dying process remain.

The self can be bolstered by new meaning in confronting and, in a sense, rehearsing its own death. For some, spiritual meaning derives from forms of nature mysticism by which the self surrenders its being into the energies of the universe, realizing the natural cycle of life and death into which each of us is born. Others find inspirational meaning by embracing their deaths as a final act of obedience to God; such trust in a benevolent deity may be further permeated with hope for life after death, with a belief in reincarnation, or with a kind of agnosticism about afterlife accompanied by gratitude for having been gifted with this single sojourn on earth. Whatever the response to the shadow of death, the aging self is summoned to grapple with the approaching darkness. Only through such nocturnal wrestling, as with Jacob and the angel, can the self experience the fullest blessing of the end-time.

Therefore, death constitutes the ultimate loss challenging the elder person. Throughout the ages, individuals have attempted to give added meaning to existence by the pursuit of some form of immortality. Some strive to live on through their achievements, leaving monuments to their memory; others seek to immortalize themselves through their children or family dynasties; still others believe in some form of life after death. The quest for immortality in the face of death can be a positive endeavor, giving hope and fostering creative energy. But longing for immortality can also become a desperate attempt to avoid confronting death.

The literary imagination warns us against the futile quest to avoid death. In *Gulliver's Travels,* Swift paints a grim picture of the Struldbrugs, that group of persons who manage to live on endlessly:

> When they came to fourscore years, which is reckoned the extremity of living in this country, they had not only the follies and infirmities of other old men, but many more which arose from the dreadful prospect of never dying. They were not only opinionative, peevish, covetous, morose, vain, talkative; but incapable of friendship, and dead to all natural affection. Envy and impotent desires are their prevailing passions . . . and whenever they see a funeral, they lament and repine that others are gone to a harbour of rest, to which they

themselves never can hope to arrive. . . . They are despised and hated by all sorts of people: when one of them is born, it is reckoned ominous. . . .

The reader will easily believe, that from what I had heard and seen, my keen appetite for perpetuity of life was much abated. I grew heartily ashamed of the pleasing visions I had formed; and thought no tyrant could invent a death into which I would not run with pleasure from such a life.[32]

Swift's story offers valuable food for reflection. The quest for immortality, understood as an infinite extension of life as we know it, is vain and counterproductive to human welfare, both for the Struldbrugs and for society at large. This literary trope dramatizes the need to encounter the natural reality of death, however intimidating. The Struldbrugs are a metaphor for our need, in old age, to make peace as creatively as possible with our end-time.

The heedless pursuit of personal survival also leads to negative ethical consequences. For the fear of death, of personal extinction, drives many to abuse and destroy their fellow humans.[33] A graphic example of this deadly will to survive at all costs can be seen in the kingly throne of certain primitive tribes, its legs mounted on the skulls of tribal enemies.[34] In the modern world of politics and commerce, the feet of corporate thrones are better disguised, but the grasping for survival at all costs sometimes destroys competitors more effectively than the spears of primitive tribesmen.

Beyond these ethical considerations, the desire for immortality, when it is an equivalent to an escape from facing personal demise, becomes an antireligious sentiment. Tennyson's "Tithonus" underscores this point. The mythical Tithonus had asked for and received unending continuance of life on earth. But his request was marred because the ravages of old age afflicted him unceasingly. He was left "maim'd / To dwell in presence of immortal youth, / Immortal age beside immortal youth, / And all I was, in ashes."[35] In this predicament Tithonus prays, "Yet hold me not forever in thine East." The east is the land of morning, of youth. Tithonus's prayer climaxes in the final verses:

> Release me, and restore me to the ground;
> Thou seest all things, thou wilt see my grave:
> Thou wilt renew thy beauty by morn;
> I earth in earth forget these empty courts,
> And thee returning on thy silver wheels.[36]

In one sense, the poem can be understood as a warning against the artificial prolongation of life when the quality of living has degenerated beneath a human norm. Such an understanding merits special attention today, when medical technology can keep the elderly "alive" in hospitals and nursing homes even when such artificial life hardly deserves to be called human. From this perspective, the disrespect for human dignity in such "immortality" constitutes an antireligious activity. Since the divine dwells in the human, such insults to human dignity are also offensive to God. In another sense, "Tithonus" emphasizes the antireligious orientation of a thoughtless demand for immortality in that the earthly immortalist is finally exiled to the cold zone of the east, unable to pass through death and return to God. Tithonus had to struggle with his own grave and "forget these empty courts," the palaces of youth heedless of death. Only then could he return to God "on thy silver wheels." The immortalist desire becomes a flight from confrontation with death.[37]

Yet only in light of such an encounter can we be graced with the deepest, sustaining religious experience. Here is, indeed, a paradox. As death-bound creatures we long for life; yet spiritual living in its fullness calls for facing, and eventually embracing, personal death. It is significant that a major (if not *the* major) theme of world religions is the problem of death. Whether we are ultimately saved from it through a redeemer, as in Christianity, or released from repeated confrontations with it, as in Hinduism, death is the great hub around which religions circle.

Indeed, our contemporary period offers its own brands of escape from old age and death. Cryonics, the freezing of the newly dead for future revival, is a concrete example of theories that look to modern and future science to deliver us from death. Our very stress on longevity as a principal concern of life can consume so much energy that little is left to devote to the spiritual quality of the years we have gained.[38] The current preoccupation with near-death experiences, with their patterned sequence of images: the tunnel, the light, the guides, the voices, and so forth, are too easily accepted as a "proof" of life after death sought in the quest for comfort.[39] Traditionally religious persons are especially tempted to take near-death recitals as confirmation of a benevolent immortality without working through the pain and mystery of their own deaths.

H. Nouwen brings us a vital message from the elderly, who remind us of "the illusion of any final cure." He tells us that the old confront the doctor with the limitations of his healing powers, the psychologist with the relativity of self-fulfillment, the social worker with the lasting ambiguities in human relations, and the minister with the undeniable reality of death. In short, they confront us all with the illusory nature of any final cure.[40] Nouwen goes on to urge caring rather than curing as the needed remedy for this illusion. Yet before we can care in depth for ourselves or others, there is a kind of cure that we must undertake. The illusion of cure can only be healed by a curing of the illusion. This is more than a play on words. Confrontation with our own limitations in old age and eventually with our own deaths becomes an essential step in healing the illusion of immortality, a necessary prerequisite to experiencing mortal existence in all its richness.

Uncertainties about the present and future, as well as personal uncertainty, offer significant challenges to the elderly. At first glance we might suppose the old, due to long experience, to be quite certain about their identities and their relationship to the world. Yet many factors conspire to make us uncertain in old age. Those who lose a spouse experience serious uncertainties, both physical and mental-emotional. At a late stage in life they must learn to cope with practical matters previously handled by a partner. On an emotional level, they miss the other's support, which sustained them for many years. Uncertainty about personal worth is especially keen among men retired from the work force.

The insecurity of poverty and poor health causes great anxiety for many older persons. Regardless of financial standing, declining physical health presents a major challenge for elders. The impact of illness in old age can have serious emotional and psychological consequences. Perhaps for the first time in one's life comes a sense of truly inevitable decline; in earlier periods sickness and disabilities were seen as temporary trials to be overcome. But in certain phases of elderhood we perceive a general decay of the whole organism, an irresistable collapse of our physical systems. With little or no promise of recuperation, the older individual can fall into depression and despair. A new level of human brokenness is experienced. In this situation, it takes extraordinary reserves of spiritual power to maintain a life of hope and creativity. Some of the elderly interviewees in chapter seven confront the prospects of failing health with both realism and courage. It is particularly important for those who minister to the elderly to be able to empathize with the various levels of distress attendant on losses of physical well-being.

A culture that exalts the young will reject the old and expect them to fail.[41] These expectations become self-fulfilling prophecies as elderly individuals become more cautious and withdraw from the wider community in order to avoid mistakes that might seem to confirm their inadequacies. All these aspects of uncertainty heighten the danger of despair in old age that Erikson stresses as the opposite of the task of integration for the old. Uncertainties tend to unravel the fabric of unity in life. As de Beauvoir notes, the old feel some continuity with an earlier identity, while they also undergo profound dislocations as the world and their lives are constantly transformed.[42]

Uncertainties among the old are linked to a sense of incompleteness. The middle-aged person must curtail the illusory dreams of youth, but life still grants a considerable span of time to finish certain chosen tasks. In old age, the time for concluding unfinished business becomes highly circumscribed. Difficult questions arise as we ponder the shortness of time in the face of the uncertainties of elderhood. Many creative writers have experienced a powerful sense of incompleteness in later life; they describe their work, as well as their lives, as "failed approximations."[43] For such writers, elderhood becomes "a tentative, half-scared, half-hopeful, nearly-compulsive time for the exploitation of a gift that at any time may be cruelly withdrawn."[44]

Yeats gave poignant witness to this sense of "failed approximation." Just as Tolstoy in midlife had experienced a dreadful unfulfillment amid all his successes, so Yeats, showered with honors near the end of his life, could write:

> "The work is done," grown old he thought,
> "According to my boyish plan;
> Let the fools rage, I swerved in naught,
> Something to perfection brought";
> *But louder sang that ghost, "What then?"*[45]

The "What then?" of the elderly, however painfully surrounded by uncertainty, can be a creative moment. As the older person moves toward unexplored boundaries, he or she is called upon to create new models for living. Precedents for creative aging amid modern uncertainties are lacking. Thus the most disturbing of times can become a season for innovative ventures. But the dreams of old age differ from those of younger periods. The very experience of "failed approximations" can lead to new forms of reconciliation within the self. It may not be important to reach our earlier goals; it may be enough to learn humility, compassion, and care from our partially achieved strivings.

Besieged by doubts from within and uncertainties from without, the older person is tempted to turn inward. This is not the inwardness of contemplation, which all aging people need as a source for creative coping. Rather, this in-turning results from fear and desolation. It is a kind of self-centeredness, as if the aging individual were closing out the world in order to erect protective ramparts around what is left of the beleaguered self. Tyrone's parents in Eugene O'Neill's *Long Day's Journey Into Night* represent sadly inturning, escapist elders, unable to cope with the reality of their losses. In some persons this movement away from open involvement in society takes the form of materialism. These Scrooge-like elders cling desperately to the things they have amassed or seek incessantly to build the hoard that they must ultimately relinquish. For them, material security shelters a hardened and menaced self. Others unite materialism with a tyrannical spirit, hoping to remain important and needed in the eyes of their families or associates by dominating others as long as possible. They share the illness of Shakespeare's Lear before Cordelia works her gracious transformation on his conscience.

Whether this self-centered phenomenon be marked by greed for things or lust for power, it contributes to a rigidity of spirit. Indeed, adhering inflexibly to set ideologies or structures may serve as a protective device. As such, it is usually accompanied by negative attitudes to the new or youthful. Distrust, envy, and resentment eat at the souls of such people, pushing them ever closer to inner despair, while outwardly they appear to prosper. Of course, we are portraying types or extremes; no one individual fully represents a type. Rather, it is a matter of major characteristics of the personality. After all, negative qualities in the aged are not always mere projections by the young or middle-aged. Moreover, these unattractive qualities may begin to develop in middle age and become fixed in later years.

What matters in our context, however, is not the mere enumeration of detestable or pitiable traits in some among the elderly. We describe these negative aspects as symptomatic of a self turning inward, threatened from without by a youth-oriented society and from within by the spectre of personal decline. Furthermore, we all participate, to some degree, in these negative proclivities. We are all on a continuum of aging. The vital issue for spiritual growth is that we recognize these tendencies within ourselves; for only after recognizing them within can we hope to understand the partial reality of their context—that is, a world that threatens the aging human—and then find the psychospiritual resources that will aid us to avoid the process of destructive in-turning.

Beneath these challenges to the self in old age flows the undercurrent of diminished time. This is the central problem of finitude and death. Many of the negative tendencies just discussed are the unfortunate byproducts of psychological defense systems erected to stave off the ultimate threat of mortality. In light of this final determinant, a chief concern is to find ways of dealing with shortened time in the face of death. From one perspective, the curtailment of our time span in elderhood is a truth not to be talked away. It is part of the hard reality of life for creatures who know that they must die, but who simultaneously long for more life. From this angle, the traditional spirituality of the West urges us to enter with faith into the dark night, while in the East we are summoned to resign ourselves to our karmic fate in the long-term plan of the universe. But from a different perspective, spiritual guidance leads us to meditate on the qualitative, over against the quantitative understanding of time in the face of a fast-approaching end. Again, the poet helps us to grasp such a transformation of time. In view of more important values, Yeats tells us to set time afire, as though duration in itself lacks true significance:

> The innocent and the beautiful
> Have no enemy but time;
> Arise and bid me strike a match
> And strike another till time catch;
> Should the conflagration climb,
> Run till all the sages know.[46]

In his poem, Yeats contrasts the youthful beauty of the Gore-Booth sisters with their elderly state, "withered old and skeleton-gaunt." Yet this contrast between youth and old age constitutes only part of Yeats's vision. Of more universal significance is the image of burning time-span concepts as inimical to a fuller understanding of human existence. The most valuable dimension of the lives of the Gore-Booth sisters was not that they managed to live to ripe old age. Rather, the true significance of these women rests in qualitative levels: the intensity of their commitment to causes for the benefit of humankind. The poet's conflagration of time reminds the "sages" that the onus of restricted duration in elderhood can be relativized through qualitative reflections on time.

The Book of Wisdom explains that the qualitative dimension of life consists of understanding and right conduct:

> The virtuous man though he die before his time, will find rest. Length of days is not what makes age honorable, nor number of years the true measure of life; understanding, this is man's grey hairs, untarnished life, this is ripe old age (Wisdom 4:7–10).

The biblical sense of "redeeming the time" focuses on two interrelated aspects: understanding, a wisdom imparted by the indwelling spirit of God to those who open themselves, and righteous living, which has both ethical and liturgical dimensions. The Israelite was commanded to act justly and to respond to other mandates arising from the covenant with Yahweh. Thus, the ability to "burn" time, to relativize it, becomes a kind of spiritual alchemy that reduces the sheer material weight and extension of our years. It is a process of refining the gold of our lives, of using the pain and the promise of our days to ennoble the golden years with the quality of soul that has been distilled.

The elderly who seek to meet the challenges of aging find themselves pulled between the two poles of time in the face of death. On one side, they can learn to "burn" time, to relativize its threats through qualitative valuing. Yet, on the other side, the specific, durational sense of limited time pulses back into awareness. The alternating rhythms of relativized and extended time form the cadence of elderhood. Both have their threats, challenges, and values. The qualitative sense of time may also be menacing because the aging self may discover spiritual, humanistic, and ethical weaknesses. A paralyzing depression can grip such persons when they juxtapose a negative self-evaluation against their remaining time to make amends. When people are thus impaled on both horns of the dilemma of time, empathetic and sensitive counseling allows the soft voice of the spirit to work its own transformation through suffering the dilemma. As one counselor remarks:

> We may try to force our own hopeful spirit onto those who have begun to reject their self-worth. By denying their real pain and despair, we run the risk of failing to affirm even the tiny amount of light that is left in their lives.[47]

Just as the qualitative appreciation of time can deeply threaten an aging individual, the quantitative sense of limited duration can have a beneficial effect on the elderly self. We have examined the negative or frightening aspects of time as limited duration in old age. Yet this quantitative side of time, when it is personally experienced, and not just a conceptual notion, can heighten our sensibilities to the beauty of otherwise ordinary events. We begin to notice, with a new intensity, the laugh or smile of a friend, the spontaneous joy or tears of children, a special gesture of caring service at the supermarket checkout. We become more attentive to the texture of things: gnarled oaks, robins' breasts, and the pleasing shape of a turn in the road or of an old house. Whether letting in the morning air or closing the shutters at night, we pause for a moment to realize that we are a part of nature and society in this place and time. The limits of our time span in older age can teach us "to experience the ordinary for what it is—part of a gift which has an end as well as a beginning—[and] new emotions emerge: joy that we have been included to receive the gift, reverence before the mystery that this is so."[48]

Challenges from the World

The issues that challenge the aging self during elderhood are not separate from the problems that society and culture produce. A mutual interplay exists between the personal and the social dimensions of elderhood, as any number of examples attest. Yet the awareness of approaching death and cultural attitudes toward aging are two different matters. The former stems from an inner biological clock, the latter from a variety of external, historical forces. Here we are concerned with questions that arise from the historical context in which we grow old and the consequences that this historical milieu has for older persons. Many contemporary social attitudes toward old age in America perpetuate negative nineteenth-century views toward the elderly. From the seventeenth to the nineteenth century, American life shifted gradually from the traditional-agrarian to the modern-technological. As cross-cultural studies indicate, older people generally experience more respect and value in traditional, tribal, hierarchical, and agricultural cultures than in those driven by industrial, pluralistic, and nonfamilial factors. The latter emphasize youth, while they denigrate or merely tolerate the old.

The American Puritans, maintaining a venerable tradition from biblical times, saw old age as a gift from God. In the family, elders assumed patriarchal roles, especially if they were still in control of property. The counsel of the elderly was often sought in affairs of church and state. John Adams could say, "I can never forgive New York, Connecticut or Maine for turning out venerable men of sixty or seventy . . . when their judgement is often the best."[49] Reversal of this traditional attitude toward old people, who in greater numbers were living beyond the period of their children's dependence, can be heard in Emerson's nineteenth-century sentiments: "Nature abhors the old, and old age seems the only disease; all others run into this one."[50] Whereas the seventeenth century assigned active roles in society to the aged, the nineteenth century tended to assume that old age was meant to be a time of repose and disengagement.

Although economic determinants can be overemphasized in this cultural shift in mentality toward the aged, the place of the elderly in industrial societies cannot be overlooked as a major factor in determining the social quality of their lives. Simone de Beauvoir paints too grim a picture of the old in modern industrial states:

> Society inflicts so wretched a standard of living upon the vast majority of old people that it is almost tautological to say "old and poor": again, most exceedingly poor people are old. Leisure does not open new possibilities for the retired man; just when he is at last set free from compulsion and restraint, the means of making use of this liberty are taken from him. He is condemned to stagnate in boredom and

loneliness, a mere throw-out. The fact that for the last fifteen or twenty years of his life a man should be no more than a reject, a piece of scrap, reveals the failure of our civilization.[51]

A more balanced perspective would take into account the various retirement and welfare benefits enjoyed by the elderly in many modern nations. But the overall image of the elderly poor, whether in Third World or in industrialized nations, as thrown on the scrap heap of humanity characterizes the plight of millions around the world. In prophetic tones she describes old age as a "calamity," which exposes the failure of an entire civilization.

In de Beauvoir's view, the economic conditions of industrialized society that have been drastically altering the position of the old for the worse reached their apex in this century. Her theme, with its Marxist overtones, is clear: The oppressive ideology that today abuses the old stems from their deteriorated place in economic systems. The social values deriving from such systems determine how the elderly will be treated. In most modern political economies, these values are duplicitous: an official rhetoric and ethic of respect for the old along with widespread actual discrimination and mistreatment of aged people as inferior beings.[52]

It is not necessary to embrace the Marxist basis of her critique in order to recognize the truth of systematic discrimination against old persons. Nothing short of a profound revolution in the political economies of modern nations, contends de Beauvoir, will improve the lives of the old. The kind of revolution or reform needed is a moot question; in the United States and other countries much that is beneficial can still be realized through political and legal processes. As we will argue in the next chapter, participation of the elderly with other age groups in social reform is a crucial aspect of creative aging.

Social trends in modern times have deeply influenced patterns of aging, with far-reaching consequences for older individuals. The family household has long since ceased to be a center of production, in which the elderly could be easily integrated as valuable contributors. The movement of production to factories leaves senior citizens behind, with the implementation of early retirement that gives rise to the "roleless role" of the elderly.[53] The bureaucratic complexity of industrial society also demands that older persons deal with massive, impersonal organizations in which the individual is merely a number on a computer card.

Modern urban patterns, responding to the needs of a technological economy, have made the extended family of agrarian towns virtually obsolete. The nuclear family, in which both spouses must often work, has neither the time nor the temperament to care directly for elderly relatives. As a result of these changes, many old persons, often those in precarious health, are forced to live in isolated housing or in communities for the elderly. For either of these latter options to be humane, older persons must have adequate economic standing.

For many elderly poor, isolated in grim housing conditions, hampered in access to shopping centers by physical disabilities, lack of transportation or of money, or fear of street crime, old age is anything but golden years in which "the best is yet to be." For these elderly poor, life in an otherwise affluent society becomes a tragedy. In this situation, religion must do more than urge resignation on the part of the afflicted elderly. Nor is religious responsibility met by a casual dismissal of the widespread problem with references to biblical statements such as "for the poor you will always have with you" (Mark 14:8–9).

In truth, this passage, properly understood, is a stinging rebuke to indifference. The constant presence of the poor, far from being an excuse for apathy, represents the summons of God. We are called to both empathy for the elderly poor and involvement in the struggle to change the social structures that oppress these forgotten and destitute persons. Religious motivation for such engagement stems from an ancient western tradition encapsulated in these biblical lines: "You shall rise up before the hoary head, and honor the face of an old man" (Lev. 19:32). It was a sin for a society to despise and oppress the old: "You showed them no mercy; on the aged you made your yoke exceedingly heavy" (Is. 47:6).

Changes in economic and social structures significantly affect the mental, emotional, and spiritual health of the elderly. After compulsory retirement, many worry about maintaining sufficient income, especially in an era of inflation. Others wonder how they will find substitute employment in order to survive in later years. Concerns about housing, safety, community services, and the use of new leisure time impinge on old people. The harvest years, therefore, are not a serene period for a majority of the old. The personal crises of ill health (which may at times be job-related, and therefore social in cause), chronic discomfort, loss of friends, and loss of status are aggravated by social issues that cause depression, anger, and anxiety. For the elderly experience the stress of lowered self-esteem, evoked not only by role loss through retirement, but also by the many ways in which societal attitudes denigrate the old.

Thus, external stress can trigger internal responses of depression, anxiety, psychosomatic illnesses, paranoia, rigid patterns of thinking, helplessness, and irritability.[54] None of these problems are unique to the elderly, but they assume a special poignance among them. In many cases, the elderly do not have the means to alter the social conditions that press down upon them. Indeed, these citizens who have served society in various ways throughout life do not deserve to be rejected and sometimes abandoned by the very communities they helped to build. Although there have been a number of commendable social, legal, and political movements in recent years to better the lot of old people, the impersonal, individualistic, and competitive ethos of contemporary society will indefinitely resist change for the benefit of the aged.

Just as it is important to struggle for reform, it is spiritually significant to realize both the limits of desired change and the intractability of social evil. A kind of Pollyanna liberalism can prevent people from confronting the depths of institutional evil, with its injustices and erosion of personal accountability for these abuses. To encounter societal "powers and principalities" is to understand that they will always be present and powerful. Only by appreciating how radically immersed we are in the darkness and pain of these powers, even contributing to their destructive energies, can we know the mystery of iniquity. In paradoxical fashion, we experience the power of light when engulfed by the powers of darkness.

A spirituality for aging calls for the courage of facing not only our own personal diminishments, but also the social network of oppression toward which we are both accomplices and opponents. It is more than the beginning of wisdom to understand this experientially as we age. This understanding of our involvement in the structures of evil keeps us from making simple divisions between good and bad. Yet it does not hamper our efforts to overcome injustices. Rather, this realistic grasp of our situation tempers our endeavors with humility, as opposed to self-righteousness. Moreover, by making us see the enormity of the problem of social evil, this vision of life makes us all the more sensitive to the need for God's grace to deal with the complexity of the problem.

The impact of social factors on aging can also be approached in a cross-cultural way. Studies of primitive or nonindustrial societies as compared with highly industrialized, urbanized, mostly western societies show important differences in the status of the elderly.[55] The key finding is that certain changes in social attitude and behavior toward the old are closely correlated to the degree of modernization experienced by a particular nation or region. "Modernization" is admittedly a loose word, but some specificity attaches to it when it is further defined by industrialized economies, urbanized cultures, high standards of formal education, greater political pluralism, developed scientific and technological capacities. All this is in contrast to more rural, patriarchal, less literate, and less scientific cultures. The point is not to judge such social forms as inferior, but rather to note the differences in the social condition of the aged. It may well be that the condition of the old in so-called primitive societies can be judged superior to their lot in modernized societies.

Although modernized societies have a larger proportion of old people, the general status of the aged is higher in primitive than in modern cultures. Older persons enjoy greater political and economic power, whereas such influence is possessed by only a few elders in modernized societies. The more intensely familial cultures that venerate ancestors enhance the prestige of the elderly, especially if the old are still in control of family farms or other property.[56] If the old constitute a small proportion of the population, as in primitive societies, their status is higher. This situation might be changed if the proportionately more numerous elderly in modern societies were more effectively organized for political and legal action. This may occur in the United States when the large "baby boom" population born during the post-World War II years enters elderhood at the turn of the century.

The status of the elderly is higher in societies where extended families prevail. Older persons can have more direct influence over relatives than in modern societies with nuclear family patterns. Seniority in the modern family ceases, for the most part, to be decisive in either familial or economic relations. Rather, the old usually live apart from their children and are unable to wield much economic or political influence. Thus the proportion of older persons who maintain leadership roles diminishes in modern societies.[57] In modern society the old increasingly become wards of the state rather than the responsibility of offspring living in their own nuclear families. While certain advantages in the modern situation could be adduced for both the elderly and their children, the overall trend is toward segregation, isolation, and impersonal treatment. Moreover, with the decline of their social effectiveness, the old experience a concomitant loss of self-esteem. While we cannot turn the clock back to an earlier era, we need to attend closely to the societal elements that have altered the life situation of the elderly in contemporary culture. A spirituality for aging must respond to the realities experienced by the old today.

From a cross-cultural perspective, modernized societies seem to be accelerating the rate of social change. Cowgill holds that the status of the old is inversely proportional to the rate of social change.[58] If this is true, the elderly are incrementally facing "future shock." The image is one of a wheel spinning ever faster; its centrifugal force propels the aged away from the center into separate and individualistic styles of life. In important ways, the elderly do not choose the separation nor the individualism of modern society. Rather, these outcomes are the result of socioeconomic forces gaining momentum for at least two centuries. The center of the wheel of social change calls for and glorifies youthful energies to keep it spinning; as a corollary old age is demeaned:

> The glorification of youth and the denigration of old age are . . . results of the growing segregation of different stages of life . . . in modern American society. The socioeconomic changes of the last century have gradually led to a segregation of work from other aspects of life and to a shift from the predominance of familial values to an emphasis on individualism and privacy.[59]

The challenge to those concerned with the well-being of the elderly, therefore, is to discover ways in the modern context to move from segregation to greater integration and from atomistic individualism to authentic community. We usually reserve the word "segregation" for racial divisions, but it applies equally well to the separation of age groups.

In light of this increasing segregation of the old in modern society, the controversial theory of disengagement was developed in the early 1960s.[60] According to the disengagement theory, it is both natural and proper for the old to choose to disengage from their earlier active participation in society. The theory holds that both the older individual and the wider community desire the disengagement of the elderly. Disengagement theorists point to signs that seem to confirm the pattern in contemporary society: The older person moves away from the rewards of more instrumental roles in the midst of social action to relational rewards; the older person tends to seek greater individuation, moving away from the general norms of society that had greater influence in earlier periods of the life span. Disengagement theory was further refined by pointing out that the elderly have a greater awareness of a shorter time to live and of reduced alternatives. Thus they are inclined to shift away from the achievement rewards of middle age toward more personal and relational satisfactions in later years.[61]

The chief criticism of disengagement theory is that it sought to make a virtue of an unfortunate necessity. The critics charge that the disengagement theorists hold simply that whatever is, must be.[62] Since industrial societies shunt the old to the sidelines, the elderly are said to want disengagement. The opponents of disengagement theory, usually gerontologists who favor an interactive theory of aging, point out that disengagement is not a naturally chosen option in primitive and agrarian cultures. The healthy old, they retort, do not desire disengagement from society: rather, they are forced against their wills to accept a less active, sideline position. Some criticize the disengagement theory of aging as a type of adjustment model that in fact covers over the depression of the old who have been compelled to disengage.[63] Others reject the notion as "sludge language" for rationalizing or disguising society's rejection of old people.[64] But the more common criticisms of disengagement come from gerontologists like Havighurst, who propose active engagement in personal and societal tasks as a vital dimension of healthy, creative aging.

Both the disengagement and the interactionist theories of aging address important dimensions of elderhood. Disengagement could be an excuse for the elimination of the old from a production-oriented social system, but there are other ways of understanding disengagement. The inclination of many older persons to further explore and activate their true identities over against collective conventions and demands may be part of the later phases of the individuation process. In the idiom of religion, the individuation process is a spiritual journey. The language of religion implies a certain detachment from worldly affairs in order to permit one's own individual religious calling to develop as fully as possible. In the metaphor of psychology, a certain disengagement from being engulfed in active pursuits allows deeper encounter with enriching forces in one's unconscious, the archetypical images that can lead a person to a fuller spiritual realization in old age. Disengagement from intense, external activity can also give the older person time to cultivate friendships and leisure activities.

Those who propose greater interaction for the elderly are also right in important ways. Both for their own self-esteem and for the contribution that their accumulated experience can make to the wider community, the elderly need to find avenues for interaction with society. Yet a life of constantly programmed activity can lessen personal growth and the thoughtful contribution the old can make to the larger community. Of course, the proportions of disengagement and social involvement differ according to individual temperaments and needs. But in the rhythm of action and withdrawal for reflection, all of life can become a prayer, a human spiritual existence in union with God.

The impact of social change on the aging process is focused, for many, on retirement in our society. The loss of a role in the world of work tends to bring with it a loss of personal power and self-esteem. Although this challenge is also encountered in mid-life career transitions, the middle-aged usually have time to reestablish their places in the occupational sphere. But with retirement, one's association with gainful employment and its ability in our culture to confer power, status, and meaning, is permanently severed for many older people. For the elderly, therefore, it is not merely a matter of role change, but of "role exit."[65]

However much those who are retiring may look forward to ceasing work and having time for other things, emotional problems are frequently linked with this passage from employment to unemployment in old age. Feelings of sadness or depression, of deprivation or uncertainty accompany this transition. Men, in modern societies, have drawn much of their sense of self-worth and potency, in the broad sense of power, from their work. With the ever-growing number of women in the labor force, more of them will be faced with the psychological and emotional challenges of compulsory retirement. The reduction or stoppage of work can undermine the very structure of personality; dignity is closely associated with some form of labor. We can see this clearly among younger persons in less privileged sectors of the population. Long periods of unemployment have an important effect on the deterioration of their personalities and also on their involvement in antisocial attitudes and behaviors.

Social forces presently afoot promise to aggravate the problem of retirement and the consequences of role loss. Earlier retirement may be demanded in some sectors of the work force, because automation eliminates various jobs or because a large younger cohort demands a share of available positions. At the turn of the next century, a very large part of the population in the United States will face retirement and its challenges. Still another factor exacerbating the problem stems from the otherwise very desirable fact that more people are now able to enjoy longer periods of health after retirement. The issue is further complicated by the needs of a highly mobile and differentiated society in which the old are isolated from avenues of reentry into the work world. Browning, looking at these developments from an Eriksonian perspective, sees a deepening conflict between options for care (generativity) and stagnation (self-absorption) for the old.[66]

Nor does it seem sufficient to simply urge less work-role preoccupation as an ideal for older people.[67] While there is great value for the elderly, as we have argued, in pursuing inner psychological and spiritual goals away from total immersion in the work world, we also need meaningful options for continuing participation in the labors of society. For, from a religious viewpoint, significant work makes one a participant in God's creation and providence. Various modern theologies emphasize human involvement in the work of building a more just and humane world. Such work knows no retirement day; loss of such work is the loss of vocation, depriving one of values and meaning.[68]

Again, the point of this discussion is not the abolition of a particular retirement age; retirement may well be necessary in some sectors of the labor force. Rather, the issue to be dramatized, for the sake of the elderly and of society as a whole, is the need for significant opportunities for work after retirement. Here "work" means any esteemed and needed contribution to the common welfare. Such work, however it is structured in terms of time or other conditions, should be remunerated, since money (or its substitute) is a significant token of respect for work in our culture. In reference to retirement, Rosow has underscored the lack of rites of passage to old age in our society, with consequent role discontinuity and ambiguity for the old.[69] For the elderly, this leads to devaluation, stereotyping, exclusion, role loss, and, in many cases, a clinging to youthful self-images. Our social demand that people grow old in this way denies the elderly the possibility of dignity and continued growth as persons. It also deprives society at large of the lively, experienced contribution of the old.

A society that drives the old into a roleless segregation also intensifies their isolation and loneliness. While everyone experiences some loneliness at any age, we do not give sufficient attention to the social factors that accentuate an especially acute loneliness for the old. Their isolation is caused, in part, by physical limitations to mobility, a handicap aggravated by lowered socioeconomic status. In short, the old who live in or near the poverty level experience not only a depressed self-image and lowered morale, but also more intense feelings of isolation and loneliness.[70] Thus, being lonely in older age is not simply a matter of personal temperament or lack of individual initiative to reach out to others. The societal roots of the problem are significant; the elderly who have more money manifest greater self-esteem and morale.[71]

In addition to their material advantages, wealthier old people have greater degrees of self-valuation, which in turn inspires involvement with others. Because they are better dressed, own nicer homes and cars, have educational degrees, these elders naturally expect to be received graciously in society. Conversely, the elderly poor face abandonment by society and a type of social death. In the eighteenth century, Rousseau succinctly described this sad condition: "And old age is, of all ills, that which human aid can least alleviate; they cease to be without others perceiving that they are no more, and almost without perceiving it themselves."[72] Although Rousseau underlines the quiet fading away of the old, he too easily dismisses what human aid might do to alleviate the abandonment of many elderly persons. A nation's provision of adequate income, shelter, nutrition, and other needs can greatly assuage the exaggerated loneliness of old age for the less economically privileged.

Literature graphically portrays the societal dimensions of segregation and abandonment in elderhood. Two figures in Chekhov's *The Cherry Orchard* exemplify a kind of loneliness caused by social forces. Aging Madame Lyubov, born to wealth, is unable to accept the sale of property that reminds her of an older family tradition that new socioeconomic realities are undermining. As a representative of the new order of things confronts her with the reality of selling her estate, we can see her retreating pitifully into the past, isolating herself in memories far from the new Russia of "efficient truth":

> What truth? You see where the truth lies, but I seem to have lost my sight, I see nothing. You settle every problem so boldly, but tell me, my dear boy, isn't it because you're young—because you haven't yet understood one of your problems through suffering? You look forward boldly, and isn't it that you don't see and don't expect anything dreadful because life is still hidden from your young eyes? You're bolder, more honest, deeper than we are, but think, be just a little magnanimous, have pity on me. I was born here, you know, my father and mother lived here, my grandfather lived here, I love this house. I can't conceive of life without the cherry orchard, and if it really must be sold, then sell me with the orchard. . . . My boy was drowned here. Pity me, my dear kind fellow.[73]

Even her wealth and breeding cannot resist the segregating and isolating impetus of social forces. She is seen by the new era as a sad fossil, clinging to outdated traditions, unable to change and adapt.

At least Madame Lyubov has social standing to somewhat mollify her pain. Firs, the eighty-seven-year-old valet in her family, is an even more tragic and rejected figure. Chekhov brings down the final curtain with a lonely view of Firs. When the others have departed from the house and the orchard, Firs is left alone:

> Firs (goes up to the doors, and tries the handles): Locked! They have gone . . . They have forgotten me . . . Never mind . . . I'll sit here a bit . . . These young people . . . Life has slipped by as though I hadn't lived . . . I'll lie down a bit . . . There's no strength in you, nothing left in you—all gone! Ech! I'm good for nothing.

(Lies motionless. A sound is heard that seems to come from the sky, like a breaking harp-string, dying away mournfully. All is still again, and there is heard nothing but the strokes of the axe far away in the orchard.) [74]

Firs represents the more extreme loneliness of the less privileged in face of social change. A similar picture of loneliness and rejection stands out in "Mr. Flood's Party." Old Eben Flood has only himself to address as he lifts his jug to celebrate wistfully what small measure of life is left to him. His friends of other days are gone and the doors of the town are now closed to him:

> There was not much that was ahead of him,
> And there was nothing in the town below—
> Where many strangers would have shut the many doors
> That many friends had opened long ago. [75]

The challenge of loneliness in old age calls for a social as well as a personal response. The social reply must include effective organizing and delivery of adequate social well-being programs to the elderly. This is both a political and a religious mission. We will discuss the politics of aging in the next chapter. The religious mandate stems from the prophetic voices raised to honor the old in the core documents of religions. Honoring the elderly today requires more than lip service at retirement time and at occasional family festivals. It must include involvement in the reform of political, legal, and social structures for the liberation of the old from isolating and dehumanizing conditions. This is a dimension of liberation theology that needs development. The theologians of liberation, especially in Third World countries, have applied biblical interpretations to inspire the general political and economic reform of nations. Such universal change toward more just structures is vital, but a specific focus on the reform needs of particular groups, such as the elderly, requires special attention from liberation theologians that has not yet been forthcoming.

Breaking the elderly out of their isolation from the wider society and the consequent loneliness they suffer also requires a change of attitude among the old themselves. In preparation for the 1981 White House Conference on Aging, Arthur Flemming criticized the churches for fostering a self-centered perspective among the elderly. Religious institutions seem to corroborate the general attitude that the old have served society enough in the past and are now entitled to retire from social commitment to spend their remaining years in private involvements. Fleming comments on the task of the churches toward the elderly:

> Our mission is to break older persons out of that self-centered attitude . . . they have just as much of an obligation to serve their fellow human beings as they had at any other stage in life . . . the older person has the obligation to serve others right down to the day of his or her death. Of course we know from experience that when an older person recognizes and accepts that responsibility it brings a joy and a satisfaction to them that cannot come in any other way.[76]

In fostering the privatized life of the old, the churches also deplete the political influence that the elderly might be able to wield for the welfare of their own age cohort. Sometimes the valid argument that *being* should be respected over *doing* is used to support the inactivity of the old. Yet being and doing, despite our culture's wrong-headed stress on the latter, are not mutually exclusive. They represent, rather, two sides of a polarity that should characterize human life at every stage. *Doing*—the active participation in political, economic, and cultural affairs—should be a part of a vital life as long as health permits.

Older Christians have no mandate to retire from stewardship of the world and from the life-enhancing struggles to better the lot of their fellows. Church leaders, on the other hand, too easily fall into a bifurcated understanding of the world and of their mission to the elderly. Emphasis is placed on the salvation of the soul, to the neglect of the fully embodied person, living in and affected by political-social networks.[77] Moreover, pastors and theologians are unconsciously influenced by a society that demeans old age and sees little value in saving seemingly spent lives. Finally, there is a mistaken notion that the religiousness of the elderly consists exclusively of private devotion and belief in an immortal soul. This is part of the widespread notion that people become increasingly pious in the latter sense as a means to conquer the ravages of time.[78] If piety or religiousness, however, is defined in a more adequate way, religious commitment to social causes, not just private piety, forms an essential part of authentic spirituality.

Although involvement in active pursuits can help the elderly to overcome some isolation and loneliness, old age will necessarily entail a certain aloneness proper to this time of life. The diminishment of physical energies, the death of friends and relatives, the sense of a shortness of time—all these elements and others add to a particular quality of loneliness in old age. Moreover, the accumulation of emotions and hurts from past life add a special edge to the loneliness of later years. However able the elderly may be to convert these sentiments into creative aloneness, a kind of emptiness and loneliness can be both frightening and depressing. Yet loneliness, if we do not run away from it, can be "the key to spiritual life."[79] By entering the doorway of loneliness with both trust and hope, we can find the spiritual energy to release the thoughts that perpetuate, in debilitating ways, emotional hurts from the past and fears about the future.

Without denying aloneness, the old can also experience "inner community," that awareness of being connected with all of life.[80] The sentiment of inner community resembles an ideal of Buddhism: the gradual dissolution of the separate, defensive ego to allow its relatedness to all things to emerge. Thus the loneliness of old age can become a spiritually enriching condition. Perhaps for the first time, the older person experiences the essential aloneness of every human being before the meaning of one's unique life and death. At long last the need to be judged by outside norms and the inclination to falsify oneself in order to please others can be laid aside. "Stripped of the masks and blinders that dimmed one's view of self before, one is forced to confront one's real self, to experience one's dignity . . . it makes one more perceptive of the presence of God who likes to speak in silence."[81] In this silence, life itself can become a prayer of gratitude and of hope, echoing the prayer of Dag Hammarskjold: "Night is drawing nigh; for all that has been, thanks; for all that shall be, yes."[82]

The challenge to old people from today's world is, in summary, to preserve and enhance human dignity in a hostile environment. Modern society has little use for the old, who are seen as excess baggage weighing down the technological vessel. Although we just referred to the importance of some activity for the old, they are particularly burdened and rejected in a society that focuses almost exclusively on *doing* over *being.* Power to get things done is respected and rewarded, but the elderly are associated with powerlessness, with lack of efficacy. Younger and middle-aged people in our culture cannot imagine that they would be happy to be old, to be in a state of powerlessness. Therefore, they resent and reject the elderly. Paul Tournier, in his theological reflections on aging, points to a radical issue for the old:

> I have come to the conclusion that there is one essential, profound, underlying problem, and that is that the old are not loved. They do not feel themselves to be loved, and too many people treat them with indifference and seek no contact with them. . . .[83]

It is very hard to struggle against this stream. The lack of love and respect for the old in our culture causes them to feel unlovable, to lose any sense of empowerment and to withdraw into the quasi-safety of isolation. In a society where the production of things is paramount, people are easily treated as things, to be discarded when no longer useful.

A change in this social pattern, a movement toward the empowerment of the old, depends primarily upon the elderly themselves. One of their most important tasks may be to teach the rest of society that heedless focus on things and on frenetic action will only lead to counterfeit happiness. We often try to conceal our frustrations and fears in acquisition and hyperactivity. But to appreciate the mode of being appropriate to every stage of life, one must learn to sanctify time rather than become a victim of space. "Most of us seem to labor for the sake of things of space. As a result we suffer from a deeply rooted dread of time. . . ."[84] Things, and laboring to acquire things, dominate space. By keeping our lives immersed exclusively in the spatial network, we seek to avoid the voices of time. For the passage of time reminds us of diminishment and death.

To show that every stage of life, in its temporal passage, can be imbued with meaning and value becomes a special responsibility for the elderly. For if they can demonstrate that in old age, the most despised time of life, zest, joy, service, and deep meaning can be found, the aged will not only empower themselves again, they will also encourage younger people to reevaluate elderhood, seeing its promise for their future, as well as its problems. Heschel knew that such living in old age, running counter to the dominant currents of society, needs prayerful communion with the divine presence in the worldly work of sanctifying time:

> He who lives with a sense for the presence knows that to get older does not mean to lose time but rather to gain time. And, he also knows that in all his deeds, the chief task of man is to sanctify time. All it takes to sanctify time is God, a soul, and a moment. And the three are always here.[85]

Challenges from Immediate Others

The older man and woman encounter new problems in relationships with family and friends. For the married elderly, retirement of a husband often means that he will spend more time at home. This can become a source of new stress, especially for relationships that have been relatively unhappy. The divorce rate among the elderly, although still lower than in younger age groups, has been steadily rising. Short of such terminations, both husband and wife have to learn to cope with unresolved problems in the other. A wife may be faced with the psychological strains of a husband unable to adjust to retirement. An older wife may desire to devote more time to organizations outside the home rather than be increasingly limited by the emotional or physical demands of her retired husband. Health problems of either partner may add new strains in the relationship.

Nevertheless, the married elderly have been found to adjust better to the changed circumstances of old age than the single elderly, especially men.[86] These findings indicate the greater mutual support partners experience in marriage. That single men have more difficulty in adjustment may be attributable to men's dependence on women for the daily needs of life; moreover, it may be that men have not learned to handle the emotions of aloneness as well as women in our culture. All of these issues may be further aggravated by poverty or by a lowered economic status. Thus the family in elderhood is beset by many problems.

A spirituality of aging seeks to discover paths toward deeper meaning and experience in and through these difficulties, without offering simplistic solutions. Old age offers a couple the opportunity to move marriage from a merely functional relationship to deeper levels of love and commitment. Many of the functional tasks of raising children and developing a career are behind the husband and wife. Opening new dimensions of communication is especially difficult if the partners have been long alienated from one another, or if they have experienced only routine, functional interchanges in the past. But through the struggles of the later years, when both partners know experientially the shortness of life, a deeper devotion and intercommunion can be realized.

Such devotion and communion unite the couple to God in each other. Augustine understood that even if physical desire diminishes with age, that which the bodily act signifies, the mutual love of the partners, can shine even more brilliantly:

> But now in good, although aged, marriages, albeit there hath withered away the glow of full age between male and female, yet there lives in full vigor the order of charity between husband and wife.[87]

Nor is a degree of "loving strife" foreign to this mutuality.[88] To be profoundly human and spiritual, a relationship need not be placid. Without entering into therapeutic literature on "fighting fair," we can assert that the energy and feeling involved in honest disagreement can be a healthy avenue of interpersonal communication.

A large percentage of older men who lose their spouses remarry; since fewer women remarry, and since women generally live longer than men, there is a very large population of single or widowed elderly women. People remarry for a variety of reasons: companionship, health, and financial motives, as well as for affection and sex. Conventional attitudes on sex for the elderly have fostered unnecessary misconceptions. One erroneous notion is that the elderly do not want sexual relations. It is an easy step from there to claim that older persons *should* not want to engage in sex, and that if they do, they are perverse. Blythe may be overstating the issue when he writes, ". . . [with] any manifestation of an old person's not being in full repressive control of these urges, he or she is seen as either dangerous or pathetic. . . ."[89] The jokes of younger people about geriatric sexuality disguise a disgust and fear. This is partly explainable in a culture that associates sexuality with youthful bodies and, furthermore, is terrified by the prospect of aging and death.

Life sciences tell us, however, that, for the elderly in reasonably good health, sex is a perfectly normal desire and activity. By uncritically embracing social stereotypes, the elderly can deprive themselves of sexuality or feel guilt or unworthiness if they participate in it. Yet the old can also help to change false stereotypes and contribute to a much-needed revision in current attitudes toward sexuality. The elderly can exercise positive attitudes toward physical sexuality and they can foster the truth of the deeper spiritual meaning of sex of which the bodily acts are symbolic. In facing the unique challenges of elderhood, men and women, through sexual love, can demonstrate devotion and commitment in supporting each other, and can thereby manifest to younger people the fuller meaning of love.

As grandparents, the elderly fulfill an important role for future generations. The extent of "grandparenting" depends on a number of variables, including proximity to grandchildren, the health of the grandparents, and temperamental compatibilities with their children and grandchildren. Some grandparents find their contact with children emotionally fulfilling, allowing them to participate vicariously in the accomplishments of their grandchildren. A sense of continuity with their family line also gives a feeling of biological renewal; the new generation, as extensions of the old, will live beyond the death of the elderly—a type of immortality. Although grandparents can spoil children and interfere with parents' plans for rearing their offspring, they may also develop special, positive relationships with grandchildren. Grandparents are far enough removed from the daily disciplines invoked by parents and from the work-a-day pressures on fathers and mothers to be able to offer a special kind of attention to children.

It is a striking fact that many college students have very positive memories of and sentiments toward their grandparents. In the best situations, grandparents become models for meeting life's problems with grace, wisdom, and courage. Thus the role of grandparent is part of the larger mentoring function proper to old age. As mentors to younger generations, whether in their immediate family or beyond it, the elderly exercise the religious ministries of teacher and prophet. This is accomplished as much by example as by instruction. Moreover, the genuine faith and wisdom of old people can have a profound effect on the future attitudes of the young toward religious living. This point is neatly summarized by Fahey:

. . . If older people view life, with its limitations and with its heart-aches, within a spiritual context and with enthusiasm, then they are giving a kind of witness to the validity of religious thought that no young person can ever give. On the other hand, if a person who is older and who has been identified with religion for many years seems to have a narrow perspective in regard to life, shows an intolerance or self-centeredness, then religious views held by that person tend to be rendered incredible in the eyes of the young.[90]

The death of a spouse, after many years of shared life, often trau-matizes the survivor. The loss of a life companion produces emo-tions ranging from grief to depression and anger. Loneliness and deprivation of affection can cause physical as well as psychological suffering. Working through such bereavement may be one of the principal tasks of old age.[91] At first the bereaved person needs to face the reality of a spouse's death within the supporting context of a caring community. Traditional Jewish funeral rituals provide an excellent model for grieving. The reality of the death is affirmed, the survivor is permitted to mourn intensely at first and more mod-erately during the year of reciting Kaddish, and then to gradually reintegrate into the wider community. To become a widow or wid-ower in contemporary society can be much more devastating than it should be for lack of therapeutic and religious rituals for grieving. People need patterned ways of mourning, of expressing even nega-tive feeling and guilts within the sustaining ambience of a caring group.

The surviving spouse, in our individualistic, unrelated society, frequently experiences isolation from former friends with whom he or she previously associated as part of a couple. The bereaved indi-vidual may withdraw all the more from social interaction because he or she feels stigmatized, as one who carries a curse or, at least, a tragedy that is socially unacceptable. Men may undergo this isola-tion even more than widows, in that the latter, being more numer-ous, can more easily discover groups of women with similar experi-ences. The elderly have the opportunity of "rehearsing," in a sense, the death of a mate because many friends and associates in the same age group will experience similar situations. It remains to be seen whether persons linked in more egalitarian modern marriages will be better able to cope with the loss of a mate. A greater economic and social independence may especially aid women in this difficult transition.

An important ministry for the elderly and for churches consists in helping widows and widowers through the loss of a spouse. Much can be learned in this area from the knowledge and experience of modern associations like Hospice and other death-therapy agencies. Assisting the surviving spouse with problem-solving, emotional guidance, and creative reintegration into the community remains a largely neglected ministry. By contrast, the role of the widow in the early church was held in high esteem as one of providing spiritual guidance. Augustine reiterates a theme evidenced in other patristic writings on widowhood:

> ... whilst charity carries the vigor of this beauty into things that are before, length of years causeth not in it a wrinkle. You have with you a holy aged woman, both in your house and in Christ, whom to consult concerning perseverance; how you are to fight with this or that temptation, what you are to do, that it may be the more easily overcome; what safeguard you are to take, that it may not easily again lay wait; and if there be anything of this sort, she teaches you, who is not by time fixed, by love a well-wisher, by natural affection full of cares, by age secure ... in such things consult her, who hath made trial of what you have made trial of.[92]

Still another area of challenge arises from the relationship between middle-aged children and elderly parents. Both aging children and old parents are faced by questions of dependency and responsibility. Earlier roles are reversed; it now becomes the offspring's responsibility to take care of elderly fathers and mothers, while they, in turn, struggle with problems of dependency, of being burdens on others. We live in a society that values independence and individuality. As persons in such a social order confront greater physical and emotional dependency, their self-esteem and sense of social worth can be injured. Most older persons try to maintain independence from their children as long as possible. Much has been made in the contemporary media about neglect of elderly parents by their children. Horror stories of rejection by children and of "warehousing" aged parents abound. Even when the more extreme cases of such neglect are avoided, there remains the more general question of what to do about elderly parents who cannot fend for themselves. A surprisingly large number of families in the United States, about eight percent, are multigenerational.[93] A number of factors contribute to the multigenerational family, including divorce, death, financial expediency, and child care.

Yet the mobile nuclear family, often with both spouses working, has considerable difficulty taking in aged parents, especially if they need a good deal of direct attention. When a history of generational conflict has alienated children from their parents, the latter become increasingly outsiders to their children.[94] Again, the impersonal, urbanized nuclear family fosters such distancing. There is less social condemnation for neglecting aged parents. Despite these inducements to abandon old parents to social institutions, many well-intentioned middle-aged sons and daughters are torn by conflicting motives and emotions. They feel responsible to give first priority to their own children and mates in an era when time for quality relationships is at a premium. But they are also motivated by love, duty, and guilt toward their own parents in the diminishments of later maturity. The parents may accuse their children of ingratitude and selfishness. Unless the situation is resolved, the sons and daughters continue to experience the direct and indirect effects of simmering guilt and resentment toward their old parents. Sadness and bitterness about their children may accompany the fathers and mothers to the grave.

The reconciliation of these conflicting sentiments is a task of great spiritual sensitivity. The parents need to gain a realistic understanding of the pressures on the families of their middle-aged children. If the elderly can communicate this appreciation with empathy and without subtle guilt messages, children will be more disposed to admire and to show affection for their parents. Perhaps the most beautiful legacy that aging parents can leave to their children is a personally lived lesson about facing old age and death with courage and grace:

> . . . you look to your sixty-or-seventy-year-old parents for your last lessons: how to go on living and how to die. If they are healthy and active and contented, you are happy for them and you seek to imitate them. If they are miserable, you try to help them, but you also hope that you will not imitate them. One way or another, they are your inheritance: your blessing or your curse.[95]

On the other side of the reconciling process, children have an important responsibility to care for their parents. I Timothy reminds Christians of the close link between genuine religious faith and faithfulness to parents: "If anyone does not provide for his relatives, and especially for his own family, he has disowned the faith and is worse than an unbeliever" (I Tim. 5:8).

Yet given the probable persistence of the nuclear family structure in urbanized, technological societies, institutional care of the elderly will most likely be the lot of increasing sections of the population. Institutions for the old will surely play a more important role in the early part of the next century, as the "baby boom" group born in the forties and fifties reaches elderhood with ever-longer life expectancies. The question, therefore, is not whether there will be facilities for the elderly apart from their immediate families, but what kind of institutions these will be. Will they be private or public or a combination of both? Will they be intergenerational places or exclusively for the old? A key issue will be how well the environment of these institutions fosters a quality of life contributing to personal growth and social involvement.

Yet whatever shape these homes for the elderly may take, the obligation of filial care persists for sons and daughters. This means more than financial support or finding a suitable retirement home for parents. The mandate in the passage from Timothy above includes the most difficult demand, that of finding time for one's parents, for their emotional and spiritual well-being. Moreover, in our society the meaning of the injunction from Timothy must be extended beyond one's immediate relatives. For there is a constantly growing portion of the population who will never have married or who in old age will be alone, without immediate family. The needs of this very large group of single individuals calls for a rethinking of the meaning of "relatives" in the scriptural passage. Although it is difficult for us to exercise care much beyond blood-related circles, the measure of one's spiritual depth may consist in precisely such a wider commitment, in a broader definition of who constitutes my "family."

The challenges from self, world, and immediate other must be seen within the pervasive social context of ageism. In all these areas, elderhood is negatively perceived as a condition to be banished from awareness or reviled as fearsome and disgusting. Ageism thereby permits younger people "to see older people as different from themselves. Thus they subtly cease to identify with their elders as human beings."[96] Butler succinctly defines ageism as "a process of systematic stereotyping of and discrimination against people because they are old as racism and sexism can accomplish this with skin color and gender. Old people are categorized as senile, rigid in thought and manner, old fashioned in morality and skills."[97] Yet the overall environment of ageism in which we grow old is not the last word, as if we could point a finger at a hostile social ambience to excuse ourselves from individually grappling with the problems of old age.

The context of ageism must be taken seriously as a realistic starting point, as a grim preface against which we shape our personal lives in elderhood. But the rest of the story will need to mark out how we resist the insidious stereotyping within ourselves and how we fight against it in the public domain. As we noted at the beginning of this chapter, ageist attitudes have been deeply seared into our civilization for centuries. While we battle to reduce this oppressive milieu for elderhood, we recognize that we will grow old and die within a relatively ageist society. Therefore, a final word beyond that of social struggle concerns our personal integration in old age, our ability to give our lives both significance and peaceful resolution as the end approaches.

We can be helped to accomplish this personal task in elderhood by entering into the process of life review. In recent times, life-review therapy has been formalized into techniques that aid "a progressive return to consciousness of past experiences, in particular the resurgence of unresolved conflicts which can now be surveyed and integrated."[98] This therapy has been conducted in an individual mode through the use of written and pictorial autobiographical material and also through group sessions. Although the life-review process has been helpfully orchestrated and systematized in modern psychological idiom, its history has roots in spiritual and secular literature from ancient times to the present.

The Bible repeatedly urges the faithful to assess their lives, not in terms of immediate joys and sufferings, but in the spectrum of beginnings and ends. Repentance for past failings, forgiveness by God and neighbor, and ultimate reconciliation with nature, fellow humans, and the divine are elements of this perennial process. This reflection on one's past choices and acts, one's injuries to others and to oneself, as well as one's creative endeavors, has constituted a crucial dimension of retreat spirituality since the Middle Ages. It is part of the long *memento mori* tradition, in which we remember or recollect our lives toward greater integration in face of death. Modern writings such as Ernest Hemingway's *The Snows of Kilimanjaro,* Samuel Beckett's *Krapp's Last Tape,* and Tolstoy's *The Death of Ivan Illych,* illustrate the process of life review.

In an article on Ingmar Bergman's *Wild Strawberries,* Erik Erikson focuses on the film's protagonist, Dr. Isak Borg, in his painful yet positive process leading toward integration of past and present in old age.[99] Erikson casts Borg's life-review venture in the framework of the polarities between despair and integration, the tension proper to Erikson's old-age stage of human development. Borg is threatened by final despair in his later years as he muses on a life of professional and material success, but also of emotional and spiritual emptiness. In Freudian language, Borg has learned to work but not to love. Erikson notes that Borg is compelled to deal with his life as it truly happened; he is not permitted to hide from despair or gloss it over with thoughts about life after death:

> Despair tells us that the time is too short, if not altogether too late, for alternative roads to Integrity; this is why the elderly try to "doctor" their memories. Rationalized bitterness and disgust can mask that despair which in severe psychopathology aggravates a senile syndrome of depression, hypochondria, and paranoiac hate. Whatever chance man has to transcend the limitations of his self seem to depend on his full (if often tragic) engagement in the one and only life cycle permitted to him.[100]

Ostensibly religious people may easily be tempted to avoid the pain involved in the process of life review and incline toward sweet forgetfulness or comforting reflection on salvation after death. In *Sabbatical,* Brita Stendahl challenges her aged and dying father to confront the unresolved conflicts of his past through writing his memoirs. Instead of humoring an elderly father with inauthentic niceness (actually a way of ignoring and demeaning the old), she urges him to engage in the struggle toward a fuller quality of life, toward greater reconciliation through a confrontation with past hurts:

> . . . . My challenge to him that he write his memoirs brought about conflict where he had already spread out a comforting coverlet. His wish had been to die in peace and at peace with everybody. A rose-colored forgiving forgetfulness. I ripped that coverlet off by forcing him to remember and, as a consequence, to suffer and feel guilty about incidents of the past. Time and time again he has said "I have to write this out of me". . . .
>
> One thing I know is that I returned him to life, to the tension that is the pulse of life. It made him unhappy, but it made him alive. These memoirs, which I had envisioned would give him pleasure, gave him also intense pain. The past overshadowed the future, and in this perspective he again was in need of full absolution.[101]

In this instance, as well as in *Wild Strawberries,* it is the daughter who challenges her old father to face the unresolved conflicts of a life review. Both of these women resemble Lear's Cordelia, symbolic of both the actual daughter and the inner feminine, the neglected voice in man drawing him toward psychic wholeness. Such integrity is never fully attained, but a person can realize a deeper reconciliation of previous and present conflicts. If one is in touch with archetypical images from the unconscious, this spiritual adventure proceeds at greater depth. This process may be a fairly brief one at the very end of life, or it can be a gradual journey in later maturity, ideally a path begun in midlife and culminating amid the peculiar challenges of old age.

In this attempt to create meaning for the whole span of one's life, the elderly person will encounter unhappy and unhealed memories. There will be moments of guilt, sadness, resentment, possibly even of remorse and the edge of despair. With time greatly shortened before death, such an old seeker will experience the descent of his or her spirit, the going down to Hades or into the dark night of the soul. The psychospiritual journey offers no easy ascent. Comfortable elevations toward transcendence are eminently suspect, resembling Bonhoeffer's "cheap grace." This greater measure of fear and hope, especially in the face of worldly standards, which attribute no future to the old, is not easily won.

Again, the paradox: "Sailing to Byzantium" is a hard voyage. Yeats understood the challenge of old age, that without the arduous path of soul-making, "An aged man is but a paltry thing. / A tattered coat upon a stick. . . ." One has to sense his or her human paltriness in depth, to wear the tattered coat in order that one's "Soul clap its hands and sing, and louder sing / For every tatter in its mortal dress."[102]

V

ELDERHOOD:
THE POTENTIALS

When a man grows old his joy
Grows more deep day after day,
His empty heart is full at length,
But he has need of all that strength
Because of the increasing Night
That opens her mystery and fright.
Fifteen apparitions have I seen;
The worst a coat upon a coat-hanger.
W. B. Yeats, *"The Apparitions"*

In these lines, Yeats invokes a positive image of old age, growing joy, and a full heart. But the poet also voices a threatening paradox. Although fulfillment is possible, "increasing Night" seems to swallow up peace and happiness for many persons in their later years. Thus his worst apparition, "a coat upon a coat-hanger," resembles the image in "Sailing to Byzantium," the old man as a "tattered coat upon a stick." Many forces, physical, psychological, and social, menace the elderly today. Consideration of possibilities for spiritual growth in the last phases of life must not take a Pollyana approach. On the physical level alone, serious disabilities afflict numerous elderly persons. Evidence shows that poor health effects negative personality changes in the aging process.[1] Yet it is remarkable how some older individuals cope creatively with the limitations and sufferings of declining health. The last chapter examined psychological and social losses that constitute part of Yeats's frightening Night. But terror is not the last word; for the Night also opens up her mystery. Mystery is the locale of wisdom, that fertile place from which new possibilities can emerge. In the last chapter we intimated that the drawbacks of old age can become thresholds for spiritual growth and significant contributions to society.

Before we pursue these possibilities, it is important to review the meaning of *religiousness* or *spirituality*, as these terms are used in this essay. This is especially valuable in avoiding confusion with much empirical research on religion and old age. Most investigations examine religious conduct and/or tenets. For the most part, such behavior and belief are construed in traditional, compartmentalized ways. How frequently do older persons attend church or synagogue activities? Do they contribute to such religious institutions either financially or through personal involvements? A broad Lou Harris survey exemplifies the polling of church-related behavior and ideology.[2] Other investigators find a slight "return to religion," understood as interest in the church, during later years.[3] When researchers employ sophisticated instruments to analyze religiousness among the elderly, they find that religious feelings remain strong even though involvement in institutions may decline.[4] Moberg's study, based on Charles Glock's five dimensions of religiosity (experiential, ideological, ritualistic, intellectual, and consequential), comes closer to the understanding of spirituality in this book. But even this approach tends to focus too narrowly on religiosity as traditionally interpreted. In general, this conventional view portrays religiousness as a separate experience associated with church practices and specific beliefs in an accepted idiom.

In light of our discussion of a spirituality of aging, this traditional understanding of religiousness is not wrong, but rather too limiting. The modern mind tends to pigeon-hole religion, as well as other areas, for purposes of organization and control. We like to be tidy, to fit events into the proper section of the newspaper or weekly newsmagazine. There is value, of course, in such compartmentalizing, for it provides focus and framework. Moreover, there is a danger of confusion, of amorphous blending, if religiousness becomes indistinguishable from other aspects of life. Yet our treatment of the aging process is more willing to run the risk of overextension than to confine itself to the scope of the usual studies on religion and aging.

In brief, we are searching for the religiousness that is intrinsic to, that compenetrates the losses and gains, the descents and ascents of the aging process. Such religiousness can be discussed in terms of the traditional idioms of major religions, but it is not confined to these languages. To be religious, among other things, is to confront the boundaries of life and death, to grapple with hope and despair, to puzzle over decisions of good, evil, and mixtures of both. It means walking to the edges of the mystery at the heart of existence. Such encounters in the midst of the challenges of aging open a person to transcendent experiences, to the numinous, with its wonder, blessing, and terror. Forty years ago, Karl Stolz spoke about one's religiousness as the "master sentiment," the organizing and stabilizing function of the personality.[5] Spirituality, therefore, is not without focus; rather, its lines mark a wider canvas.

The Elderly Self

With this concept of religiousness, we pursue in greater detail the spiritual potentials of elderhood. How can later maturity be a time for distinctive, in-depth, personal growth and indispensable contributions to a more just and peaceful humankind? In the chapters on midlife we argued against the prevalent cultural bias, saying that the middle years required an inward, contemplative movement. Technological society would have the middle-aged, now at the height of their productive powers, compete and strive in the manner of the young. On the other hand, the same social forces are all too willing to encourage the elderly to separate themselves from the centers of political and economic decision making. Whether the older person disengages from the centers of societal life for private diversions or inward reflection makes little difference to younger decision makers.

In opposition to this centrifugal hurling of the elderly to the periphery of life, we will call for a new coalition of elderly persons to resist the fragmentation and dispersal of the old to the pastures of disengagement. A new politics of the elderly needs to take shape and to find a significant voice in the strongholds of power. The mere state of being elderly confers no special wisdom or talent. But if more persons in midlife and elderhood could embrace the spirituality and commitment under consideration, older persons would be in a specially privileged position to make unique contributions to important issues vexing nations, communities, and individuals. We will stress this social involvement as a crucial part of elderly spirituality in the second section of this chapter. It is first important to explore potentials for spiritual growth on the level of the self. Without such personal development, with its insights and transformations, there would be little motivation to foster political and social involvements among the elderly. Furthermore, without spiritual renewal of the self, the contributions themselves of old people to humanity would suffer in quality.

A primary task for older people is to divest themselves of negative stereotypes of what it means to be old. This is no easy chore, as an ageist culture surrounds us with harmful images of old age. Throughout life we subliminally take in these images and make them part of our own belief system about elderhood. The elderly, therefore, become victims of their own negative conditioning. In trenchant language, Alex Comfort delineates the destructive stereotypes still prevalent in western culture. Although his statement is exaggerated in some ways, it serves to highlight the ageist environment that is either overt or lurking just beneath the surface of social interactions:

> He or she is a white-haired, inactive, unemployed person, making no demands on anyone . . . docile in putting up with loneliness, rip-offs of every kind and boredom, and able to live on a pittance. He or she . . . is slightly deficient in intellect and tiresome to talk to . . . asexual, because old people are incapable of sexual activity, and it is unseemly if they are not. He or she is unemployable, because old age is second childhood and everyone knows that the old make a mess of simple work. Some credit points can be gained by visiting or by being nice to these subhuman individuals, but most of them prefer their own company and the company of other aged unfortunates. Their main occupations are religion, grumbling, reminiscing and attending the funerals of friends. If sick . . . they need not be actively treated, and are best stored in unsupervised institutions. . . . A few, who are amusing or active, are kept by society as pets. The rest are displaying unpardonable bad manners by continuing to live . . . when society has declared them unpeople and their patriotic duty is to lie down and die.[6]

If this picture is extreme, it also contains important truth about the environment of aging. Comfort's statement indicates that the old need financial security, medical care, and useful work; but implied by and underlying these requirements is the even more significant need for dignity. The potential contributions of the elderly to their own development and to society cannot be realized if such internalized stereotypes continue to hamper self-image and self-esteem.

In the difficult work of changing the image of old age, the elderly must first recognize the degree to which they have incorporated this image into their own way of seeing themselves. Positive, in-depth reflections on the possibilities for significant living amid certain physical diminishments can also help to restore dignity. The elderly can also be inspired by outstanding examples of old persons who lived fully in their later years. Models can be drawn from artists, inventors, statesmen, and persons of distinction in other fields who continued to contribute greatly to society despite physical impairments. There is danger in holding up brilliant models in old age, for figures such as Picasso, Edison, and Whitehead can produce discouragement by contrast. Yet each individual must look to his or her gifts, which can be stymied by the stereotypes of old age or facilitated by enhanced dignity through reflection on the lives of great old persons. Still another way of fighting the stereotype of advanced age is direct engagement in the political issues of the aged. Maggie Kuhn, who founded the Gray Panthers when she was sixty-four, claims, "One reason our society has become such a mess is that we're isolated from one another. The old are isolated by government policy."[7] Each of these methods fosters pride in age among the elderly. The transformation of destructive stereotypes will have to commence in the minds and hearts of older persons themselves: "Until there is a pride in age by the aged, it will continue to be treated as a punishment and as if it were some terrible sickness."[8]

Yet for the elderly self to sustain its dignity in a profound way, the issue of death must be faced. Without such a recurrent encounter with mortality in older age, potential for psychological-spiritual growth in the soul is lessened. For even positive growth qualities, cited by developmental psychologists of old age, can become futile if they are cultivated in order to escape confrontation with personal death. We will discuss these positive traits of growth in elderhood only after, and in light of, the prior facing of death. Furthermore, grappling with death can lead the elderly person to a new degree of faith, hope, and freedom that will affect social involvements and friendship building. It may seem exaggerated to take up again the topic of one's own death, since we spoke of it as a crucial dimension of midlife transitions. But death influences persons differently in the later years; middle age brings home to us the reality of our mortality, but old age makes that reality more concrete and proximate. The sense of a truly limited lifetime pervades; there is a special intensity of awareness about the final departure. Yeats captures some of this feeling in his poem "Death":

> Nor dread nor hope attend
> a dying animal;
> A man awaits his end
> Dreading and hoping all;
> Many times he died,
> Many times rose again.[9]

The poet focuses on the experience of dreading and hoping at once: the dread of losses, sufferings, and the unknown, and hope for survivors, for the earth, and for oneself. Some, armed with sociological inquiries, argue that the elderly fear death less than younger people. To some extent this is true, as we see in the interviews of the next chapter, and as is clear in various quotations below. But such claims of acceptance of death among the elderly must be examined more critically. Is this alleged acceptance a mere resignation before brute facts? Or is it a subtle way of taming the terror by issuing brave statements, like a lone person at night whistling a gay tune while walking through a graveyard? Or is the claim of being at peace with death the outcome of a serious and repeated meditation on personal demise and its meaning for enhancing the quality of inner life and outward commitments?

As intimated in the Yeats verse quoted above, death gradually educates the person who faces it with sincerity. It teaches its lessons and reveals its potentials by repetition: "Many times he died, / Many times rose again." The influential Lutheran theologian Joseph Sittler discusses this pedagogy of death, linking it to the ancient church tradition of *ars moriendi,* the art of dying learned by many rehearsals: "We are instructed in the fact and the inevitability of our own death by the little deaths in our personal world."[10] The elderly Sittler becomes aware of the losses of theological partners and friends. But these small deaths also lead us to struggle in elderhood with a basic paradox of being human. This paradox has been stated traditionally as the battle between *eros* and *xanatos,* with *eros* representing the life forces and *xanatos* those of dissolution. Fiedler describes this paradoxical situation as the "absurdity underlining both comedy and tragedy."[11] He further explains the paradox as "an absurdity which arises out of the conflict between the desire we cannot deny without denying the very wellspring of our existence (Eros) and the fragility of the flesh upon which the satisfaction of that desire depends."[12] Fiedler wonders whether this absurdity can be transcended by an act of faith or a renunciation of the passion for life or both. Ever-deepening faith in the face of death not only refuses to renounce the life passions, but transforms and heightens their meaning.

Rather than seeking to escape or disguise the paradox of old age, that is, the inevitable conflict between *eros* (as life desires) and *xanatos* (the weakening vessel for carrying out those desires), we need to enter more fully into the paradox in order to discover its new meaning and promise. The way into this final phase of personality transformation has been aptly described as growth through diminishment.[13] The paradoxical phrase "growth through diminishment" does not mean that the all-too-real diminishments of age are good in themselves. The concept is not a slogan for a kind of ascetic mysticism bordering on masochism. It does, however, move beyond the view of traditional discussions of old age, such as Cicero's *De Senectute,* which focus on the positive qualities of old age left over from younger years, as well as new satisfactions found in elderhood. These good points need to be cultivated, but their deeper meaning is lost if they are not also understood in the wider context of diminishments. To find significance in diminishments calls for faith and hope. One has faith that beneath, through, and beyond the diminishments there is a life-giving power that will draw special good for humanity and the world of nature from the diminishments.

An analogy from nature can be transposed to the spiritual realm. The seed decays in the ground while it also takes on new life-giving properties from the nuturing forces of the earth. Civilizations decay and give rise to unsuspected cultural and political developments. It is not the decay as such that gives birth to the transformation, but rather the unrecognized, unbidden forces released in the process. These analogies more closely approach the spiritual zone in the example of biblical Israel. The nation could not be saved, nor become an instrument of world renewal as long as it relied on the power of armies and kings (traits of youth). Rather, in the days of diminishment, of exile and misfortune, Israel returned to its faith in Yahweh, whose life-giving power was able to effect renewal and blessings.

It is as though the unmitigated qualities of youthful power interfered with the subtle, deeper energies of divine transformation. Paul echoes this truth when he speaks of the power of God made manifest through weakness. This is a mystery, in the sense of being a process that we can only partially comprehend, but it is not mystification. "Growth through diminishment" is not a magic phrase that achieves goals by its own incantatory repetition. The analogies to nature and history provide some insight into the reality signified by the phrase. But to ultimately embrace the diminishments of age as avenues of personal development and even public benefit requires faith and hope in a finally benevolent force sustaining the world and working inscrutably in the dynamic of rebirth through decline.

Yet this strange alchemy of personal deepening, with imporant social ramifications, through diminishments is in no way automatic. Rather, it calls for active participation by those who would follow its path. The physical and mental sufferings of the elderly make diminishments an easy source for bitterness and despair. These attitudes are understandable, but from the perspective of Teilhard de Chardin, when they become a person's dominant stance, they impede the work of grace in the world. Teilhard spoke eloquently of "the divinization of our passivities."[14] Passivity in this context is akin to diminishment. But the term *passivities* could be easily, though erroneously, interpreted as being passive amid the hardships of elderhood. This would amount to no more than a religious disengagement theory, in which the elderly retreat away from life into a quiet faith in God and possibly a hope for afterlife.

But the Teilhardian vision involves a more complex fusion of the active and passive. In the very act of embracing the diminishments of age through faith, one continues to contribute to the development of the world. In the Christic idiom of Teilhard: "If Christ is to take possession of all my life . . . then it is essential that I grow in him not only by means of . . . the supremely unifying amputations of suffering [the diminishments], but also by means of everything that my existence brings with it of positive effort."[15] It is as though the diminishments themselves serve as a purifying catalyst to allow a deeper transformation of the personality and a consequent worldly endeavor of greater value. The passivities, as "providential diminishments," are intimately correlated to "collaborating passionately in the human effort."[16]

For Teilhard, the diminishments themselves can assist us in making the radical sacrifice of egoism. As exaggerated self-interest or selfishness is purged away through sufferings of elderhood, a reversal or "ex-centration" takes place. Teilhard sees that which is more divine, more Christ-like, occupying the center of our being. With this Christic energy at the heart of our efforts, the activities of elderhood, even though less energetic or fast-paced than those of the younger years, have a richer quality and power for developing the world. The divinization of our passivities, therefore, signifies a spirituality of less egocentric activity. Teilhard's ideal for elderhood is equivalent to a worldly mysticism. As the elderly increasingly influence the world around them, both the quality of their insights and goals and the means for achieving them will be enhanced by such a spirituality of growth through diminishment.

This theme has been voiced in various ways in the religious literature on aging. Nearly a century and a half ago, in a quaintly titled book, *Euthanasy or Happy Talk Towards the End of Life,* the author expressed a spiritual value in the diminishments of age:

> Is your eyesight dimmer? Then the world is seen by you in a cathedral light. Is your hearing duller? Then it is just as though you were always where loud voices and footsteps ought not to be heard. . . . Yes, for twilight and silence . . . old age makes us like daily dwellers in the house of the Lord; and a mortal sickness does this sometimes, as well as old age.[17]

In our own time, similar voices are heard among the aged. In an interview with a very elderly Anglican priest, Father Congreve, the view of old age as a time for centering and loving stands out:

> God is making all things dark and silent around me. . . . I must begin to long for home. I seem almost asleep, but my heart is awake. It does not think, or plan, or labor to remember, but it loves; it is with-

drawn from the surface to the centre. . . . My God, I would not die as the unconscious things, the frozen sparrow under the hedge, the dead leaf whirled away before the night wind.[18]

Father Congreve expresses less potential for direct activity in the world than does Teilhard de Chardin's mysticism of diminishments. The latter, however, develops a general spirituality for the whole period of elderhood, while the Anglican priest relates his personal experiences of extreme old age. Yet even in this phase of greatly curtailed activity, important movements are at work in his life. He notes the pattern of centering, or the reintegration of self and the supremely valuable ability to love. These thoughts are reminiscent of a statement by an old Mexican-American interviewed by Robert Coles in New Mexico: "There are some joys to old age, but none greater than realizing that finally you are learning about the really important things. Perhaps God reveals some of His mysteries to us at the very end before He receives us. . . ."[19]

A person of mature faith can enter the final phase of life with a spirit that enlivens elderhood and makes peace with death. This wonderful potential does not minimize the physical sufferings and mental doubts of this period. The old, more than most people, understand personally the Pauline statement, "We have this treasure in earthen vessels" (II Cor. 4:7). But amid these hardships, the older person of faith faces death not with stoic resignation, but with a firm hope in the power of God to sustain the self in its ultimate trial and to give it courage and insight to serve humanity to the end. Such people give others an invaluable testimony that the weight of years, rather than deteriorating the quality of life, can infuse it with unsuspected riches. The dialectic of being active and passive, of fulfillment and emptiness in the diminishments of age that lead to death, is a mysterious paradox. Yet, as Leo O'Donovan writes:

> The paradox does remind us . . . that there is a trusting surrender at the heart of life without which it all too easily becomes a mockery of autonomous self-assertion; there is a passion of obedience to a greater good without which any action of love can quickly become self serving and empty.[20]

This faithful surrender to God amid the sufferings of old age constitutes a profound act of obedience. It testifies to the belief that powerful human effort alone will not save us as individuals or as collectivities. Older people who deeply understand this message are in a unique position to be responsible and free persons. As they are freed by faith and hope from the terror of their own deaths and the need to defend themselves selfishly against it, they will be better able to serve others. Their insights and commitments will be less distorted by the myopia of self-interest. The older person with such an outlook will take a broader perspective on individual and social problems. For he or she is in the world as a place to be loved, not selfishly possessed. Such a one is already both of time and eternity. This elder can become a "wounded healer," whose personal experience of suffering and death unleashes healing compassion and vision for others.

It is important to avoid glibness in urging the old to make friends of their infirmities. These diminishments are frequently onerous and painful. Yet a faith-inspired attitude toward handicaps as part of the life-long dialogue with a suffering God who accompanies our journey can become the spiritual basis for an old age that blesses both self and others. The time-honored aphorism that only the wounded physician heals bears directly on this point. This notion of making-well-again pertains both to the old themselves and to those influenced by them. On the physical level, evidence increases today about psychosomatic healing through transforming one's attitude toward illnesses and other handicaps.[21]

Psychological healing of one's own spirit requires an energetic but faith-filled encounter with personal wounds. Our physical and mental hurts can become teachers of understanding and empathy. Scholars have noted the gerontomorphic images of God in our cultural tradition, that is, God portrayed in the figure of an old man. God or the gods are described as old, wise, and powerful.[22] Simmons speculates that the old have traditionally been the custodians of religion, and thus have shaped positive pictures of divinity in their own best images. A more authentic image of God in the guise of the old, however, is that of a wounded healer, of one who has suffered the wounds of life's ages, whose wisdom and mercy are healing precisely because these qualities have been forged in the crucible of the world's suffering.

The elder as wounded healer can be seen living out a most productive part of life. For a variety of reasons, the old often choose or are forced to withdraw from involvements that could be beneficial to other individuals or groups. The elderly are too quick to internalize the cultural stereotypes of old age as a less productive period and indulge in self-fulfilling prophecies of disengagement, of going or being put out to pasture. Robert Louis Stevenson strongly protested such waste of the elderly. In his little known work *Aes Triplex,* he vigorously emphasized the contagious wisdom and courage of old people amid personal disablements and the threat of death. He underscored the special contribution of those who struggle to be creative in spite of wounds and menaces:

> By all means begin your folio; even if the doctor does not give you a year, even if he hesitates about a month, make one brave push and see what can be accomplished in a week. It is not only in finished undertakings that we ought to honour useful labour. A spirit goes out of a man who means execution, which outlives the most untimely ending. All who have meant good work with their whole hearts have done good work, although they may die before they have time to sign it. Every heart that has beat strong and cheerfully has left a hopeful impulse behind it in the world, and bettered the tradition of mankind.[23]

There is an important aspect of faith that pervades this passage. Stevenson implies that those who begin their folios despite pressing threats of illness or death trust in a purpose larger than themselves. It goes beyond the limits of our normal calculations to believe that the work of a year or a month will "leave a hopeful impulse behind it in the world." Indeed, this optimism is all the more surprising in light of the disabilities that people face with declining health.

Such faith in the value of struggling against diminishments, confident of a positive result for society, even though they might not live to see those results, has marked the lives of well-known elderly people. For some, this faith was more explicitly expressed in a profound trust that God blesses the special endeavors of those whose work is purified of self-seeking amid the hardships and shortened time of old age. In his late seventies, Pope John XXIII, much to the surprise of many observers, launched the Second Vatican Council, which initiated far-reaching reforms in the Catholic Church. Mahatma Gandhi was seventy-two when he led the final movement for Indian independence just a year before his death. Both of these men were steeped in religious faith that relied upon a greater power and wisdom to supplement and to carry out their seemingly weak efforts. In the arts and sciences, in medicine and social services, many names could be cited of older persons who began "new folios" in advanced years.

For many of these elders, the physical limitations of old age served to refine their vision of beauty and value and strengthen their resolve to leave contributions to posterity. Without trying to force him into a religious mold, we can note that Bertrand Russell's campaign for nuclear disarmament and his other social commitments, lasting into his nineties, portrayed an implicit faith in the ability of social protest to tap sources of good will and conscience in fellow humans. Russell was a man of passion, and passions move us beyond what can be rationally expected to what is hoped for even in the face of great opposition and hardship. Just before his death, this secular philosopher summarized his philosophy of life as a reaching for goals that imply faith: "Three passions, simple but overwhelmingly strong, have governed my life: the longing for love, the search for knowledge, and unbearable pity for the suffering of mankind."[24]

We have stressed the theme of growth through diminishments, with its roots in a profound faith, be it explicit or implicit, because such growth provides the undergirding motif for the self's creative potential in old age. Nevertheless, there is a danger in focusing exclusively on positive mental-health scenarios for the old, as though these psychological formulae could be applied without a searching assessment of the true context of old age. Put yet another way, the diminishments of old age, physical, social, and psychological, deeply affect the human person. Elderhood is not the same as the younger stages of life, as though one's aging organism were merely an accidental aspect of an unchanged soul or spirit. On the contrary, we are deeply affected by our bodies in decline and by the prospect of final dissolution, with its attendant losses, fears, and enigmas.

Unless we enter into this web of diminishments with a sense of faith and hope, it is easy to affirm superficial solutions to the problems of old age. We might list, for example, the desirable traits of the creative self in elderhood, as though these qualities could be learned and expressed by a kind of individual or communal self-help program. But this would only layer over the fundamental issues of old age with a veneer of popular nostrums. On the other hand, stressing growth through diminishments is not an appeal for a sad and gloomy old age in which one concentrates in an almost morbid way on deterioration and death. Rather, growth through diminishment, based on a willingness to encounter the inner demons of old age with faith, can lead to authentic joy even amid hardships. It is by facing the terrors of one's own old age, by launching out on the final night-sea journey, that a person finds the courage and insight to be profoundly wise for others in elderhood. Again, D. H. Lawrence says it with inspiration:

> And if, in the changing phases of man's life
> I fall in sickness and in misery
> my wrists seem broken and my heart seems dead
> and strength is gone, and my life
> is only the leavings of a life:
>
> and still, among it all, snatches of lovely
>   oblivion, and snatches of renewal
> odd, wintry flowers upon the withered stem,
>   yet new, strange flowers
> such as my life has not brought forth before,
>   new blossoms of me—
>
> then I must know that still
> I am in the hands (of) the unknown God,
> he is breaking me down to his own oblivion
> to send me forth on a new morning, a new man.[25]

The diminishments, then, are not a bringing down to oblivion only, but a descent to a place whence odd, wintry flowers, "new blossoms of me," can spring. This is the bedrock paradox, the faithful embracing of diminishments, led by a largely unknown, but trustworthy guide to a place of fulfillment for self and others affected by myself. This is the sense of Jesus' warning to Peter after the test of his faith and love: "When you were young, you girded yourself and walked where you would; but when you are old, you will stretch out your hands, and another will gird you and carry you where you do not wish to go" (John 21:18).

In old age, the elder is called into a new phase of the essential human condition in the face of death and its foreshadowing signs of decline. Some ignore or deny the predicament; others may seek to escape it with a schedule of constant diversion. Still others may gloss over its reality with the sanguine tones of modern psychologies of lifelong growth and learning. It is not that these therapies are wrong; rather, they are in danger of superficiality unless they spring from a deeper matrix. Such a place is one of paradox, of the final dialogue between fear and trust, between the risk of losing life only to find a new quality of life restored.

Against this background we can consider some aspects of self-development in elderhood. The concept of self-development, or adult growth, needs clarification. Self-development is a misleading notion if we take it to mean the expansion of personal potential through energetic acts of the self. Such an idea of development through volition alone ignores the complex influences of internalized life experiences on conscious and unconscious levels. Moreover, a volitional concept of self-development neglects the profound influences of social networks and cultural systems on the personality, influences ranging from one's family of origin to one's national milieu. Therefore, to avoid superficiality in thinking about self-development in elderhood, we must first recognize the social and intrapsychic networks in which growth occurs. The metaphors that dominate our minds in an age of high technology are often those of mechanical, linear causality. It is easy and erroneous to transfer this mind-set to understanding personal development. This technological mentality holds that with enough internal power, one can boost one's personal rocket in any chosen trajectory.

An even more difficult problem related to self-development or personal growth in elderhood surfaces when we reflect on the direction or purpose of such development. Will any growth pattern suffice? What kind of worth do we ascribe to one path over another? Personal development implies judgments of value. Is it better for older persons to live quiet, withdrawn lives, protecting themselves against economic and other dangers? Should their lives focus more intently on immediate family involvements and socializing with elderly friends? Or would it be more valuable, as a pattern of growth in elderhood, for persons to involve themselves, even at some risk, in humanitarian projects and ethical causes? Answers to such questions must differ with an individual's needs and desires, edu-

cational background, health, economic condition, and a variety of
other factors. But, however we decide to choose goals or tasks for
optimum development in elderhood, the question of values is crucial.

Religiousness is central to defining goals of development for a
spirituality of aging. Aging is more important as a spiritual than a
biological process. Spiritual development does not aim at religious
goals conceived of in narrow, conventional terms. In a broader
sense, spiritual becoming in elderhood consists of a "lifelong
growth in creativity and wisdom."[26] Yet creativity and wisdom are
best understood through consideration of the overarching values to
be found in the lives of great religious geniuses and in the highest
aspirations of the movements they originated. If one considers personal development in this light, creativity and wisdom take on distinctive value orientations. Development in old age focuses on at
least these three areas: interior growth through psychological and
spiritual methods, a deeper bonding of love and service with other
persons, and a commitment to the great causes of justice, peace,
and ecology among humankind.

Dynamic growth in any life phase calls for the interaction of
challenge and insight.[27] If the challenge is too severe it may lead to
unhealthy regression to earlier defense mechanisms in the personality. But if the challenge is such that ego strength can still be
maintained, new insight can dawn on a person, suggesting modes
of behavior that were not thought possible previously. A kind of dis-
equilibrium in social roles, relationships, responsibilities, and reward systems can provoke a significant change in personality.[28]

Requisite to this dynamic of growth is the assumption that development is both possible and desirable; moreover, a certain willingness to examine one's self critically in light of the challenge must
precede the emergence of new insight. A number of factors in old
age contribute to an environment where the growth process of
challenge and insight can take place. Older persons are frequently
less caught up in the routine responsibilities of earlier years, when
they were raising families and hemmed in by the requirements of
the work world. The old can be less worried about what others will
think of them, since job advancement and possible repercussions
on children are no longer central to their concerns. Furthermore,
the elderly have more discretionary time at their disposal, a situa-

tion that may allow more occasions for activities leading to personal growth.

These positive conditions for development are complemented by other elements of elderhood that appear negative at first glance. Changing social roles and responsibilities upset familiar and somewhat comforting patterns of life. Retirement is a classic example of such alteration in life-style. Yet this apparently negative challenge may be just the thing necessary to dislocate rigid, ingrained patterns of behavior. Painful self-assessment sometimes gives way to new insights about creative uses of time and energy for private enjoyment and social enhancement. The breaking or shifting of old relationships to family and friends can provide the challenge to seek involvements with new people. As the monetary and psychological rewards of a career diminish or come to an end, the older person may be challenged to adopt new values and priorities. The reward system that seemed so important in earlier years may be replaced by new avenues of satisfaction. Yet for the older person to accept a major shift in priorities requires a deep change of heart, an interior spiritual reversal. It entails swimming against the cultural stream both in terms of accepted social values and expectations of how the elderly should behave.

To illustrate this dynamic of challenge and insight in elderhood, with its requirement of a deeper spiritual revolution of the self, we can examine some of the traits and tasks of old age. Important studies in the developmental psychology of aging and in related fields ascribe certain characteristics to persons in advanced years, traits that appear to be constant in both traditional and modernized cultures.[29] The studies indicate that aging persons, especially men, "seem to move from active involvement with the world to more introversive, passive, and self-centered positions."[30] Thus the three main traits are interiority, passivity, and concern for personal satisfaction.

Interiority, as a movement from outer-world to inner-world interests, is an ambiguous notion in reference to the potentials of elderhood. It could simply mean a retreat from the world, an unwillingness to integrate a wide range of stimuli, a refusal to deal with complicated issues. In this sense, the interiority of old age becomes an escape from responsibility, a fearful withdrawal from commitment to the needs of society. This kind of interiority results in the

192 · *Elderhood: The Potentials*

rigid, dogmatic judgments that some old people make about the challenges of contemporary society. There is good reason to believe that modern technological society fosters precisely this kind of interiority. Because social pressures and expectations hamper the development of a beneficial kind of inwardness in midlife, the older person, almost forcefully disengaged from technological culture, easily falls into a narrowing style of life. Interiority is thus little more than flight from the process of challenge and insight that brings about new behavior in old age.

In contrast to this type of interiority, another inward route, ideally begun in midlife, can unleash new potential in elderhood. It involves a process of disidentification and reidentification. Just as in midlife the seeker of new identity had to revise the one-sided ambitions of youth, so also in elderhood a person must disengage from identification with social roles, whether imposed or chosen. In some ways, this disidentification is more radical in the later years, because retirement almost forces a break with earlier personality-enhancing roles. Yet this process of disidentification is but one moment of reidentification. As we surrender less authentic appraisals of ourselves, we can begin to draw together, from our personal depths, unfulfilled longings and untapped reservoirs of being appropriate to this unique self.

This process involves reminiscence in a spiraling or circular way that recognizes the unrealized desires of our souls from the past and separates them from the mere memory of past facts. Thus this circular action of the spirit is not the endless repetition of previous experiences in the boring "living in the past" characteristic of some elderly people. Rather, it is an inward, meditative mode of locating the yet unsatisfied desires of the heart and of finding ways to give these yearnings and needs new expression in the world. As one author puts it, "There is great need, as one comes to the closing part of life, to find the shape, not of the things we did so much as the self who did them in the midst of such rapid change and discontinuity."[31]

Such reidentification in elderhood elicits a creative, continuous process of becoming other than we were but, at the same time, becoming more authentically what we were meant to be. This inward work can be done individually or with the help of a qualified counselor or with the aid of a small group. For some persons, the inner journey of elderhood is shaped by artistic dimensions, the arts opening for them interior, imaginative resources. For others, the traditional idioms of religion may assist in the reidentification process. For still others, a psychospiritual route, possibly combined with those above, unfolds an authentic direction of the soul through dreams and fantasy.

Interiority of this sort is not easy. Unlike escapist interiority that narrows one's choices and engagements to protect the threatened self on the level of business-as-usual, disidentification and reidentification in elderhood challenge the self. The elder must be willing to question former modes of self-definition and risk new ways of self-understanding and action in elderhood. This can be a disconcerting experience. Earlier role identifications, though not fully satisfying, offer the comfort of familiarity. Family, friends, and society picture this elder according to older images. Embarrassment, even hostility, may attend the older person who disrupts his or her own stereotyped self-image, as well as the images that others have fashioned of him or her over many years.

If healthy interiority in old age leads to reidentification, what sort of new identities will be beneficial? Not all changes in self-understanding or new commitments are necessarily good. The process of disidentification and reidentification is different for every individual. Two general guidelines, however, may serve as criteria for judging the direction of change. One must first get in touch with one's true inner voices, which may have been stifled or ignored in the busy years of youth and midlife. What are the unmet needs of the psyche that could be addressed in elderhood? These may include exploring areas of knowledge, seeking deeper and wider friendships, engaging in stimulating travel, or fulfilling various other personal desires. Some persons can decipher these needs and wants without outside help; others benefit from individual or group therapy. A second guideline for creative reidentification in elderhood springs from the ability and desire to serve others. Turning to a life of service may encompass direct aid to needy individuals or dedication to worthy social goals or movements for the betterment of society at large. The first guideline—that of inner exploration—is a prerequisite for rewarding social service. Interiority allows us to grasp more fully our true inclinations and motives, in light of which we can make intelligent and more genuinely altruistic choices about societal engagements.

Thus the elderly person who takes up the rewarding but arduous road of reidentification through interiority reaches for a greater integration of the whole person. The path inward, when it is not merely an escape from menaces to the self, helps us to encounter those deepest forces and needs of the psyche, that ultimate personal "withinness" that at once opens the self to the transcendent experience of God-within and unites the person with others in the struggle against social evils. As Erikson suggests, such interiority is the route to fuller integrity in old age, over against the stagnation and despair that afflict those who refuse to grow. The words of Reuel Howe ring true: "You don't grow old; when you cease to grow you are old."[32]

In addition to interiority, passive mastery is a trait found among the elderly of many cultures.[33] Younger people deal with the external world through instrumental-productive styles. They strive to achieve results by directly influencing events and circumstances around them. The elderly, by contrast, employ passive-receptive modes, in which the self, rather than the world, is altered to adjust to the demands of situations and authorities. Passive mastery can degenerate into "magical mastery" in later years; the old person moves away from instrumental revisions of world and self into unrealistic styles of projection and denial. These appear to be defense mechanisms, shielding the elderly from the threatening demands of social change. One wonders whether "mastery" is not too positive a word; passive mastery often means mere conformity to events. That many older persons adapt themselves to oppressive circumstances without protest is hardly a mastery of life. It is, at best, mere coping. We have all known sad examples among the old of magical mastery, a meaningless style of making rigid judgments unrelated to the actual world in its ever-shifting complexity.

In what ways can a spirituality of aging that seeks to maximize the potentials of elderhood address the issues of passive mastery? This spirituality can distinguish between two forms of passive mastery, and stress the importance of a personal, spiritual revolution to the realization of a beneficial mastery. The first kind of passive mastery is capitulation before the relentless onslaught of the instrumental-productive ethos in our culture. The dominant way of achieving goals in a technological society is through the manipulation of persons, things, and events. The forms of such control are varied and subtle, but they are clearly directed toward change in the external world.

The elder who falls into conformist passive mastery may do so because he or she believes that the instrumental-productive style is the best, and possibly the only, way to manage the world. He or she would like to compete with the young on their own turf, but the personal and social diminishments of age force him or her to settle for whatever small parcel of ground is left. The older person, relegated to the margins of society, can only conform in order not to lose out completely. The elder seeks to make do, without understanding the need for an interior conversion that allows the individual to embrace positive styles of passive mastery.

Such positive mastery radically questions the uncritical acceptance of the instrumental-productive mode as the only, or the best, way of dealing with the world. Movement into elderhood may teach a person that significant inner change in mind and heart is crucial for the very purpose of effecting worthwhile changes in the outer world. This older person will come to realize the limits of outward, instrumental styles of remaking the world. The inward revision of the self, therefore, is not a mere conformity, out of necessity, to external pressures. Rather, it is an understanding with conviction that certain passive styles are essential for improving the world. The passive mode entails a willingness to listen to and learn from autonomous movements within the soul that wisely challenge ideas and actions based on heedless pursuit of the goals of the active, instrumental ego.

A passive style of mastery also allows the older individual to empathize with the needs and intentions of others, rather than impose his or her own desires on them or presume to know what they want. Finally, the passive mode of mastery can sensitize the elder to ecological needs, to a reverence for nature's rhythms and beauty. But such development in old age demands, especially in our society, a kind of religious conversion, a turning-around within oneself of the dominant instrumental-productive ethos of the age. For the elderly trait of passive mastery to become the counterweight that it should be to the external instrumentalism of earlier years, the old must enter with faith into the diminishments of elderhood and welcome the challenges that produce new insight during this final phase of life.

Gerontological research, in addition to delineating common traits of old age, has listed tasks for successful elderhood. The notion of tasks to accomplish underscores the modern emphasis on old age as a time of personal development. This is a positive reaction to a conventional view of elderhood as, at best, a holding operation, a clinging to the remnants of earlier developments. But the idea of successful aging and its appointed tasks must be understood with a certain relativity, and with an eye to the subjective component of such assessments. What may be deemed successful aging in one culture or class may not be so esteemed in another. Individuals also differ in their assessments of success or its lack.

Moreover, the tasks, components, and patterns of successful aging should be scrutinized in the context of a fuller spirituality of aging. Do they foster soul-making, that is, the fullest expansion of the inner potentials of the elderly person? This development of total potential has both inward and outward aspects. On the one hand, it means the encounter with transcendent forces within the conscious and unconscious psyche. This is the inward phase of the individuation process, whereby the elder continues to reconcile inner opposites in the light of the central unifying principle of the soul, what Jung calls the Self or the God-image at the core of each psyche. The soul-making process also has external dimensions, relating to other persons and to the great causes of humanity. The inner person cannot develop in a solipsistic vacuum, but flourishes through interpersonal exchange of mind and affect.

Nor can true soul-making go forward without serious concern for and involvement in major human endeavors. Such enterprises might include efforts to alleviate world hunger, to protect the ecology of the seas, to advance learning in the arts and sciences, to struggle for human rights, to work for the reduction and elimination of nuclear weapons, or many similar matters of vital concern to the community at large. What a single individual can accomplish will be limited in scope. Yet the spiritual process of soul-making in elderhood must not be confined to inner or interpersonal dimensions alone. The fullest spirituality encompasses a dynamic interrelation, a circular flow of all these aspects in a mutually enriching manner.

If we agree with Stevenson that a chief task or objective of elderhood is the sharing of wisdom with others,[34] this wisdom must embrace all three of these levels. A person of wisdom understands human responsibility to the inward, the interpersonal, and the worldwide facets of existence. This complex and ongoing experience in elderhood makes the difference between being a person of knowledge or one of wisdom. Knowledge pertains to clarity of thought, perception, and information, but wisdom signifies a profundity of discernment and judgment. Such discretion and prudence entail, in addition to sufficient knowledge, a multifaceted experience on all three planes: inward, interpersonal, and worldwide.

Knowledge has been more prized than wisdom since the emergence of modern science and technology. We are profoundly impressed, even dazzled, by the advances achieved in many fields through scientific experiments. Yet we are also distressed by the prevalent lack of wisdom in the way we treat interpersonal relationships, as well as in our way of dealing with the global problems of war, famine, and oppression. Our era is characterized by degenerating personal relationships, dangers of massive starvation in large areas of the world, and the ominous menace of nuclear weapons. No one will be able to speak and act wisely on these matters simply by reason of age. Authentic wisdom flows from an ever-deepening spirituality that grapples with the human condition in its inward and outward complexity. Moreover, finding ways of effectively sharing wisdom with individuals, groups, communities, and nations calls for greater organized political and social effort than has been exercised by the elderly in the past.

Several gerontologists underscore the task of maintaining midlife activities for those in advanced years.[35] This advice is based on the partially valid assumption that physical and mental wellbeing are preserved by maintaining a certain level of activity. Counseling for elderhood also militates against the tendency to retreat into a disengaged and sedentary life. Yet there can be an insidious undercurrent in the activity theory of successful aging. It can mean that an elderly person will be judged successful only to the extent that middle-age activities are sustained. This becomes another way of claiming that elderhood does not have a legitimate pace of its own, that it is decline and deterioration unless the faster tempo of the middle years prevails.

In this guise, activity theory can be little more than a subtle way of glorifying youth at the expense of old age. Elders who incorporate such thinking into their life-styles may be forced to live on the treadmill of action, without retaining time for, and developing interest in, the inward tasks of this phase of life. Moreover, the prescribed activity may simply be that which is dictated to the elderly by social convention. Indeed, this may be restricted to such approved activities as involvement in recreational and social organizations. If the elderly were to organize politically and take energetic action on public issues, such activity might well be condemned by society. On an individual level, the older person who breaks out of stereotypical conduct for the aged is sometimes ridiculed or otherwise insulted by younger people. Thus it becomes crucial to ask what *kind* of activity is appropriate as a task for successful aging. Older people who choose to follow a more religious path, as we have been discussing it, will establish a different list of priorities for action than those led along by social convention.

Another commendable task in elderhood is the pursuit of new interests, possibly a second or third career. Older persons can learn new skills and hobbies. Some have found new ways of working in the community, performing valuable services and enhancing their own self-esteem. Both as volunteers and as paid personnel, many older citizens have found rewarding work. Others have found themselves excluded by age from entering new fields. This is partly justifiable, in order to allow younger people a chance to find a place in careers with limited openings. Yet many elders have been frustrated in their attempts to start new careers in fields with genuine needs for personnel because of rigid retirement and hiring rules based on age. Other elders, although enjoying good health, have become apathetic about life and have hedged themselves in with familiar, though unproductive, routines. Much depends upon the individual's personality development, especially from middle years.

Some, unable to overcome secret fears of taking risks, protect themselves with a rocking-chair old age. Others use the socially permissible excuses of lessened energy or other physical disabilities to armor themselves so that new options and activities need not be chosen. (It is important to keep in mind, however, that researchers who classify the old in categories such as "rocking-chair" or "armored" types are ordinarily younger persons, who may be projecting their own value system onto the elderly.[36] It may be that persons who, in the eyes of more active investigators, have made a rocking-chair accommodation to elderhood have, in truth, slowed down just enough to allow time for neglected dimensions of life.) Another pattern of old age that destroys the potential for new involvements is found in angry and self-hating types. These people have been embittered by past experiences, and face their advanced years with resentments and self-deprecation.

Of course, such typologies have limited relevance, in that actual persons usually manifest a combination of the positive and negative traits; it is a matter of predominance, of the style that generally rules a person in old age. The most desired pattern is that in which older persons foster in their lives a rhythm of reinvigorating withdrawal and active pursuit of new interests and new meaning in life.

Gerontological research also indicates that people, for the most part, continue into old age with the personality patterns developed in earlier years. In an important study of elderly persons, Neugarten and her associates concluded that "characteristics that have been central to the personality seem to become even more clearly delineated, and those values the individual has been cherishing become even more salient."[37] Rather than sharp discontinuity of personality, there seems to be greater consistency in old age, unless some major physical or mental disability has intervened.

H. Nouwen and W. Gaffney concisely summarize a desired continuity between earlier phases of life and elderhood:

> It is indeed the task of everyone who cares to prevent people—young, middle-aged, and old—from clinging to false expectations and from building their lives of false suppositions. If it is true that people age the way they live, our first task is to help people discover life styles in which "being" is not identified with "having," self-esteem does not depend on success, and goodness is not the same as popularity. Care for the aging means a persistent refusal to attach any kind of ultimate significance to grades, degrees, positions, promotions, or rewards, and the courageous effort to keep men and women in contact with their inner self, where they can experience their own solitude and silence as potential recipients of the light. When one has not discovered and

experienced the light that is love, peace, forgiveness, gentleness, kindness, and deep joy in the early years, how can one expect to recognize it in old age? As the book of Sirach says: "If you have gathered nothing in your youth, how can you find anything in your old age?" (Si 25:3–4). That is true not only of money and material goods, but also of peace and purity of heart.[38]

The above reflections combine psychological and religious dimensions related to the tasks of elderhood.

From the perspective of a spirituality of aging, how would we assess these studies on tasks and patterns in elderhood? Continuity with one's past habits of mind and action underlines both the need for spiritual renewal in midlife and the sober recognition of resistance to change in old age. We have especially discussed many aspects of religious potential for the middle years that can be further refined in elderhood. The issue of resistance to change in elderhood prompts further reflection. To a certain degree, resistance to change in the personality is a positive trait. It can connote steadfastness in pursuing significant values, for self and others, without succumbing to social fads and pressures to conform in old age. In this sense, resistance is a graced event, a struggle against odds to follow a worthwhile life path. Examples of the choice not to swerve in elderhood from commitments and life-styles established earlier are Mother Teresa, in her work for the Asian poor, and Dorothy Day of the Catholic Worker Movement, in her dedication to peacemaking.

Resistance to change is positive with regard to spiritual development from another standpoint. It underscores the limits of human endeavor in self-development and the need to open the soul to God's grace for significant change to occur. Such resistance reminds us of the intractability of the fearful human psyche, hedging itself about with protective defense mechanisms that hamper growth through the phases of life. Only the divine spirit working within us and operating through outside factors can relieve these self-insulating fears, permit a break in the dam of resistance, and foster a creatively enhanced personality in old age.

In light of a spirituality for aging, research into various personality types in elderhood highlights the need for relativity of judgment, the place of religious stewardship, and the vital role of healing and forgiveness with the approach of death. A religious attitude means that we recognize and respect the directions of grace in others, directions that may defy outward appearances and scholarly classifications. The person of developed religious sensitivities should be less prone to judge others solely on the basis of outward conduct. Although outward behavior is the main source for the scientific researcher, the person of spiritual acumen will reserve final judgment about elders who evidence signs of apathy, anger, frustration, guilt, and even self-hatred.

On one level, these traits are usually not beneficial. But on another plane, these seemingly negative qualities may indicate an individual's inner struggle as a kind of spiritual alchemy whereby the soul, in dialogue with God, is painfully working out a deeper mode of personal growth. Not all negative attributes of elderhood are evidence of this difficult spiritual alchemy. But a spiritually sensitive observer will maintain a certain relativity, or perhaps better, a respect for complexity, in assessing the various patterns of old age. For he or she is aware of another conversation going on in the human spirit between inner, transcendent presences and the observable world.

Other factors to be taken into account in evaluating the tasks and patterns of elderhood from a religious viewpoint are stewardship and service. This religious perspective can be considered in relation to what gerontologists have termed the components of life satisfaction, which ideally mark successful aging both in reference to accomplishing tasks and demonstrating optimal aging patterns. An important study on life satisfaction in elderhood has provided the foundation of much speculation in social gerontology.[39] The aspects of life satisfaction, according to these authors, are zest (versus apathy), resolution in accepting personal responsibility for one's own life without blaming oneself or others, a balance between desired and accomplished goals in life, a good self-concept, and a general tone of optimism, happiness, and spontaneity. Another study of elements of high morale among the elderly would add to the above such factors as physical comfort, financial security, productive activity, and a good social life.[40]

From the standpoint of a spirituality of aging, all of these facets of life satisfaction or high morale are positive, but too limited in scope. Lacking are the religiously vital qualities of stewardship and service. Most gerontologists stress individual or private satisfaction as keys to life satisfaction among the elderly. The major world religions, especially in the West, would not be content with such a privatized view of what constitutes satisfaction in life. A sense of stewardship pervades the teaching of these religious movements. Stewardship implies a broader understanding of social responsibility toward fellow humans and the world in general. Service is the extension of stewardship in such activities as the doing of justice, peacemaking, and other works of love toward neighbor and nature. The word "satisfaction" suggests fulfillment and the taking of pleasure in some form of completion. A life is not fulfilled, even after many years, if its general tenor has been one of only personal satisfaction. This religious emphasis on stewardship and service has its own dangers, for it may needlessly impose guilts and scruples on people for enjoying private satisfactions. Such moralism is not an authentic focus of the social imperative of religion. Rather, stewardship and service represent, for the religious mind, the intrinsic interconnection and coresponsibility of all creation as an expression of divine involvement and responsibility in the world.

A final task of elderhood consists of finding healing and forgiveness by reviewing one's life and preparing proximately for death. We have already discussed life review at the end of chapter five. In that section we stressed the challenge of facing in depth one's life, with all its successes and failures. Something must still be said about the positive religious potential in a serious process of life review. No life lived into elderhood is without memories of hurts inflicted or received, and of sadness over roads taken in the past. These memories are balanced, in part, by the blessings and achievements of one's years. Yet, on both the negative and positive sides of the ledger we encounter the limits of finitude. Spiritual insight into this experience suggests that the events of our lives and their outcomes depend on more than our own efforts. On both sides of the ledger in a life review, we find the influences of others, for good or ill. Moreover, we know through faith that, just as God assists us in our accomplishments, so, too, the Holy Spirit endeavors to draw good out of the failures of our lives.

This is neither a pollyanna view of the human predicament nor a facile way of pardoning our own irresponsibility and even malice. Rather, the person growing in spiritual sensitivity experiences the truthful humility that comes of recognizing the multiple influences of grace that sustain any accomplishment. Such a one further recognizes, without exculpation from misdeeds, that the Spirit of God never ceases to struggle with us against evil, trying in unforeseen ways to promote the welfare of creation, restraining its bent toward destructiveness.

In addition to this potential for humility and recognition of grace in a life review, the elder can learn the compassion and forgiveness of the wounded healer. He or she can experience God's healing forgiveness, often through the forgiveness of an offended person. Again, this assurance of forgiveness is not an excuse for shirking responsibility in doing what is necessary to make amends to an injured party. But the elder who learns experientially that close human relations need forgiveness to survive and prosper will be able to act as a genuine healer toward others.

The last task of old age is proximate preparation for death and progressing through the final stages of one's life with significant others. We have reflected on the meaning of death, of facing finitude in the context of midlife and older age. Without repeating, we can here consider more immediate matters in the preparation for death. On a practical level, it is an act of caring to leave one's affairs in order so that others may benefit from legacies without difficulty. Concrete matters such as wills, appointing an executor, leaving clear indications of where important documents are located, become important. On a more personal plane, the older person faces the twin tasks of engaging personal feelings and needs as death becomes more imminent and communicating with family and friends. Contemporary research on death and dying indicates the value of open communication of emotion and thought between friends and intimates.

Although this communication will take place over longer periods of elderhood, it is intensified during the very last phase of life. Death therapy seeks to heighten the quality of life as much as possible during terminal stages. Among the many dimensions of the process are the sustaining of hope for recovery or hope for a quality time period before death, respect for positive and seemingly negative emotions, the grieving of losses, and expressions of love and care for significant others. Death therapy also focuses on the needs of survivors: anticipatory grieving and adequate mourning after death, expression of authentic feelings, and community and individual support before and after the loss of a loved one. The modern Hospice movement has become a model of caring for the dying, attending to their physical, psychological, and spiritual needs.

The spiritual and religious needs of the dying are too often ignored. The clergy must improve the content and means of ministry to the terminally ill and their families. But the enhancement of spiritual meaning cannot be limited to more traditional modes of religion. Persons who do not consider themselves religious in conventional ways also have spiritual longings and needs. Such dying individuals may find peace and insight in art, music, and literature. Whatever uplifts and ennobles the spirit is crucially valuable in the dying process. Certainly attempts to cure or arrest a disease and to relieve pain remain important. But our society's overemphasis on physical medicine deprives the dying person of the spiritual comforts that can lift life towards an otherwise unrealized integration in the final period.

A discussion of preparing for death in elderhood might seem to support the notion that the old have little or no future. Frequently enough in the literature on aging one encounters this theme. For instance, S. Philip Brown writes, "Having lost many former roles, while facing the onset of chronic diseases and the presence of death, the older adult must zero in on the basic issues of life. The person is not concerned about the long-range goals but has such a sense of immediacy."[41] Paul Pruyser, in his essay on personal growth in aging, advocates living in the present.[42] Again, the implicit message is that the old have no future. When this attitude is accepted, advice to the elderly focuses on making the most of the present moment and forsaking future goals. There is value in stressing attention to the here-and-now, to relishing the immediate. There is a tendency, especially among the old, to live in the past through reminiscences that block out the present. (Although, as we noted above, recollections of the past can be brought into the present to enlighten and enhance it.) Moreover, we incline toward the postponement of fuller living by projecting and anticipating greater joy or fulfillment in the future. From this standpoint, the counsel to stop postponing life and live in the present makes good sense.

But the generally accepted view among writers on old age that the elderly do not, and even should not, have long-range goals also has very unfortunate consequences. It becomes a subtle way of saying that life is over, that the old person should curtail future-thinking and settle for the pleasures of the moment. This outlook becomes an implicit denial of a very basic quality or need of being human. As the German thinker Ernst Block emphasized in his philosophy, humans are by nature future-oriented beings. To be truly human is to hope, that is to believe that we are not trapped in the present, but rather can look for and work towards something better than the present. This "better than" means more than quantitative, material betterment. It also includes the quest for a more just, peaceful community in the social sphere, and for fuller immersion in the rich mystery of living on the individual level.

Elders do have a future. The relative proximity of death does not negate this truth, unless discussion is confined to a merely individual and quantifiable measure of time. If we understand our individual lives as organically and inextricably joined to those of others and to the ecological systems of the planet, the future of the world is our future. This vision of reality is all the more true for a spirituality of aging. For the wisdom of the old consists precisely in a less self-centered commitment to the care and integration of the whole human project. One could almost say that the elderly, as custodians of the wisdom of the race, should be even more future-oriented than the young and the middle-aged, who are typically enveloped in immediate concerns, establishing or developing a career, providing for families, and rearing children.

From a Judeo-Christian perspective, both the organic and the futurist aspects of this argument are paramount. The Hebrew emphasis on the corporate or organic dimensions of Israel as the People of God assumes the intimate interlinking of the lives of all Jews; if Israel is likened to a corporate body, as in the vision of Isaiah, individuals are not independent, separated atoms, but cells of a greater organism. These "cells" are personal and gifted with freedom, but they are mandated to work for the good of the whole body of Israel, which, in turn, is commanded to be a vessel of service and salvation for the wider organism of humankind. Jewish messianism is intrinsically vectored toward the future. Believers are enjoined to live according to the ethical and religious requirements of Torah in order to hasten the coming of the messianic era. Whether this is understood in a historical or a more symbolic sense, its futurist dimension is paramount.

Organic and futurist aspects are also central to Christianity. Through baptism, Christians are incorporated into the body of Christ, the Church. The Pauline vision of the Christian community as organism (I Cor. 12:14 ff.) has inspired images of bodily unity in the Church for two millennia. The liturgy of the Eucharist continues the conviction of incorporation into Christ and into the believing community through the consumption of the bread and wine. Christianity is an eminently eschatological, or future-oriented, religion. The kingdom of God, though already partially present in the believer and in the world, is yet to come in its fullness. The decisions and actions of the Christian, at all stages of life, contribute to or detract from the coming kingdom of justice and peace.

The organic and eschatological dimensions of Judaism and Christianity, therefore, stand firmly against the notion that the old have no future. On the contrary, the elderly believer has a special mission to contribute to the organic welfare of the community and to shape the future. Freed from some of the narrower concerns of earlier years, the old can think and act for universal purposes. W. Beardslee recognizes the central link between Christian hope and the future, while acknowledging the ever-unfinished dimension of the kingdom to come as it struggles against the forces of despair:

> Nevertheless, despite its perversion and its erosion, hope that is not just passive, but involves enlistment in the future, is the basic form of Christian hope which the Christian tradition can offer to the present world. . . . Today we see that the final end toward which hope reaches will have to be transformed, in our grasp of it, into an endless movement into the future, . . . the new life for which one hopes will never come to be the prevalent reality in a total way, though real changes and achievements are possible. . . . Hope will be real on the boundary between hope and despair.[43]

Futurists in our own time, through their literature, organizations, and activities, have highlighted the importance of dwelling on what may yet happen. One of these scholars, E. Brewer, has focused on the value of future-orientation for the elderly.[44] Brewer warns against the debilitating effects of the assumption that the old have no future. This presumption can lead to deterioration of self-image in elderhood and consequent depression when the old conceive themselves as useless or irrelevant to the future. Life review for the elderly is not sufficient; they must also engage in a "life preview."[45] This involves the fashioning of images of the future for themselves, their families, and society in general. Although their own biological time, on a horizontal plane, is curtailed, the old can intensify their existence in the present and toward the future in the sense of a richer vertical temporality. Within the limits of health, the elder needs to explore ways of enhancing the personal future and improving the wellbeing of close relations and of the community at large.

Various conceptions of life after death can inspire the elderly self with a sense of immortality. For some, immortality means a continuance into God's future, either with a personal consciousness joined to an individual, spiritual mode of existence, or with a blending into a cosmic, universal consciousness. Others, in the tradition of eastern religion, envision their personal future as a process of rebirths evolving toward a more enlightened consciousness and a more perfect earthly world. Sri Aurobindo is a modern Hindu proponent of such a vision. Still others may formulate more mundane conceptions of immortality through the continuance of their works or through their progeny. None of these motivating images of a personal future need be a fearful denial of death or an escape from responsibility to the world. While these subterfuges are possible, images of immortality and of the future of the human community are necessary and beneficial for self and others.

The vision of elderhood with a mission toward the future offers a needed framework for examining the social and political potential of the elderly. Rather than withdrawing into the past or to the periphery of the present, the elderly have a profound responsibility and vocation to build the future, both for their fellow elders and for the whole human community.

Elderhood for the World

We have examined some of the potentials for a deeper selfhood in later life. Although we stressed personal, spiritual growth in the last section, it was always seen with an eye for the wider social context of elderhood. Emphasis on interiority should not suggest withdrawal from the world in elderhood. Rather, the interior life becomes, in part, a preparation for contributing the authentic wisdom of age to the central concerns of communities and nations. At this point, we need to look directly at the social and political ramifications of a creative old age.

Modern western cultures almost universally relegate the elderly to the periphery of society, where they live as isolated individuals or in social groupings of their elderly peers. The old are increasingly removed from the centers of decision making that influence the welfare of all. This exile of the old from the sources of social power results in large part from their separation from other aspects of life, and from an ever-stronger emphasis on individualism and privacy.[46] Life, like work, is segmented into rigid stages in which age groups are divided from each other according to the perceived needs of an industrial-technological economy. In this process, the elderly become more completely excluded from the realm of social and political power. Recreational and social communities are built for the elderly, but such retirement communities lack direct political impact on the larger society.

This polite banishment of the elderly from the world of politics, economics, and civic life generally has two negative consequences. First, it deprives the middle-aged and the young of the talent and insight of the old. For the elderly can offer the wisdom of experience in a more honest, altruistic way because they have fewer familial interests to protect and less need to hedge their views for the sake of job promotions and peer prestige. A second unfortunate result of the social disempowerment of the elderly is its depressing effect on older individuals. Some resign themselves to life in the separate environment of retirement communities or to the forgotten existence of isolated persons in a community run by younger generations. But many suffer from *Torschlusspanik*, the panic of the closing of doors.[47] As the elderly see opportunities for social, economic, and political involvement denied them, they develop depreciated self-images. They tend to see themselves as nobodies, has-beens, or as burdens to others.

The irony of the situation is that *Torschlusspanik*, with its damaging psychological consequences, seems to go hand in hand with an increasing range of services for the elderly:

Our western, industrialized, materialistic culture in our particular moment in history seems to have created a *Zeitgeist* which produces acute and prolonged psychological and spiritual *Torschlusspanik* for an increasing proportion of the aging, while at the same time creating an increasing range of programs, agencies, and situations to care for physical and financial needs and problems of the aging.[48]

These contradictions make it very hard for an older person to shape a new identity for old age, a self-concept with meaning and integrity. A spirituality of aging, therefore, must stand against the social tide that would confine the elderly to society's periphery. Just as the middle-aged need to cultivate deeper interiority, moving against the cultural stream that pulls them into the vortex of activity, so the elderly must find ways to break through the walls of kindly social banishment to find their own voice and energy at the center of events.

A religious attitude in old age calls for more, not less, concern for and commitment to the world. This is not to deny the right and need to withdraw from certain intense activities in later years. It could very well be that the kind of action demanded in earlier years is foreign to the spirit of an enhanced old age. Such undesirable activities might include the unabated efforts to accumulate wealth for oneself and one's family. The greedy old person, as depicted in the various literary forms of Scrooge, is a particularly disagreeable character. Moreover, the choice of a quieter, less hectic life by an older person should be respected. But a careful exploration of Judeo-Christian sources reveals the abiding responsibility of stewardship for, and commitment to, the wellbeing of the human community and the earth itself. Part of the stewardship of the elderly may in fact be the "responsibility to help free others from the belief that frenetic activity is the measure of life. . . . By maintaining their integrity and value, the aged bear witness to the undiminished worth that God attaches to human life itself."[49]

This sense of the stewardship of life itself, apart from its utility and function, becomes a vital mission of old age. The elderly, therefore, have the special role of cherishing life itself for its own intrinsic meaning. Sometimes they may exercise this care toward children and younger persons. It may be even more important for the elderly to care for one another, sustaining the intrinsic value of life for their peers, who are often afflicted by loneliness and other suffering. Thus this primary religious activity of the old, directed toward the world through care for life itself, is a countermeasure to the heedless activity that dominates contemporary existence. Reflecting on this dimension of elderhood, W. Hogan writes, "Man misses so much of his own meaning and worth when he fails to grasp a sense of the life which he has taken for granted."[50]

Yet, even beyond this testimony to the value of being, not just of doing, the elderly are called to what P. Tournier terms a "passage to universal commitments."[51] This passage entails the continuing development of an attitude optimally begun in midlife. It means, in brief, a search for new ways of human bonding, wider forms of love, commitment to the universal concerns of humankind. This universalizing of concerns does not abandon the particular or individual need. Rather, it seeks the transcendent dimensions harbored in specific actions. The kingdom is here in this concrete deed, yet the kingdom in a specific place also points beyond, to universal, unrealized horizons. The concrete and provisional are closely linked to the general and fulfilled.[52] In this process the elder experiences detachment from possessive relationships to things and a broader attachment to people. He or she becomes less a consumer, and more a sharer of material and spiritual resources.

The religious elder struggles against the modern trend to disenfranchise the old, to remove them from the seats of power. But the goal of this effort is not the attainment of more power, in the sense of domination and control; rather, the old desire to stay at the center of events in order to transform power from its oppressive uses to a resourceful energy that works for universal betterment. This new kind of power resembles the biblical image of the appearance of God's might to Elijah as a gentle breeze (I Kings 19:9–160). Such spiritual and human power is a far cry from the power of marching armies or churning machines. It is the power of insight and persuasion, which does not ignore evil and ignorance in the world, but believes that wisdom and goodness can prevail.

This turning toward the world in elderhood, rather than away from it, rests on firm theological moorings in the Christian tradition. C. Curran (see also my book *Reconciliation: The Function of the Church* for a general perspective on the same theological point), speaking of aging, underscores the transformational aspect of the Paschal Mystery of Jesus' death and resurrection, with its sense of partial continuity between this world and the next, and the consequent need to work for the development of this world in order to bring it to fuller completion in light of the Christ-event. He contrasts a transformational with a paradoxical eschatology, also derivable from a Christian perspective. The paradoxical eschatology stresses discontinuity between the kingdom to come and this world, this veil of tears, "as a place of light in the midst of darkness, joy in sorrow, and power in weakness."[53] Pushed to its logical conclusion, the paradoxical view might incline the elderly to forsake this world, marked by sin, suffering, and death, for deliverance by God into an existence not marred by these hardships.[54] Curran opts for the transformational view of the world as more adequate to Christian theology.

Yet I would argue that both standpoints, the paradoxical and the transformational, must be maintained in creative tension for Christian elderhood. Indeed, both facets are experienced, especially in midlife and old age. To hold only to a transformational theology could cause the elderly to naively embrace human wisdom as fully adequate for building a more peaceful and just world. This kind of humanism has its own pitfalls: It fails to recognize the depths of fear, suspicion, greed, and hatred in human affairs. Disregarding the brokenness of the world and the limits of human achievement, a purely transformational theology may lead to even greater disillusionment in old age, when the humanistic ideals of a lifetime may appear ineffectual in the concrete circumstances of a still very sinful world. Holding to the paradoxical aspect of the Christian mystery at the same time allows a more authentic appropriation of both the limits of worldly transformation and the difficult reality of the diminishments of old age. These are part of what Curran terms the "downward curve" in elderhood, the diminishments of pain, loneliness, and isolation for many old people.[55] He wisely notes the balance of this decline with an "upward curve" in old age among those who experience deeper self-understanding, more meaningful relations with others, and a calmer acceptance of life's vicissitudes.

On all these levels the elder of faith encounters God. It would seem, therefore, that to maintain in creative polarity both the downward and the upward curves of elderhood, it is necessary to embrace both the paradoxical and transformational theologies of the world. Only in this complex, but truer attitude toward the world can the older person resemble the noble picture that Curran sketches of one

> ... who, through years of experience and accumulated wisdom, having seen the beauty of human existence and its degradations, having experienced the love of other human beings and known, as well, hatred and vengeance, now serenely and peacefully views human existence and strives for meaning and intelligibility. Now, less dependent than ever on the vicissitudes of time and space, and purified in the struggle of human existence, the aging person comes to grips with him/herself in an ever-deepening encounter of acceptance of who he/she is and how life should be lived.[56]

Curran sees this positive task of old age as one of giving meaning and intelligibility to one's life. Although this is surely one worthy goal of elderhood, it would, if taken as the sole task, be too individualistic and isolated. More is required of elders who pursue a full spirituality of aging. They are still responsible for the world in its concrete needs. Their lives can achieve heightened intelligibility and meaning if they continue to struggle and work in social, political, economic, and cultural realms.

The Gray Panther movement is a contemporary example of the involvement of the elderly and their younger supporters in the world. They stress political and educational activity to combat ageism in society and to improve the lives of older persons and others. For example, they monitor the media to detect and expose stereotypes, distortions, and omissions concerning old people. Print and electronic media sometimes present images of old age that demean or ridicule older persons; old age may be depicted as idyllic or moribund; the life concerns of elders are frequently excluded.

The Panthers also stress better ways to negotiate various stages of the life cycle. In this sense, the movement strives for alternative lifestyles and opportunities for older *and* younger people. A particularly important aspect of the Panther program is its awareness of the effectiveness of forming coalitions with other groups in order to influence public policy. The coalition approach to problems also broadens the spectrum of Panther concerns, extending beyond issues directly affecting the aged to those focused on eliminating discrimination in social institutions at large. The public mission of the elderly, in keeping with the passage to universal concerns, is to work for the widest possible good of society; it is not enough to militate only for the causes of the elderly. Perhaps more than any other age cohort, the elderly are called to care about the needs of unborn generations and the future status of the planet. This emphasis on posterity seems natural as the last parenting function of the elderly: From care for their own few children in early life phases, they move toward a preparenting of tomorrow's many children.

Another element of the Panther program merits special attention: the conviction that political, legal, and economic changes in society require the formation of local, regional, and national networks as effective bases for social change. This is still the power of persuasion, not coercion, but it has the added force of organization and focus. The elderly, in general, have not yet fully realized the political effectiveness of organizing themselves into interest and pressure groups. In this regard, the Gray Panthers may be a harbinger of things to come, perhaps by the end of this century, when the aged population will be much larger than it is today. A recent scene symbolic of this politicization of the elderly was the octogenarian Congressman Claude Pepper leading a group of elderly delegates from the 1981 White House Conference on Aging to plead their cause before a congressional committee.

In the politics of aging, the Panthers represent only a single type of movement, one which is generally critical of other organized groups for the elderly. Among these other organizations are such important groups as The American Association of Retired Persons, The National Council of Senior Citizens, The Gerontological Society, and The National Council of Aging. The Panthers have criticized such established groups for excessive attention to organizational maintenance and for failing to enlist the elderly themselves in the political process. The goals and activities of these groups depend in part on their membership bases and professional directions.[57] Some are oriented toward organized labor, others toward the welfare community, and still others toward researchers, planners, and gerontological professionals. The various constituencies and purposes of these organizations provide a pluralism of approaches to problems of aging, but they also give rise to divisiveness within the movement as a whole and lack of cohesiveness in influencing public policy. There is also a question of how adequately the leadership cadres of these organizations represent their membership. As public funding for needs of the elderly becomes tighter in the forseeable future, a more unified advocacy among these organizations seems imperative.

Governmental expenditures in the area of aging have risen dramatically in the past two decades. Current expenditures for the elderly amount to about a quarter of the federal budget. Social Security, Medicare, federal grants to states in Medicaid, expenditures for the old under the Veterans Administration, retirement and insurance benefits for federal civilian and military employees—these major programs, combined with others, totalled over 130 billion dollars in 1979. Although these public efforts have improved the living conditions and general wellbeing of many older persons, "severe and widespread problems continue to exist among major aging subpopulations."[58] Median incomes for older persons are lower than those of younger groups, especially among minority populations. Greatly increased health problems, coupled with economic hardship and loneliness, combine to produce a dismal old age for many. Increases in Social Security benefits have not kept pace with the inflated cost of living, especially for those whose base income was low during their working years. With a growing population of older citizens and the emphasis on restrained governmental spending in the decades ahead, much study and debate needs to center on public means of raising and distributing funds for programs for the elderly.

This brief reflection on some political issues is included here in order to indicate the complexity of bringing about needed social changes. Those religiously motivated to engage the real world of aging cannot be content to deal only with the abstract. The Older Americans Act of 1965 set forth a list of national objectives, which have only been partially met by legislation to date. These goals touch upon many aspects of an older person's life, and are worth enumerating in order to sketch out the extent of the issues involved. In addition to adequate income in retirement, the objectives call for the best possible physical and mental health, without regard for economic status, suitable housing, at affordable cost, in keeping with the preferences of the elderly, restorative services for those who require institutional care, opportunity for employment without age discrimination, retirement to health and dignity after years of service, pursuit of meaningful civic and cultural activity, efficient community services, immediate benefits from the knowledge gained by research, and finally, independence and freedom in planning and managing their own lives.[59]

Another particularly important dimension of elderly wellbeing is the need for living environments and support systems. Such systems may be formal or informal. Formal support systems range from major governmental programs for the elderly, such as Social Security and Medicare, to local organizations like labor unions and churches. Informal support networks consist of kin, friends, and neighbors. Although the elderly need and are grateful for the aid of larger bureaucracies, they strongly prefer the assistance of informal, primary relations.[60] Older Americans are generally very independent, turning to social service agencies only when family and friends are not able to sustain them. It is only when frailty or sickness incapacitate elders that the responsibility for their wellbeing shifts to formal agencies.[61]

This desire for primary communities of support among the elderly relates to the ministry of churches and synagogues toward the aged. For many older people, these religious institutions stand somewhere between primary relationships and bureaucratic social services. Religious heritage is tied to spiritual sentiments and hopes that are closely related to feeling for family and friends. Church professionals and lay ministers are often ideally suited to act as intermediaries between formal agencies and the elderly or to cooperate as coworkers in secularly sponsored programs for the elderly.

Churches are also, for this reason, in a unique position to foster alternative environments for elderly living. (Many retirement homes and communities are sponsored by religious organizations. While some of these retirement centers meet a variety of human needs, others simply replicate the environments of their secular counterparts.) In addition to the usual requirements, such as shelter, nutrition, health care, and recreation, religious centers and outreach programs are in a particularly good position to foster intellectual, psychological, and spiritual growth among the elderly. Although many older persons prefer to live alone, with a spouse, or with other members of their extended family, many others find exciting challenges, new joys, friendships, and ways of being of service in a communal environment. The best of these religious centers combine community orientation with respect for independence, services for the elderly, and the opportunity for older persons to take initiative in determining the policy of the community.

Both gerontologists and older persons have criticized the sequestering of the elderly in old age communities, because such environments lessen the advantages of integenerational encounters. While this is a serious objection, it is possible to structure communities of the elderly so that contacts with younger persons are sufficiently fostered. This can be done through easy access to the retirement community by outsiders and proximity to the surrounding area for the elders.

It has also been cogently argued that groupings of the old in exclusive, self-reinforcing settings are very important for an adequate socialization to old age in America. In a culture that rejects the elderly, Americans are so poorly socialized for old age that they need the added support of their peers in order to sustain new roles and ventures.[62] I. Rosow supports this idea, noting a variety of negative aspects of old age in America, including social losses, exclusion, stereotypes, discrimination, and role discontinuity. Both generational integration and special communities of the elderly are mutually compatible and desirable values. The question then becomes how to provide options for integration, as well as age-group cohesion.

Religious institutions have a special responsibility in fostering vital eldership. In recent years churches and synagogues have become more aware of the need to minister to and with senior adults. Until comparatively recently, churches tended to emphasize ministry to youth as a special age group; adulthood was simply the general period following youth. But today church specialists in aging stress the need to consider the elderly as a "distinct but not separate group."[63] Since many elderly persons maintain or renew ecclesiastical adherence, opportunities for a ministry to the aging are manifold.

This ministry, however, must not be limited to a doing-for the elderly. Rather, churches need to expand their ministry in new ways in order to foster a doing-with and a doing-by senior adults. As a preliminary step toward enlisting the participation of the elderly, church leaders at all levels need to preach and act against false and harmful attitudes about elderhood in the minds of their congregations. Moreover, some elders feel pushed aside and ignored by younger members of congregations.[64] A prerequisite, therefore, for a creative ministry to the aging is the clear understanding that such a mission has three dimensions: services for the elderly, involvements with older parishioners, and contributions by older persons to the rest of the congregation. As a preliminary step to insure the success of this threefold ministry, representatives of the elderly must be included in the planning and decision-making committees of churches and synagogues.

Churches can provide a number of services for older persons on a physical, as well as psychospiritual level. Able-bodied and knowledgeable elders can also contribute in these activities. Examples of such ministries include home services for shut-ins, such as providing meals, helping with shopping, and home repairs. Many senior persons may also need assistance in communicating with social or financial agencies, whose benefits may be lost to immobile or sick elders because they lack knowledge of such options or are unable to contact these organizations. In these ways, church ministry to the elderly will strive to coordinate its services with secular agencies; the goal is to avoid duplicating or substituting for services already supplied by private and public organizations. Rather, ministers to the aging would act as facilitators and liaisons, directly providing only those services not provided by secular agencies.

Some churches have developed friendly visitors programs to the old who cannot leave their houses and to those in nursing homes. Others have linked their ministries with such organizations as Hospice, caring for terminally ill elders and their families. Poorer older people may not attend church because they are embarrassed by their limited ability to contribute financially; they may also be ashamed to go to church in worn or outmoded clothing. Transportation, whether to religious services or to other destinations, is also an important facet of ministry to the elderly. Churches may need to explore the best use and adaptation of their physical facilities to benefit the elderly. Religious institutions can also sponsor research about aging and other education programs as a part of a wide-ranging and future-oriented ministry.

Meeting the psychological and spiritual needs of the elderly is a crucial function of ministry to the aging.[65] Bible study and continuing education programs can involve the elderly in enlightening and

218 · *Elderhood: The Potentials*

inspiring intellectual ventures. Preaching needs to be conscious of the spiritual needs of the elderly. Counseling for crises specific to old age is still another possibility for this ministry. The churches can become significant places for fellowship, allowing elders to enjoy the companionship of their peers and of younger members. One of the principal roles of the church in the minds of older persons is to provide a locus for community life where feelings, needs, and hopes can be expressed.[66] Various forms of recreation, including drama, singing, music, and library facilities, can involve the elderly in parish life. Corporate worship, as the spiritual center of the congregation, should involve the old in visible ways. It is important for the elderly to be a part of the liturgical life of a community, giving concrete evidence of a multigenerational family of worship. Older persons who are qualified to preach might share some of the wisdom of age with others in the parish.

Finally, churches can include the elderly in "social gospel" activities, those religiously inspired efforts to influence laws and institutions in matters pertaining to justice and human rights. Elders may have more time than younger people, and less to risk in terms of status and position in working for social causes that follow from religious commitment. Moreover, older congregants, with wider experiences in life, should be better able to understand the moral ambiguities involved in taking political-ethical stands on issues. Younger persons addressing morally significant legal and political questions may be self-righteous in their views. Several factors contribute to this lack of moral tolerance and ignorance of ethical ambiguity among younger persons: a conviction that moral positions are divinely sanctioned, the need to win or succeed for the sake of individual power, and a lack of personal experience of the ambiguities of ethical issues.

An elderhood turned constructively toward the world, whether inspired by religious institutions or other movements, becomes an art of living the final phase of life. Some of the world's great artists stand, in old age, as models for others in turning suffering and the temptation to despair into creative events for humankind. The story of the aging Venetian master, Titian, is one of freedom and courage. While his students were in a nearby room lamenting his impending death, Titian, in his last hours, had risen from his bed and gone to his easel to work devotedly on a final painting.[67] A few days before his death, Michelangelo, nearly ninety years old, "was working on a radical new vision as he altered completely the Rondanini Pieta."[68] Henry James encountered professional setbacks and personal loneliness in his life; yet through these sufferings he struggled for artistic fulfillment in his later years. Writing to an aging and depressed Henry Adams, James notes:

> You see I still, in the presence of life (or what you deny to be such), have reactions, as many as possible—and the book I sent you is proof of them. It's I suppose, because I am that queer monster, the artist, an obstinate finality, an inexhaustible sensibility. Hence the reactions—appearances, memories, many things, go on playing upon it with the consequence that I note and "enjoy" (grim word!) noting. It takes doing—and I *do*. I believe I shall do yet again—it is still an act of life.[69]

Although most of us do not possess the creative genius of great artists, from them we can learn an attitude and a vitality that keeps elderhood alive for the world. In some ways, we too easily decide to withdraw from events, to become old in conformity with the cultural stereotypes of old as useless, sad, and decrepit.

The aging artist is not oblivious to diminishments and the tendency to despair. Yeats expressed frustration at his old age: "I am tired and in a rage at being old. I am all I ever was and much, much more, but an enemy has bound and twisted me so I can plan and think as I never could, but no longer achieve all I plan and think."[70] Yet it is precisely at the moment when the elderly artist confronts and transcends his or her sufferings that unique insights are bestowed on younger generations. Again, Yeats encapsulated the active blindness of youth, caught up in "sensual music," but not conscious of "monuments of unageing intellect." However, this gift of the old seer—Sophocles' Tiresias, Shakespeare's Prospero, Mozart's Sarastro—is essential for the wellbeing of humanity:

> That is no country for old men. The young
> in one another's arms, birds in the trees
> —Those dying generations—at their song.
> The salmon-falls, the mackerel-crowded seas,
> Fish, flesh, or fowl, commend all summer long
> Whatever is begotten, born, and dies.
> Caught in that sensual music all neglect
> Monuments of unageing intellect.[71]

It may be that in the crucible of final sufferings, the elderly artist experiences a union with the sufferings of the world and a rare purification of ego that opens it to the truth of things. With literary exaggeration, Yeats writes:

> Through all the lying day of youth
> I waved my leaves and flowers in the sun.
> Perhaps now I may wither—
> Into the truth.[72]

At their best, aging artists manifest an amazing energy. This is not the strenuous energy of youth: full of activity, hedged about by social expectation, and fearful of failure. Rather, the old artist possesses a more subtle dynamism that combines truth-speaking, playfulness, and a degree of liberating insight that pierces into the mystery of life. For such a one, doing in and for the world does not cease with elderhood. Rather, the old artist seems better able to unite with the world in an accepting way. The alchemy of years produces a gentle, but profound union with the joys and sorrows of existence. In one of his last poems Rilke admonished:

> From what experience have you suffered most?
> Is drinking bitter?
> Become wine![73]

The light shining from the self-portrait of the aged Rembrandt or the prayerful oneness of an old Rubenstein with his piano depict the spiritual potential of elderhood to enhance the world.

Elderhood, therefore, is not a time to withdraw from the world, but rather to make a special offering to fellow humans through a deeper involvement in the worldly sphere. We do not agree that "the last time is for oneself."[74] Throughout this section, we have stressed the theme of an old age more fully committed to the great needs of humanity. This stand against conventional views of old people retiring from the center of public life is not meant to deprive elders of solitude and time away from the hectic pace of modern society. Rather, our insistence upon an old age moved from the periphery of social life to its center stems from the unique and needed contributions that the elderly can make to younger and to future generations.

The elderly who have been following an inward path from their middle years will have experienced a greater sense of the wilderness of existence. "Wilderness is to nature as wisdom is to consciousness."[75] Just as the untrammeled wilderness of nature contains subtleties and complexities in an ecological oneness, so true human wisdom requires that a person make the long journey into the wilderness of life's joys, sufferings, possibilities, and uncanny unities amid diversity. To accomplish this, the elder must go beyond mere cleverness and self-seeking to a nonpossessive relationship with the mystery of natural and human ecologies. When this state of soul has been attained, a kind of wisdom surpassing mere calculation can be brought to worldly deliberations and decisions. It is not that the old are more likely to know the technical answers to problems, but that elders are able to offer the wisdom of context from their own experiences, an ambience in which the technological choices may serve a greater, long-range good.

It is not a matter of energy, but of vision. Sophocles, himself the revered elder playwright, portrayed the old, blind Oedipus led by Antigone through long wandering back to Colonus, his birthplace. Sophocles did not mitigate the tragedy and the suffering in Oedipus' life; nor did he maintain that Antigone and the others who received Oedipus into Colonus would be spared their own confrontation with suffering. Yet there is a wisdom of vision about things human and divine that only the physically blind, old man can give. Oedipus reflects on his life:

> For when he [Apollo] gave me oracles of evil,
> He also spoke of this: A resting place,
> After long years, in the last country, where
> I should find home among the sacred Furies:
> That there I might round out my bitter life,
> Conferring benefit on those who received me.[76]

Sophocles' Oedipus returns in his last years to be a source of insight and courage in the center of the city. He becomes Tiresias, the blind seer, reborn. The paradox of the blind one who sees points toward a new kind of power, a force of selfless wisdom that is needed to counterbalance the power of those with normal sight. These are not usually able to see as far or as deeply because their vision is bound by the immediate, the material, the literal. More-

over, their vision is blurred by greater self-interest. Physical blindness allows the old Oedipus to cultivate a mythopoetic vision, an
ability to see the many-layered symbolic realms of existence with
the clairvoyant insight of Tiresias.[77]

Thus the old Oedipus, now open to the gentler, feminine side of
himself—Antigone—returns to the place of his birth with a new
wisdom for Colonus. It is as though the hidden purpose of his tragedy and long exile was to bestow wisdom on the people of Colonus
about the meaning of personal and communal life. He seems to
embody the poetic thought of T. S. Eliot, who ends "Four Quartets" with these intriguing lines:

> We shall not cease from exploration
> And the end of all our exploring
> Will be to arrive where we started
> And know the place for the first time.
> Through the unknown, unremembered gate
> When the last of earth left to discover
> Is that which was the beginning. . . .[78]

Oedipus mirrors an old age for the world. His return from distant
wandering to his native place symbolized a type of fulfillment, the
closing of a circle. From the vantage point of his age, he is able to
"know the place for the first time," that is, encompass a fuller
meaning for all the seasons of life. The younger citizens of Colonus
cannot attain Oedipus' knowledge in an experiential way because
they have not yet passed through the "unknown, unremembered
gate." But by accepting Oedipus into the center of their lives they
will receive the benefit, the fruit of his wisdom, for facing their own
lives with courage and hope.

Major world religions corroborate this ideal of an elderhood involved in the world, rather than retreating from it. In the Jewish
tradition, the Hebrew word *zakayn* is a synonym for "wise." This
wisdom is an understanding of Torah, which the elder who has
lived long according to God's mandates was thought to possess.
Thus, when Leviticus commands Hebrews to honor the presence of
the aged (Lev. 19:32), it is only partially because the faithful Israelite elder is personally more surrounded by God's love through
years of fulfilling *mitvot*. Indeed, younger Hebrews rose before old
age because the elder's experiential knowledge of Torah was the

most valuable wisdom about life for the whole community. The Talmud assumed that one who reached old age probably had an understanding of God's role in and for the universe.[79]

The great Asian traditions also echo the theme of a spiritual elderhood redounding to the welfare of society. In the Confucian Analect, the old were thought to have progressed toward a worldly wisdom of moral learning and practical conduct. Long years of study and experience were required to master the complexities of Confucian teaching and to gain expertise in the conduct of state.[80] Old age was especially sacred because only the elderly could have a secure grasp of the golden mean on which the good life of individuals and groups was founded. In this pragmatic Chinese tradition, the elder was not dismissed from the center of society to seek private spirituality in an isolated way. Rather, the old were viewed as essential to the collective wisdom of the whole community, acting as capstones and guides for Confucian understanding.

The word *lao* (old) in China also bore an honorary meaning, referring to the specially revered or wise, even though the person so named might not be old in years.[81] The ancient Taoist heritage of China, not as pragmatically oriented as the Confucian tradition, sought to help adherents to live according to the *Tao,* the natural and yet mysterious order of reality. The key concept of *wu wei* signified a spontaneous or unplanned response to challenges. One deals with persons and events in adaptive but effective ways, just as water naturally conforms itself to an obstructing rock by going around it. The taoist elder, who has learned to enter into the life of *wu wei,* became a model for others. As a teacher and paradigm, such an old person served the community, showing others important turns on the path to wisdom.

The Brahmin culture of Hindu society would seem at first consideration to encourage the old to seek deeper spirituality away from civic and social life. For the *Manu Smitri* declares: When a householder sees his skin wrinkled and his hair grey, and when he sees the son of his son, then he should resort to the forest.[82] Alone, or together with his wife, the Brahmin is exhorted to leave the active and pragmatic world of the householder and pursue spiritual wisdom through various forms of yoga. In some ways it is true that the Hindu elder, through detachment and asceticism, transforms the losses of aging into spiritual insight.[83] Yet a closer look at the

Manu Smitri indicates that the mandate to leave the social sphere for inward pursuits applies to persons that we would regard as middle-aged: "when he sees the son of his son." The contemplative stage, therefore, begins in midlife. By the time of elderhood, as we know it, the person would ideally have attained the state of *sanyasin,* or one who renounces social status for transcendent ends. Some elders, as *sanyasin,* live apart from society, while others return with a heightened degree of compassion and unity with all creatures. Such a one is eminently in the world, though not of it, in the sense of serving the human and spiritual development of others (as does the Bodhisattva in the Buddhist tradition), not dominating the world for self-aggrandizing ends.

Similarly, in Korea persons move at sixty through an important rite of passage, called *hwangap,* into old age. Family and friends celebrate this event, after which the elder retires to seek serenity and expand his or her spiritual life.[84] But in the Korean life-style, such an older person usually remains close to an extended family in a place of both honor and influence. He or she is not sequestered away from younger generations in a group of the old. In addition to having some worldly influence through the family, the Korean elder, according to the purposes of *hwangap,* becomes a model for others in facing the challenges of old age. In a pursuit of serenity and wholeness, such an older person teaches others how to face the doubts and uncertainties of the last phase of life.

Let these concluding remarks about elderhood for the world underscore the great potential that older people can and should exercise in the public sphere. There is no contradiction, but rather a complementarity between the quest for wisdom and spiritual wholeness in old age and active involvement in society. The social order itself, as well as the elder, is impoverished by being deprived of the active participation of the old in the major concerns of the world.

VI

REFLECTIONS ON ELDERHOOD: INTERVIEWS

The last two chapters explored the challenges and potentials of the later years in an attempt to delineate a spirituality of aging. Some of the major problems of growing old were examined in the light of a wide-ranging literature on aging. Amid these real difficulties, we tried to locate and develop a theological outlook intrinsic to the challenges themselves and to their possible outcomes. Recalling a theme stated at the beginning of this book, we sought to find a religiousness at the center of the aging process, not a spirituality externally imposed or even grafted on to the experience of midlife and elderhood. Traditional idioms of religions were interpreted in the context of aging itself. Throughout the chapters on midlife and elderhood we also emphasized the double and interlinking themes of the need for a contemplative middle age and an old age turned back toward the service of the world. The dominant culture of our time stands against both of these orientations. It would have middle-aged persons compete all the harder according to the "success" patterns of youth, while our social ethos encourages the elderly in various ways to withdraw from society's major issues. Yet all these discussions were conducted in theoretical modes, in the general concepts we must use when developing overall positions on individual and social dimensions of aging. But, in fact, we all age in the concrete, not in the abstract. Theory is useful, even essential, but we must also consult specific human experiences of coping with elderhood.

In this section we return to listening to the voices of older persons speaking about their own experiences in elderhood. In chapter three, these reflective elders took us back into their memories of early formation and the ensuing developments to middle age. We now hear them commenting on their present experiences in reference to old age, death, and afterlife. The following remarks, therefore, are not assessments of the past, but attempts to grapple with the present and the future. These men and women, from their sixties to middle eighties, must face negative aspects of aging and seek to draw from elderhood meaning for themselves and others. They ponder the proximity of death, probing their attitudes toward it and the place it takes in the last phase of life. Finally, they examine their beliefs about life after death and the impact of these tenets on daily living.

Reflections on Elderhood

Early preparation for old age is important advice that the interviewees give to younger persons. In chapter six we noted that a number of gerontologists find that patterns set in middle age continue into the later years. Education for aging well should probably begin in youth by dispelling negative attitudes toward old people and studying examples of elders who manifest a productive and inspiring old age. But midlife would seem to be the most crucial preparatory time for elderhood, for the challenges of the middle period are directly related to those of old age. John Tracy Ellis reminds us that people do not enter abruptly into creative elderhood:

> Creative aging is not an abrupt thing. It comes on day by day in a gradual evolution, and the state of mind in which aging leaves people is conditioned by their past and their native endowment. Some have been resourceful and imaginative persons from their youth, and these, I think, are better able to face old age with serenity. Others find old age a severe burden, since they have little or nothing to occupy their time in anything like a positive way. Aging "creatively" depends very much on the individual man and woman and what they are able to make of it. I think of Monsignor James Richardson, now retired at Saint Joseph's Seminary here, who fills his days with visits to neighboring hospitals, where he cheers the sick by prayer and a brief chat.

Ellis implies that with imaginative preparation the later years can allow one to continue certain activities that were always part of a career and to initiate new involvements.

He speaks about "slowing into the terminus" in a gradual way, keeping alive his many interests and his friendships:

> I have often said of late that I borrow a phrase read long ago in the life of Henry Edward Manning, Cardinal Archbishop of Westminster, when he had grown old and described his status in these words, "I am slowing into the terminus." I, too, am "slowing into the terminus," but I thank God that it has proved to be so gradual a process as to cause no sharp interruption in my daily life or routine. Inevitably with advancing years one's attitudes change. For example, I am more than content to remain at home. In fact, I find myself less and less inclined to wish to travel either within the country or abroad, which, I suppose, is part of the aging process. And then, as I remarked before, there have been the many devoted friends, most of them years younger than myself, who have seemingly not lost interest in me because of my "antiquity." And that has been a factor in keeping me alert, for I have not lost interest in life by any means. I thank God for the good eyesight that enables me to read and thus to remain abreast of developments in the church, the state, and society in general. The combination of all these has made aging a quiet and painless experience for me, a process that has brought with it no sharp and unpleasant breaks with the past.

Academics, like Helen Hole, find themselves blessed with a variety of continuing engagements that they can tailor to fit the needs of old age. She underscores the value of developing many interests along the way; also, she notes the importance of finding a rhythm of action and ease that is most satisfying:

> You need a lot of interests. You can't wait until you retire then suddenly develop your interests. You've got to have them. And I always had a lot of interests, and so when I retired, I had a beautiful time. I enjoyed it thoroughly because now I had a chance to do all the things I hadn't time to do before. Being an academic, I invented a plan to divide my life into terms. One term I would do writing and research, and one term I would do teaching. That's when I went to the Earlham School of Religion, for instance. Or Pendle Hill, teaching graduate students. And one term I did what I called Quakerizing. That is, I visited Quaker Institutions, educational institutions usually, but not

228 · *Reflections on Elderhood: Interviews*

necessarily. I visited meetings when I was asked and led retreats and all that kind of thing. And then, in the summer term, I went to New Hampshire and did nothing with great enthusiasm. And it worked beautifully because it had variety and it wasn't too long.

Lawrence Jones reminds us that we prepare for old age by the perspectives on it imbibed in earlier years. Some people program themselves to be "old" in decrepit or hypochondriacal ways in order to gain sympathy or attention and to excuse themselves from the effort of squarely engaging life. Jones discovers in anticipatory imagination ways of continuing his religious ministry through writing, child care, and counseling:

I may be whistling in the dark, but I don't intend to get old. George Burns in a little article that I was reading in the *Readers Digest* the other day said that many people even start at the age of thirty to prepare to get old. I was out with my wife the other day when we saw a car drive up. Two men got out with about four women, two of whom were widows. I said to my wife, "When we get to that stage, do not be asking me to go to dinner with old people because I am not going to go. I know what they talk about. How are you feeling? How are your legs feeling? This, that, and the other."

When it comes to aging, I have my thing all laid out. If I am physically able to do it, I intend to stay alive my whole life. My mother did it. My father did it. Both of them stayed alive all their lives. What I mean is that they were engaged in life. Mother entered into the life of her grandchildren much more vigorously than she entered into our lives. When and if I retire, I have three things that I want to do. One, I plan to finish the book that I have on my desk in its first draft. It is a history of the black church in America. Secondly, I am going to the nearest nursery school, and I am going to say, "You have just acquired a resident grandfather. I am going to be here a couple of days each week. I just want to love the children."

A third thing is that I am going to go to some church, probably here in Washington, and say to the pastor, "Now, I am an experienced counselor. I just want to join your staff for a couple of afternoons a week. You tell people that if they have problems they want to discuss with somebody, somebody is here to listen. I will listen to them and try to help them to the degree that I can, but I am only going to be here a couple of days a week." Then if things were to work out like I hope they will, I will find a little church somewhere with about two hundred people where I can preach, which I love to do. I love to wrestle with the word of God.

In the above remarks, and in those of John Bennett to follow, preparation for old age is marked by intentions to become involved at the center of things, not to withdraw to the periphery of life. Bennett talks about certain disengagements for the sake of reengagement in the world. His own life is an outstanding testimonial to flexible and creative reengagement. Bennett, in his late seventies, continues to teach part-time and to write penetrating articles on social ethics. like Jones, Bennett holds that we should expect more, not less, from those in older age:

> Well, disengagement theory was dominant around 1960. But now people realize that while there have to be various forms of disengagement, there have to be reengagements. Disengagement is no adequate formula for aging. Obviously, when you retire from your main job you don't hang around trying to make trouble for your successor. You are disengaged. And you're somewhat disengaged as people in your generation tend to die before you do. But I think reengagement is very important as well. Now, I've been fortunate because I've had so many things to stimulate me, to keep alive. And everybody doesn't have that. I have been fortunate in my health at seventy-eight.
>
> Now elderly people are classified as such at sixty-five, but they still have a good deal of vitality. I don't think that we should let them sing their last song. We shouldn't put people between sixty-five and eighty in the same category as people who are older than that. We should have great flexibility and think of people as individuals, and expect a lot more from them.

Cultivating a spirit of contemplation constitutes a vital preparation for old age. Much of chapter two emphasized a turning inward in midlife in order to cope in depth with the peculiar challenges of that period; the ability to maintain a meditative life in elderhood both enhances one's contributions during the last years and helps a person deal with the diminishments of age. It is particularly interesting that William Monihan speaks of contemplation as a mode of overcoming isolation and loneliness in old age. Monihan sees himself breaking out of self-confinement through contemplation. It leads him to a sense of oneness with nature:

> I feel that the so-called wisdom of the old finds its inner point in contemplation—contemplation taken totally, taken through nature, the universe, and all of these things. If the intricacy and perfection

that we see in the realms of human learning are so magnificent, why aren't we exploring the worlds of the spirit, which are so full? Anyone who reads the literature of the mystics can see what worlds are within them, what personalities come into conflict with the divine, what it means to walk with God and converse with God. Are you just talking about hot air, or are you talking about the real things? During my year at a Benedictine monastery in France, I wanted to get my hand on the shoulder of a contemplative and say, "How are you doing? What is happening?" I would say that through osmosis I get a feeling, a sense of what they had, and it was something very, very rich. It was a familiarity with the divine, as the Lord guiding and teaching us in a classroom: "Now you do this. Now you do that." That exchange is what it means to speak and walk in the Spirit.

Now I am coming to the essence of older age. The so-called wisdom of the old finds its full flower in contemplation in a full sense, so that you really can look at the universe and be glad and learn and be refreshed, but not be confined to the inner life only in the sense of "my life." Every poet of any quality has been reaching out for that mystic element, that sense of the divine, whether he sees it in the granite or in the hawk, as Robinson Jeffers saw it. Every poet has been reaching for that. Great music has been trying to grasp that in some way. Let us divert for a moment to Beethoven. I did a symposium on Beethoven in '78. Beethoven in the last years of his life, through greater suffering, produced the string quartets which today are of much excitement to scholars, for this was the fruit of contemplation and suffering. Beethoven began to see how his suffering could be a component part of his creative ability. He died a peaceful man.

The above passage also indicates that a contemplative life does not come about automatically in elderhood; it must be pursued, sought out, as Monihan intimates when he asks the monk what is happening. Finally, contemplation will not keep one from pain, as seen in the Beethoven example, but it can help transform suffering into spiritual depths and selfless service.

A prayerful attitude seems to be connected with the development of a more tolerant stance toward other people. Lavinia Scott makes this connection in her own growth from judgmental and puritanical positions in youth to respecting the decisions of others who differ with her. A person who is in touch with an authentic spiritual journey will recognize the numerous and surprising ways by which God leads others:

But I've always believed in prayer and meditation, though I'm not terribly good at meditation. And in the inspiration of great preachers and writers. I think I mentioned Harry Emerson Fosdick as being an inspiration when I was young. He still is. Of course, in my student early life he was one of the great liberal Christian leaders. And I think I'm less moralistic about my religion than I was. I was pretty puritanical as a young person. And I still am somewhat puritanical, I think. But I'm less judgmental, I think, then I used to be, and feel that other people have a right to their own decisions. I mean, I don't drink, but I do not condemn people who do. And while I regret the lack of church attendance and Sunday observance by many people, I don't pressure even the young people in my family to believe as I do or to practice as I do. I try to be a help to them, but sometimes I wonder if I'm as much help as I should be to them. So I think I'm more tolerant, less judgmental.

A religious preparation for old age seems to entail a willingness to be led to new theological understanding. This does not, as Blumenthal notes below, mean an easy shift of opinion with every novel wave of thought; for he claims that it takes a lifetime to formulate with care one's religious philosophy. One is brought gradually through the myriad experiences of life to reshape basic positions. Blumenthal sees his own movement to be one away from fundamentalist tenets toward more limited, but for him authentic beliefs:

> It takes a lifetime to formulate a religious philosophy, and it serves in all phases of life. Old age gives one the opportunity to take stock.
> One cannot discuss God without a basic definition. To me, God is involved in the power and the purpose of the universe. I don't know anything about him, but I am convinced of this presence. I surrendered the fundamentalist concepts of him long ago. I have lived without them, and I shall die without them as well.

In subsequent comments on death, the rabbi will indicate that his "modernist" views preclude an afterlife. Although this outlook may be less comforting than more traditional understandings, he maintains a firm conviction about God's presence in this life, especially as orchestrated in the rhythms of Jewish religious existence:

> For myself, every service in which I participate now is a recreation of the thousands that I have attended in so many places. Each is a reaffirmation of all that have preceded it. It is good to know that it will survive.

In a similar vein, O'Hanlon registers a changed understanding about God, stemming in part from his own experiences as a Christian thinker who turned toward the Orient for spiritual wisdom in later life:

> Well, I suppose that from the very early years of my life down to the present, I guess there has been a mellowing of the image of God. I think that in my early years, because of the way in which commandments and moral principles were taught, it was very natural to think of God as the big eye in the sky. God is watching you and that means that you had better behave. That has not entirely disappeared but has moved more and more into the background and mellowed. The idea of God who is gracious, the source of goodness, the One whose primary concern in everything is to make sure that you get as enriched and fulfilled as you possibly can be . . . that is the general image of God in my later years.

In addition to a readiness to alter one's views with new experiences, preparation for old age requires that we learn to confront the psychological and physical injuries or limitations referred to throughout our theoretical analysis of the topic. It is important in younger years to envision as best we can the coming impact of negative social attitudes about the old. In this way they will not take us by surprise, nor will we be crushed by them, letting ourselves too easily become society's victims. Greenberg strikes a balance between awareness of discrimination against the elderly and excessive dependence on the efforts and thoughts of others:

> There is no doubt that there are many things that we do to older people that are vicious and harmful. That ought to be avoided as much as possible—for example, the notion that if they're around you can't have a good time, that they put a damper upon it. That is why you don't keep them in your home. I think that is terrible. The sense of showing love to those who showed love to you has been lost. That is a terrific loss to those who don't show the love, and not merely to the older people. That is what we are suffering. On the other hand, unfortunately, too many old people have made themselves dependent upon what others are going to do for them, or what others are going to think of them. I wrote way back in 1919, "Contentment and gladness / Are often in sadness / Sought where they are not / And hence sought in vain. / To ask of another / A friend or a brother / For that which is in you / Can bring only pain."
> But that goes back to another thing, to your own sense of status.

What are people going to say? At one point or another you have to make up your mind not to be bothered by what others will say. I said it in a jocular vein, but I always thought that I could make a living shining shoes. It all depends upon what and how much you want. I wasn't scared of not having things that other people think are important to them. If you set high material or social goals, you have to pay the price for it. I am not worried if I don't have a car. It doesn't concern me.

The last point, about one's sense of status deriving from material things, is particularly important in our culture. Such a high premium is placed on financial success that those of modest means in elderhood might see themselves as failures. Greenberg's sense of values, stemming from Jewish religion and ethics, does not allow materialism to lead to despair in old age.

Although O'Hanlon enjoys his entry into elderhood, he, too, perceives the damaging influence of social attitudes on the elderly. He contrasts prevalent outlooks in the West to those of Japanese society:

> First, for myself, I am really relishing the process at the moment. I am not finding it problematical. Fortunately, my physical condition is good. I am active and all of that. I have a pattern of life which is fruitful and energy-giving for me. My feelings about the general way in which the culture treats old people is that it is pretty crummy. Take as an example the expression "senior citizens." Now what does that mean? That means that it is really a bad thing to be old, so we need to get a more indirect name. We do not want to call them old, because old is really an awful thing. There is this endless series of euphemisms. Pretty soon "senior citizen" is not going to be any good. You will have to find another one. The basic reason is the feeling that being old is not a good thing. These are useless people. They are worn out, and they are ready for the ash heap. We try to be as nice to them as we can. But they are of no real help to us anymore.
>
> I remember talking to a Japanese whom I was interviewing a couple of years ago. He had lived in this country for some time and so was familiar with both countries and cultures. I asked, "What do you think about these two cultures? Would you like to be part of this culture or would you like to be Japanese?" The answer was, "I think that when my parents get old, I will take care of them; I think that I will be a part of the Japanese culture." That for him was the decisive difference. In our culture being old is not a respected position which has authority, wisdom, and meaning. In his culture it is. That is something that is so deeply rooted in the value system that I do not think

that it will easily change. However, I would think that, quite apart from what older people want, we should focus on their value for the rest of the culture: we should prize, relish, and respect their resources of wisdom and experience. What it amounts to is that activity, knowledge, and quickness are great values in our culture, but wisdom and related things are not.

A final lesson from both of the above interviewees focuses on the primary significance of reverence for persons. Greenberg speaks of this as loving the old who in their earlier years cared for us. O'Hanlon approaches reverence for persons in a different way, urging us to respect the experience and wisdom of the old as an intrinsically valuable dimension of who they are.

Many persons in old age suffer not only from damage inflicted by social attitudes, but also from remorse and self-recrimination for their own decisions earlier in life. Clarice Bowman long regretted her choice to retire early; this decision became a source for self-hatred. Perhaps one of the most difficult achievements for a sensitive person is not to forgive others, but to forgive oneself. Without self-forgiveness one can stagnate in despair during elderhood:

> My message about aging would be to struggle to keep growing and to keep from getting bitter and resentful at being rejected. I resented my own decision to retire when I did. I said, "Why'd I ever do that?" I was hating myself. One can be consumed with remorse at wrong turnings made, at failures and all kinds of things where one wished one had lived differently. I have gone through agonies of soul-searching, seeking not only forgiveness, but self-forgiveness. And one can get mired in one's own thoughts. One can wait too much on the sidelines for invitations from others, without straining and struggling to go do things that keep one alive. One has to do one's own stirring the waters, in a way, or else one stagnates.

Benjamin Mays offers still another clue for creative aging against social odds. For he has had to struggle against the twin liabilities in our culture of race and age. Part of his secret for success in elderhood is living toward the future; Mays corroborates in his own life our argument in chapter five that the old have a future:

> I really have never had time to think too much about aging. I lived in crisis all the time. The main crisis in my life was how I was going to develop to be a man of respect and decency and how was I going to

make it in a world that was determined that I was not going to make it. I beat the system. I know quite well that I am an old man, but I have kept busy on the things that I have to do in the future rather than looking back on what I had done. When a man looks back and can see only the great things he has done in the past, he is through. I say sometimes that I do not have time to get older or have time to die. I am trying to see what the next thing is. I was determined that education administration would never keep me from doing some scholarly work. With a Ph.D. I think that a man ought to produce something. I have produced seven books. The eighth one is coming out soon, and I am working on another one. I have always felt that it is better to die on the job rather than go somewhere, sit down, and wait to die.

As we move into the later years of life, physical limitations and possible disabilities increase. Brewer's reflections on his own handicaps in old age help us anticipate such difficulties and temper activities in order to cope with these new shortcomings:

> Another side of this growing older has been declining health. This has two parts. One is a generalized decline of energy. I involve myself in less work time and more in rest or leisure time than I used to. I guess I was something of a workaholic in an earlier day. And that's been balanced out some. I need to spend more time in restful types of activities. I expect that my energy level will continue to decline gradually. And I will have to really relate to and compensate for that. But the other has been a more dramatic type of thing. I have had difficulty with bodily functions. For example, I've had cataract operations on both eyes, and that's an older person's problem. However, I'm pretty well fixed so far as sight is concerned. So the disability is not very serious, but it's there. I have faced, in the last year or so, difficulty with teeth and gums. That's pretty well under control, but it's been a very handicapping factor. And I'm facing shortly now a prostate gland operation, which again is an older person's kind of thing, so that in addition to the gradual decline of energy and having to relate to that, I've had these specific sorts of things. Now aside from that, my health has been good. I've had no handicapping condition of any significance—nothing that keeps me from doing my work in a relatively normal fashion. And I'm certainly grateful for that.

Another very active author, Professor Albert C. Outler, echoes the latter experiences in reference to physical energy. It is particularly interesting to note the role that stimulating events and persons perform in rejuvenating the energy of this talented man:

I think you are talking about an inevitable rhythm that becomes most important as age comes on and as the shadows lengthen and our work on earth is done. In the first place, I find that, given my normal energies, I turn very much more apathetic unless there is somebody there, somebody asking me to do something. Given another person's presence at home, your coming, or having to speak to a class or something or another, arouses vitality that isn't there naturally. On the other hand, you have to have these blockers for adrenalin stimulus in order to take care of coronary constriction. So I use a chemical pacemaker to block the adrenalin stimulus. What this means is that other people stir up more vitality that I feel like I have before a lecture, before a sermon, before an interview. Often I feel like, "Gee, I can't pull it off this time." Then from somewhere the resources come, vitality surges up, and I get on through. Then I collapse again. That is what getting old has meant for me so far.

In spite of these drawbacks, both of these men maintain a full schedule of activities; they seem to have been able to face bodily decline as a challenge, making certain accommodations in their work so as not to abandon it. Brewer remarks that he may be doing some of his best teaching and writing in elderhood. It could be that having to slow down, to assess the truly valuable areas on which to expend time and energy, has had a creative result:

Yet I'm involved in projects of research and writing, including different and new ideas in teaching. I think, for example, that I'm probably doing the best teaching now that I've ever done, and I anticipate that the next two years will continue that. I'm certainly much more interested in teaching than I have been in the past. I know I'm exploring new areas in my research and writing now. And I expect to continue that from now on, as long as I'm able to do so.

Finding joy in one's present phase of life can also act as a deterrent to physical diminishment and suffering. Jack Boozer speaks of an immense compensation in experiencing the values of a particular stage of life rather than looking nostalgically backward at youth:

I find that the happiest stage of life is the stage you're in at that time. It may be that I'm more a victim of *machismo* than I think, but I don't think of myself as being old. I can't play tennis as vigorously as I once did. I have a back problem and I haven't played golf in a number of years. But I can still ride the bicycle and walk, and I like to use the sledge hammer for splitting wood. And I really enjoy working in the soil, physical work. I think life would be different for me if I were not able to walk and if I were in pain every day. I cannot say what that would be like. I just hope and am reasonably confident that there are opportunities and graces and activities that are available then that aren't available now, because I'm in a different pattern of life now. That has certainly been the case so far. I think that there is an immense compensation to what one learns in a certain stage. In other words, I don't think that I would want to live through my adolescence again, not knowing any more than I did as an adolescent then. I cherish that time, but I also cherish things I know now that I didn't know when I was an adolescent. There are dimensions of pleasure, of care, of work and activity that I didn't even know; I wasn't aware. And I know those now.

Although part of preparing for older age involves self-initiative, religious and secular institutions need to explore alternative living environments to enhance elderhood. The octogenerian artist L. Jenkins speaks forcefully about the need to establish centers for the old in which spiritual, social, and physical requirements could be met. As an artist, she would like to have her own studio within walking distance of a chapel and other facilities. She urges the importance of meditation in the life of the old, as well as the overcoming of isolated existences:

> I would hope to see somebody having retreat centers or even homes, where women like myself and men—it would have to be both sexes—could go. They would be able to walk to a chapel. They wouldn't have to get in an automobile. They would be in a quiet place where they could carry on their own work. I would have my own studio. But I would have a central dining room and a central place for the Mass and prayer and meditation. It would be a center where aged people could come. And in stages they would make this transition from the active to the death experience. I could have a daily Mass. I could have a liturgy which I cannot have, situated here. Then, a place like a hospice, where they wouldn't have to go into intensive care, but could meet death in that environment. And there we could help each other to contemplate, to combat this whole thing of our culture that everything should be success, everything should be outside—the fast pace of America. And we don't know where they're going at this fast pace even. We could turn this life in and bring it together. This would be an introduction to death. And death would then be a glorious step into the next life. Now, I have to try to do this alone. And I have to combat all these outside influences . . . it's very difficult. Of course, I have this little room. I have my friends who come here to meditate,

which is a big help. I have many young people who come and tell me their experiences in India or at the Zen Center.

An old person is no different from any other person. They want meaning in life. The Catholic Church should spend a great deal of time and thought and energy on the education of persons who have been very active and teach them how to turn, how to be a contemplative, because the real meaning is there. You find it here in Carmel, a tremendous percentage of lonely old ladies who are alcoholics. The alcoholic problem is very high here, simply because there has been in this culture no way to educate them to be and not just to do. I would like to see the Catholic Church spend time, money, and effort in educating people in meditation.

Mildred Cranston[1] is fortunate enough to live in a church-related retirement community that offers some of the options desired by Jenkins. Although Cranston is critical of the churches' lack of care for the old, she underlines the significance of the Pilgrim Place community in Claremont, California, where she has lived for a number of years. The communal meal was a special source of support at the time of her husband's death:

I think that the churches have a good deal to do in finding out how to take care of the old. I remember some years ago we were looking at a church building over here, studying a nursery they had for children. We were invited to go up a stairway. In the corner of the room, with not much light, were four ladies licking envelopes to send out for the church. They were bored to death and needed to have a drink of water, as if they were licking too many envelopes. The woman showing us said, "Well, these are such dear old people. They do this for us every week." And I thought, "To hell with it."

We do a lot of laughing over here in the Pilgrim Place Retirement Community. We do it around those tables. That meal saves us. When Earl died, I walked over within twenty-four hours and I said, "Put me down for four days for the common meal." It saved my life. Your grief makes you turn in like this. If I stay away from the community meal a week, I am awfully glad when I come back. I like it. There are some that get on my nerves, but it is probably true that I get on theirs. We do not fuss.

As an educator and civic leader, Benjamin Mays has been in the forefront of those who influence public policy. This octogenarian stresses the preparation of the young for elderhood by including them in institutional planning for the old, and he also affirms the role of government in providing varied programs for the elderly:

> I am a member of the White House Committee on Aging. I think one thing we must keep in mind is that there is no gap between youth and age. You move, you grow into old age. Age and youth belong together. When age is not willing to listen to youth, it has lost its right to leadership, and when youth is not willing to listen to age, it is not ready for responsibility. You have to have young people in the White House Conference on Aging. The government is going to appoint so many from each of the fifty states. One thing we emphasize is that you have to have young people in all of these conferences so that they will understand that they are part of it. Where we are, they are going to be, so you might as well enter into it sympathetically, because unless you die early, your time is coming. We want to help them to live and die in peace and gracefully. They all don't need the same prescription. Some people should live in their own home. The government ought to see to it that those who need to live there can get all the services that they need. There are others who ought to be in the best nursing home possible. There again this conference is to take care of things so that those who ought to be in their homes will be in their homes. Others ought to be in first-class nursing homes with television and services every Sunday morning. Contact the churches and make sure that they can go to their own churches if they are in the neighborhood. Get buses and take them there. They need to live a happy life and die in dignity.

In the last chapter, we emphasized the value of an old age turned back toward the world in service. A number of comments in the interviews center on the contributions that the old can make to one another and to the general wellbeing of society. The ability to rise above the physical and social liabilities of old age and again to become involved in worthwhile projects seems to be a key factor in creative elderhood. M. L. Tobin expresses her vital concern for major social issues such as nuclear weapons and militarization; her personal growth is linked to opposing movements that are judged destructive to the human community:

> People could be doing in their final years things that they never had a chance to do before. All kinds of new things. I am trying to grow in love, friendship, an effort to do something about the perilous situation that we find ourselves in as a world, the whole nuclear threat. If I believe that human life is good, then I have to affirm that. Because I affirm it, I would like to see other people have it and enjoy it, and I don't

want to see them destroyed in nuclear blasts. So that is very much on the top of my mind. We are exploiting people, not only in our own country, but around the world, in order to build up a fantastic military arsenal that is ridiculous on the face of it. It is so ridiculous, you think, "How could reasonable people do this?"

Anne Bennett is another elderly woman who has been in the forefront of causes such as Christian feminism and world peace. While she believes that it is important for the elderly to organize and exercise political power for their own needs, Bennett wants older people to militate as well for changes that will benefit the next generation:

> In the last years of the sixties, before John retired in 1970, I was working with a group of women who were all facing retirement. I was the only volunteer person in this professional group. And our concern was to get an organization going in which we could keep in touch with each other and continue to work on the great public issues. Now, that group later became the Gray Panthers. But the Gray Panthers' main emphasis has been on advocacy for the elderly. That's very important and it needs to be done. I noticed a report recently from our United Church of Christ about their aging program. And again, it is advocacy for the aging in housing, health, etc. I feel that, as an elderly person, I also have an obligation to the next generation. And I think the emphasis should be on advocacy for the elderly to fill needs, but emphasis should be on working for and with the coming generation and not just for the elderly. It's the great public issues. We have more time. We have no hostages to fortune. We don't have any jobs to be fired from.

In confronting these major world problems, the elderly can remind the younger persons that the seemingly overwhelming issues are not entirely new; similar matters have been faced before. Such counsel, Bennett affirms, can prevent discouragement:

> I know a lot of people are grateful when I remind them of things that happened before, that the problems they face today aren't unique. And I think this is very good for people to realize. The result is that people get an apocalyptic view of things too quickly if they look only at present evils. It is helpful if they realize we've recovered from similar things in the past. Things are not quite the same now, as the threat to the environment and the threat of nuclear annihilation are definitely new. But a very large part of the frustrations about things are not new. I think it is important to remember that.

The contributions of the old need not be only in the area of great world issues; they can also reach out to their peers, working to enhance the lives of their elderly friends. Clarice Bowman presents imaginative examples of such activities in recreations that elevate the spirit and in creative writing projects. The latter help older persons integrate their lives through autobiographical reflection:

> My sister and I have been working with what's called the Spare Time Club, which is a group of interdenominational elderly people. The one thing we've done that went over big was singing for fun. I went back on all the fun things we used to do with the crazy songs, folk songs, and especially love songs. And when we began to open up those things, they sang them with such joy and, I'm sure, memories. They were very happy. Older people need a lot of that kind of thing, a lot of humor. Maybe that jogs them out of too much moroseness and bitterness. And we had a creative writing course here last fall. We're having another one on life journeys this fall. I was surprised at the requests to participate which came from some of the elderly people. And I didn't dream what in the world we'd do on creative writing with a group of the elderly. But you know they got to trying their wings. Some of them had wanted to be writers all their lives and never had a chance to do it. And a number of them were writing up their experiences for their grandchildren, for the future generations, and writing about their roots.

Another service of the elderly is one of counseling younger persons. Bowman describes her experience of empathizing with the doubts and hardships of such a group:

> The word "experience" is too abstract for telling young people about old age. Rather, how it feels to weather through hard times and somehow be aware that you've been helped to come through. And the young people can sense that maybe they can, too. It's an affirmation at the other end of the dark valley that older people can make. Young people don't appreciate the warnings we give them. They think they are quite sufficient without warnings. But to know that one can find one's way through some dark valleys is a help. And I think that when we say words of belief or faith and affirmation with younger people, we should say them quietly and reverently and almost with awe. Not glibly. There's too much glibness going on. It's not being wrested out of us with pain. In this young adult group of mine, some terrific problems have been faced. In a small group that grew from six to twenty, there've been two losses of babies. There's been some very serious illness, also deaths of near relatives. I think it's been meaningful to

them to have an older person. Gradually, not at first, they've come to a point where they can dare ask me about doubts concerning God and things like that. I think they need older people who have suffered and who are not glib.

Implied in this account is the insight that the attitude of the older counselor is important for gaining the respect and trust of the young. If the elder avoids glibness and speaks from the matrix of his or her own sufferings, the artificial barriers of age fall away and the spirit of the experienced old communicates with the spirit of the needy young. Sylvia Heschel underscores this point by reminding us that some of our language about old age sets up artificial obstacles between generations. Beyond these preconceptions, the personhood of the old can share valuable wisdom with the personhood of the young:

> Words are deeply affective, yet are used so blithely and carelessly. Categories are for "things," not human beings. When one has lived a number of years and become a designated "senior citizen," all at once one is caused to look upon oneself as someone else. One can feel shunted, shelved, and obliged to reevaluate oneself in terms of what others think. The inner life has not changed, only the outer shell has. When one has sown well from one's early life on, one then continues to grow, amazingly, until the end. Let us not categorize by groups, nor call them names, nor set up number of years as the guidelines. Let us liberate ourselves from the machinations of this age of mechanics.

Lawrence Jones, who earlier in this chapter produced an impressive scenario of planned activities for his old age, eloquently sums up the overall goal of an elderhood for the world. He speaks of the tragedy of social circumstances that hamper persons from realizing their potential. In light of this, his purpose in life and his mark of success in elderhood would be to help others come to full flowering. He notes also the reciprocal benefit of finding nurturance toward his own growth in helping others to attain their potential:

> I have the feeling that I ought to touch people's lives for good. I'll tell you what I am trying to do, Gene. I believe that it was God's intention that people actualize the possibility with which they were born, so that it can come to full flower. The degree to which I can help do that will also nurture me to full flower. That is what makes racism and all the other kinds of "isms" so terrible, because they rob people of their futures and therefore frustrate God. Aging, then, can be a process of nurturing people to the fullness of their being.

Confronting Death

Throughout the chapters on midlife and elderhood, we have stressed the importance of coming to grips with one's own finitude and its many ramifications. In this section we listen to older persons speak about their personal reflections on death. In general, this group of interviewees is able to find significance in the face of death; a calm courage and a spiritual hope pervade their remarks. Yet they are also acutely aware of the negativities associated with the final decline. A sense of the shortness of time in which to complete certain tasks stands out in the following passage. Albert Outler experiences death as a nearby shadow or a nuisance that could rob him of time to finish various projects. He feels a certain relief in being able to accomplish the major goals he had set for himself:

> At least since my first gastric ulcer, which, you see, is normally associated with stomach cancer, I have had the sense of death as a shadow. Most of the time I have thought of it as a nuisance. Yes. If it had come earlier than now, it would have interrupted something that desperately needed getting done—or I thought it did—and that it was fairly crucial for me to get done. I guess one of the most interesting moments was when I put almost the last touch on the main draft of the four volumes of Wesley's sermons. I thought to myself, "Now, no matter what happens, here is the job—and the most important job that I would like to leave done—done." So if I were to die now, it wouldn't be as much of a nuisance as it would have been if I had had to leave this project in somebody else's hands. Without boasting, they couldn't have finished it. All of that work would have gone for naught. So I have not feared death so much as feared what it would do to these interlocking projects. The great boon of my life is that now I am at a place where all these projects are relatively on their own, with whatever contribution that I made to them. Now the question is how much more is there to be done that I could do. That doesn't seem to matter an awful lot; it doesn't matter as much as I thought. I thought that I would have a priority of things that I would like to get done before I die. I guess I do in a vague sort of way, but no longer with a sense of urgency. If I were to die now, a lot of things would go undone, but none of them would seem to me to be as regrettable now as it would have been.

Whereas Outler associates death with loss of time to complete one's life work, John Bennett sees this loss in terms of a future that he will not experience. Unlike the past, social change is so rapid today that he experiences some disappointment at not being around to see how things will work out:

> I think the sense that there's less time to do something is very important. And also the sense that you will not know how things are coming out. If you lived in the day where it would be more of the same, as far as you could see, for the next hundreds of years, death would have a different meaning than it has now. Now there are such tremendous, catastrophic changes, and you just don't know how it's coming out. That's one thing. Of course, also the loss of the person is very great.

Outler picks up on the last line of the above quote concerning the loss of the person as related to feelings of aloneness. In one way, the death of friends deprives him of desired company and constitutes a real loss of some part of his own selfhood. This experience focuses on the interlinking of lives; we are more than our individual selves; we are part of all that we have known and loved. Yet even in solitude he can summon up in memory the presence of persons who have died; in this sense, he does not die totally alone:

> There is a kind of glibness in talking about how I could face either the death of my wife, my own death, the death of my children. I might very well fall apart, and would certainly be devastated in any case. I have had now over the last ten years a steady succession of close personal friends fall away, and every one has been a substantive loss of my own selfhood. The problem of how alone I am, or how much a part of all that I have seen and been goes back to the earlier discovery that solitude is not being alone. It is a different sort of social experience. When I am in a room by myself, there is still a selective company summoned at will and truly present. The notion of dying alone, I should think, means the constriction of summonable company of spiritual companions and friends, and then the disappearance of the lot. This would be deprivation.

A recurring theme among this group of elderly persons is the fear of losing one's mental capacities as death approaches; this fear becomes stronger with the prospect of a long period in such a condition. Outler talks about the matter in terms of how to assure a graceful exit:

Death is, I take it, the ultimate deprivation. I worry a great deal, for I do not see how to insure a graceful exit. That is the remaining problem. All the other things, somewhat ungracefully, have been managed. But what is the chance of a graceful exit? The degree of indignity that comes with old age and helplessness, the dependence upon and bother to others seems to me to be graceless. This I dread more than anything else I can identify as an honest dread. Getting out of life is more difficult than getting in—certainly for the person himself or herself. But as for what it will take to insure this, I do not know.

The same worry stands out in the following comments of John Bennett, who reflects on observations in his retirement community. Some may even enjoy good bodily health, while their minds are unable to remember the past hour; others with serious afflictions become destructive toward other people:

> But one of the things that does come out very much when you live in a place like this is that you don't want to survive your mind or your memory. I mean, there are people here who have pretty good health, who are no great problem to anybody else, but they don't really remember what happened the last hour. That's a very sad thing. Or there are people who've had strokes. They may turn against the people closest to them. They're miserable and they make everybody else miserable. This is a worse situation than death, I think. When one sees that, it has an effect upon your whole attitude.

Lavinia Scott tells the story of a woman at the retirement center who was unconscious as far as anyone could know; no extraordinary measures were used to keep her alive. This situation causes personal anxiety in the old, who fear a similar ending, and it also raises the more general question of the meaning of such a subhuman existence:

> Death itself does not worry me at all. The one thing that I would dread, and I again don't spend a lot of time worrying about it, is mental deterioration. Because seeing people who were once fine, able, intelligent people lose their grasp on life, as some here in our health center have done, is to me the most tragic thing. I think suffering pain is far preferable to that deterioration of the mind. And I must confess I question the purpose of that. I can understand the purpose of illness, or even of pain and sorrow—as a testing and maybe a chance for maturity and spiritual insight and so on. But this mental deterioration,

just existing, is sad. I remember one perfectly beautiful woman whom I had known years before. A few years before and a few years after I came here, she was, as far as anybody could tell, completely unconscious. She was beautiful, she was well cared for, she didn't obviously suffer, but she didn't know what was going on—had no communication. Well now, what is the purpose of that kind of existence? And it wasn't the case she was being kept alive by drastic measures. She wasn't. She was being fed and sustained but that was all, I think.

Some would argue that respect for human dignity demands that such persons be kept alive. There is also the crucial ethical matter of consent: Did the person make a clear choice at an earlier, lucid time to be kept alive or to be terminated in this limbo existence? Would she have left explicit directions for others to act in her behalf? These issues are further complicated by legal strictures. Earl Brewer, reflecting on the possibility of personal involvement in a similar terminal state, opts for inducing death:

I think that if I had my druthers, I would rather face those handicapping conditions up to a stage and then induce death rather than becoming a vegetable, entering death at that level. I hope to die with some degree of dignity, and in order to do that you need to have your wits about you, so to say, when you die. I think that the arrangements that we have for death, medically, and in the culture, the feelings that we have about it, make it dismal, disappointing, dark, and really not to be thought and talked about much. I hope to face my death not as a morbid sort of thing, but as an exploration in a continued liberation.

Bennett strengthens the argument for the "suicide of the dying" as a permissible form of euthanasia, inasmuch as it allows previous consent. He tempers this position by opposing suicide in general:

I think it's very important to distinguish between the suicide of the dying, those who've got no future in this world, and the suicide of despair. I remember hearing Arthur Rubenstein say that when he was twenty years old, he tried to commit suicide. And then he said he thought he was the happiest person in the world having lived. That's a very good illustration of how the suicide of the young is a very tragic thing. Whatever is said about the suicide of the dying, it should never become a model for others. I stress that very much in my article "Ethical Aspects of Aging in America." Not that I advocate suicide for the dying, but I think it does become in some rare situations the most defensible form of euthanasia because there is consent in it.

In addition to the physical and mental disabilities associated with dying among the elderly, an important psychological anxiety is emphasized by Lawrence Jones. He is convinced that fear of death is closely linked with deeper anxiety about an unfulfilled life, the sense of not having used God's gifts well:

> I told my wife that it was like being in parade. You start out at the back end of the parade. Everybody is up in front. You are now the grandfather. You were the father, but now you are the grandfather. In the orderly processing of things in your life, you are next in line. But the parade is illuminated by the conviction that the fear of death is anxiety about an unfulfilled life, that the gift that God has put into your hands you have not used well. Therefore, as death approaches, life has been a sound and a fury. That intensifies your anxiety.

Ellis reiterates this feeling of omitting to do what should have been done in the unusual phrase of being "ashamed to die." Both of these men bear a strong sense of responsibility to use their talents well; without such a life, the prospect of death carries a note of sadness into the later years:

> A friend remarked, "I am not afraid to die, but I am ashamed to die." I recall remarking that I frequently felt the same, in the sense of my consciousness of all too many sins committed in the past and, too, of numerous opportunities for increased grace in one form or another that I had allowed to pass unfulfilled.

As these elders approach the end of their lives, a number of positive thoughts and experiences flow from meditations on death. On a very practical level, Jack Boozer has set aside a folder for his family indicating provisions he has made for them. Having one's worldly affairs in order for loved ones can bring a kind of peacefulness to an older person. These actions themselves manifest love for one's family:

> I've really enjoyed every stage of my own life. And although I've not been ill for a long time, I carry flaws in my body, and I've had to face death. I've gone in for an exploratory operation twice, not knowing what was there and knowing that something might be detected which would be terminal. I've had to reflect on the question of death long ago because of my relation to the military. I've had to put my personal affairs in order. And there's a folder in the file cabinet at home for my wife and the children to read when I'm killed or when I die; I thought

that was likely, years before in my life. I say there that I've confronted this question, and I am at peace about that. And they should not be concerned about me. And I say other things about provisions that I've made for them and hopes that I have for them.

Contemplation of personal death can also cause a fuller appreciation of life in the present. For Daniel O'Hanlon, such meditation acts as a spur to make the most of the present hours of existence:

> Sometimes I will begin—not very often—a meditation on my own death, not as a fearful thing, but as a reminder. The net result of it is to really relish what is here right now. It is not something that I look forward to. Maybe some people reach that stage toward wholeness and wisdom where they are yearning for that great moment. When I think about death and reflect on it, it acts as a means of reminding me, "Let's get going here."

In the characteristic mode of a rabbi, Aaron Blumenthal examines the same theme by telling a story. He at once reminds a child not to squander time and stresses the value of the time remaining in his own life. But in an even more moving way, the rabbi focuses on the emotional quality of relationships with his own children; each hug and each "goodbye" has a special poignancy because it may well be the last:

> I once was teaching a class. And I was trying to tell the kids not to waste my time. I said to one kid, "How old are you?" He said, "Thirteen." I said, "How much longer do you think you're going to live?" He hadn't given it a thought. "Well, let's assume that you and I are going to live to be seventy-five years old. You have sixty-two more years in which to live. That's a lot of time. I'm seventy years old. I only have five more years left. Now, you little stinker, don't waste my time, it's too precious."
> Death makes living even more precious. It makes people even more precious. I've just seen my daughter. I've just seen my youngest son. I have four children. I have seen five of my ten grandchildren on this trip. I see them grow; they're a little bigger. I'm happy to see them. And when I put my arms around my youngest son as he took me to the plane today, I was moved a little bit by the thought, "Am I going to see him again?" Because I find myself thinking about dying.

Some of the interviewees have arrived at a point in their spiritual journeys where they look at death as a new venture. William Monihan tries, like his theosophist friend, to greet each new day as a novel opportunity, leaving behind the hampering scars and memories of the past. This is not a denial of one's history; rather, it is a quest to be free of the crushing or paralyzing happenings of that past in order to begin each day anew, even the day of death:

> I try to look at death as I would look at a new day, a new experience coming. I have a very dear friend, a very elderly lady, ninety years of age, who many years ago spoke of her discipline—she is not a Christian, but a theosophist—in trying at night to empty her mind of that day. She would try by discipline to open her mind for the following day. As she would try to go to sleep, she would clear her mind, unclutter and clear it out. I would like to be able to so live each day as to welcome new experiences, to drop my old angers, to drop my compulsiveness and passivity toward formal projects and say, "This is a new day." Hopefully, when the hour of death comes, I can say, "Well, here it is." I think that one has to cut off the past every day.

Clarice Bowman recognizes her fears about illness and surgery. Yet in the midst of these trepidations, she holds to a sense of new possibilities through the door of death. Particularly interesting in the following passage is the vital polarity in the Christian experience between the "trembling" before the reality of suffering and the trust in God that permits the soul to enter the valley of death in a spirit of adventure:

> I've had several surgeries myself, never too serious, but I always face the possibilities before going under anesthetic. Sunday week I go in for surgery and I'm more frightened than I've ever been before. It may not be malignant, but we don't know. And I've had skin cancers already. My father died of cancer. All of this is very, very frightening. And, as I say, I faced it to some extent previously, but never fully. The imminent death of all people just seems to close in on me. I think it's not so much fear as trying to hold to a trust in the power that made us all and who wills our good—and even daring to sense the possibility of further adventure ahead. Life has opened up to me some of the most wonderful adventures really. This leads me to feel that death may be another door. I can't think of it as a stopping of life and of fellowship, but rather a continuing. I'm trying to hold to this while at the moment I'm inwardly trembling.

The single dominant chord among these people of faith is a profound trust in God in the face of death. The images of this trust take on different nuances, reflecting varied life experiences. Dean Jones sketches in a graphic and touching way the tableau of father and son portraying an earthly trust that in faith mirrors his confidence in divine care:

> Down at Fisk University we had a stone wall that ran the length of the campus. My son used to like to get up on that and run. Sometimes he would run along in the evening near huge oak trees that hung over Eighteenth Avenue. There was light in between, so that there was light and shadow. He would get up on the fence and run along in the light. Then when he got to the darkness he would jump down and take my hand. We would walk through the darkness together until we got to the light again. Then he would jump up on the wall again and run. That began for me to be an analogy to our relationship with God. My son knew the father that he saw in the light and whose hand he held in the dark would not change because the circumstances had changed.

None of us like the shadow or the pain that surround death, says Professor Outler, but death is part of the natural, God-established cycle of things. To overcome death through science, as some "immortalist" writers project, smacks to him of *hubris,* that Greek sense of pride by which humans inflate their egos in destructive ways. Outler concludes with a statement of confidence in God's providence, the divine foresight that does not determine human outcomes, but rather gently accompanies our journeying, luring us toward good from beginning to end:

> To overcome death? No. This seems to me to be *hubris,* for death is a natural and inevitable thing. It seems to be in some important sense a constructive part of the whole experience of existence. I'm scared in the sense that I don't like pain, and it upsets me mightily to have things and my family upset. If there were any assurance that I would die with my boots on, or go out quietly with peace at the last, then it seems to me that death is neither friend or foe, but simply God's way of bringing to be and passing on into whatever is provided by his providence.

After nearly a century of experiencing what it means to be black in America, Benjamin Mays knows the small deaths of this long struggle. Mays, who will surely become for posterity one of the model black leaders of our time, admits his fear of pain and other disabilities associated with the final decline. Yet underneath these anxieties is the conviction in faith that the God who walked at his side through the long journey from slavery and discrimination can be entrusted with his soul at death:

> I think about death, but not enough to worry me. My views in religion have not changed in this sense. I do not believe necessarily in a burning hell, nor in a place in heaven where you fly around and wear crowns. That would bore me to death. It isn't like me. But I have faith enough to believe that God has taken care of me through all these years. In all of my ups and downs, struggle and strife, he must have been with me. Had to be. I could not make it by myself. If I trusted him while I was living, I would trust him to do with my soul. I am in accord with what God would with me. I am not afraid of death. I am afraid of pain.

The experience of trust in a larger, benevolent presence surrounding one's life and, therefore, one's death may result from years of meditation. Helen Hole expresses such contemplation-induced serenity in the trying circumstances of life-threatening surgery:

> When I went up for this by-pass operation, they told me I might not survive it. We discussed whether it was worth taking the risk. They said they thought I was pretty active, especially mentally. And it might be worth trying, and I agreed with that. My children agreed with that, including my son, who's a doctor. I discovered that I was not upset or frightened. I was not frightened at all. I didn't even have to take something to make me sleep the night before the operation. A pattern of meditation which has fed my life over a period of years helped me face the crisis. I mean the kind of meditation that gives you a sense of being in touch with something bigger than yourself that cares.

This mystic sense of belonging to a greater whole, of being part of a trustworthy purpose in the world can sometimes come suddenly while one is engaged in a very ordinary task. Jones recalls an important contemplative experience that happened while he was tending his vegetable garden. Close to the earth, he realized himself as part of a chain of being. Just as fertilizer affects the new life of plants, he envisions his own life as a catalyst for the future growth of the world. Underlying this significant insight is a sense of the trustworthiness of God's plan:

I thought about death a good bit. I was working in my yard one day. I was trying to grow some beans . . . a rabbit or other animal took care of that. The hill of beans never made it. I was working there in my garden and I had an experience. I had the experience of my identity with everything there is, that is, in a sense the beans, the manure, the soil, and all the rest . . . you know, Lovejoy's idea of the chain of being. I had the sense that we were all a part of a whole.

I haven't forgotten that, and I sometimes wish that I could recover it, because it was an experience that conferred the greatest peace. I don't know how long it lasted or anything, because I was just working in the garden. Suddenly you are at home. I recognized that at my own death, in some sense, my own existence will have fertilized the world for what comes after. You know, it is all gathered up in God's plan.

For another example of trust in the face of death, we turn to a rabbinic expression. Simon Greenberg demonstrates the feisty Jewish trait of almost debating with God about the outcome of events. He will bless the God who gave him life and who takes it away. Yet he does not know if he will be led to a point where he will be ready to go. Like John Bennett, he would enjoy living another fifty years to see how things will turn out; it is almost as though he were bargaining with God for more time. In the end, however, he listens to the Psalmist's admonition to embrace his finitude, not to live in a fool's paradise. Just as members of his family support one another in the last leave-taking, God will sustain him:

In Psalm 88, verse 16 the Psalmist says, "I have been dying since the day of my birth." People who live in a fool's paradise don't understand this. That is one of the prices that people pay for living in a fool's paradise. But every day of my life I have said, "O Lord, the soul that thou gavest me is pure, thou has given it and thou will take it away from me. As long as I live I will continue to bless you." People approach death as if they have never heard about it. That is what really happens. Leave-taking is a family thing. Now we are taking leave of our sister. Somebody is with her all the time, not some stranger—my sisters, or I, or a niece are always there. It is an opportunity, as a matter of fact, to show great love and great concern. I can't say that I will die with joy. Maybe, however, the Almighty will lead me to a point where I will say I will be glad to go; I do not know. It will not be due to the joy of expectation of being in heaven and getting a bigger reward. I would like to be around and see what is going to happen fifty years from now, but if you live with a minimum of reality, you know that you just can't do it.

The last affirmative expressions concerning death are ones of celebration or gracing. Beyond the naturalness and inevitability of dying, Jack Boozer finds grace operative in one's demise. Although death should not kill us before we die, in the sense of immobilizing us with fear and apprehension, unlimited continuance of life in its present form would encounter ungracious limits:

> I guess I'm trying to say that I think that I carry to a considerable degree in my own consciousness, not only the inevitability and naturalness of death, but what Buber called a sense that death is a gracing. But it should not kill us before we die, paralyze our use of the opportunity of joy, or meditation, of being with one another, of thinking, of reading and seeing colors each day we have.
>
> Death for a person who has reached, so to speak, three score and ten, or something like that, is no problem for me theologically or any other way. That's not part of the problem of evil, that's part of the problem of goodness or grace, it seems to me. Because life that one expects to continue on forever in its present form just has important limitations in terms of quality.

One of the greatest of graces is the ability to celebrate life as one approaches its end. Anne Bennett, with failing sight and other diminishments, knows personally the losses of old age. Yet rather than regret these losses, her faith voices celebration for what is and has been:

> And I think you come more and more to have a sense of the celebration of the life that has been and is, rather than thinking too much about the loss.

Life After Death

The doctrine of the resurrection of Christ has traditionally inspired convictions about life after death, as well as various interpretations of it. In a truly representative sample of Christian beliefs in heaven or life after death, the spectrum of replies would surely be more extensive than those given in these interviews. In the wider spectrum, the answers would probably range from very simple images of the next life to highly sophisticated understandings of the doctrine. There would also be a good number of persons who claim to be Christians, but who have abandoned belief in a personal continuance after death. The individuals interviewed in this study are highly educated people who have reflected on the traditional teaching about life after death in the context of science and other dimensions of modern learning. The result is a general tendency to reject simplistic representations and easy answers concerning life after death. Yet they also wish to hold open the sense of mystery, of possibility, and even hope for some kind of continuance beyond death. At the core of the attitudes expressed is a strong sense of trust in God: Their faith in a divine presence that supported life appears to extend toward similar possibilities after death.

In the following comments of Mildred Cranston, we see at once a denial of literal descriptions of heaven and yet a definite sense of mystery, even the possibility of surprise beyond death:

> Death and beyond is a mystery. I have not changed much from my childhood. I think about my father walking along the road with me and talking, and my asking him questions and his answering. That has been very good for me, and it has kept me from pondering too much on what is going to happen and what is not. I remember one other thing he said when my mother died. We did this more in my days than we do now. My father took us into where she was lying in the coffin there. We were just three little girls. He said, "I want to tell you that this is not your mother. This is the battle ground on which she fought." That is beautiful, isn't it? I was only ten years old, and I have always remembered. I think that we are not deserted by God. That is about all that I think that I can say. My husband and I went to a funeral here. As we were walking home, I asked, "Do you believe all these descriptions about death and heaven?" He said, "No." I asked, "What do you believe about dying?" He said, "I do not know. I think that I will be surprised."

Anne Bennett echoes the latter views in rejecting bodily resurrections, although other theologians, upholding the teachings about "spiritual bodies," might find her words too literalistic:

> I think it's a mystery from where we came and it's a mystery where we go. I just leave it at that and don't worry about it. As I said before, I don't believe in these bodily resurrections. There wouldn't be space in the universe! I just think it's mystery.

Her husband, John, underscores the problem of imagining any meaningful content to such an existence. He employs the symbol of the future life as a statement affirming the worth of life as we know it; the futurist symbolism seems to be still another way of confessing one's faith in God, who cherishes all of creation. Yet he refuses the label of "secularistic," because his position leaves open the door of mystery, or transcendence:

> I think the real problem there is even imagining any content to a life under circumstances that have none of the conditions for serving the purposes that give one's present life meaning. The purposes of life depend upon certain conditions that we're familiar with. Now, a mystical union of some sort would perhaps for some provide an adequate substance for a future life. But if that is not our orientation, it's very difficult to think of any substance. I think the future life as a projection becomes a kind of symbol of a "yes" to life. Death is not cause for despair. A certain trust in God is involved that transcends what we experience. We can't say much more than that. Now I know that wouldn't satisfy very many people if you preached it, although I do think there must be a very many people who finally think that way, but who wouldn't put it that way. A person can believe in God even though the mysteries about death are such that no traditional doctrine about it is very satisfying. That isn't necessarily secularistic. I think to be secularistic is really to deny the mystery, or to close the door to transcendence.

Daniel O'Hanlon speaks about a spiritual continuance not defined by our usual sense of time. It is not merely a matter of believing in afterlife on the authority of the scriptures or of church doctrine. Rather, he refers to a presence of God, an abiding reality experienced now in life that will continue in some form after death:

> I do not think so much of afterlife as a time. I think of the reality of God as a present reality and as an abiding reality and of my connection with that as something that is basic and will remain. I think of reality not as a place but as a way of being. I do not have particular images of it. It is my feeling that there is spiritual continuation. The nature of that awareness and what form it will take I do not know. It seems to be more than faith in the sense of believing something because someone says that it is true. Just in terms of the experience of being in touch with a level which is beyond time and which has a certain kind of independent existence, there is spiritual continuance. There is the sense of that deep part of my being which is in touch with the deep reality of the divine, and there is no reason why that should cease to be just because my body wears out.

When Clarice Bowman reflects on this sense of continuance, she links it with the trust in God learned in the trials of her family of origin. The experience of many years of trusting in a benevolent God makes it incredible for her to think that continuity would cease with death:

> Some continuity seems credible to me: That all of this investment in God and life would go out like a light seems incredible. How the going on might be, I have no rational explanation of or symbolization whatever. But perhaps because of the very early experiences of my parents' trust in God, with all of their precarious economic life and the crises they faced, I caught my contagion of that trust. So I think I still have some in spite of all the ups and downs of my life.

Does this spiritual continuance imply personal consciousness in the afterlife? While the above respondents leave the answer cloaked in the mystery of the beyond, Louisa Jenkins faces the question directly. Her reply, based on a statement of Teilhard de Chardin, reveals a kind of selflessness about the whole issue. It does not seem to matter whether she is conscious and happy in the next life; it is enough to have lived, experiencing God's presence, and to know that whatever was of value in her life will be gathered up into the divine existence forever. These thoughts about immortality are very similar to a Whiteheadian vision of eternal preservation of the individual self's value in the mind of God:

> Does the personal consciousness continue after death? This is the big question. Let's see, in that book about evolution here on the table, there's a quotation of Teilhard. And I think this is very interesting because this is about where I am. And I think that he answers it! "The problem of personal survival per se doesn't worry me much. Once the fruit of my life is received up into One who is immortal, what can it matter whether I am egotistically conscious of it or have joy of it. I am quite sincere when I say that my personal felicity does not interest me. To be happy it is enough to know that the best of me passes on forever into One who is more beautiful and greater than I."

Rabbi Simon Greenberg voices a Jewish approach to life after death. In addition to the sentiments of trust in God, assurance of some continuance, and inability to describe the beyond expressed by Christian commentators, a strongly Jewish ethical note pervades his reflection. Mystic union with God is not enough, Greenberg asserts; the good or evil that one does in this life is closely linked with the world to come. Moreover, this ethical connection appears to warrant some form of personal continuity:

> When I was much younger, I actually believed that the problem of resurrection of life after death did not constitute a necessary aspect of my thinking. But there did come a time when I said, "You must formulate some kind of a presentable statement on these basic things." And I did that. I feel now more positively than before on the question of life after death. I have formulated my position on the basis of Jewish tradition and rabbinic texts. I quote three texts that I feel I need for a complete rationale. One is, "The grave is not the final end." Number two is, "What we do here is related to what happens afterwards." Number three is, "What happens afterwards is what no one can speak of with any assurance." So the only thing that I can say is these three things: "The grave is not the end," because if the grave is the end, Isaiah has said all that needs to be said on that: "Eat, drink, for tomorrow we die." The rabbis have a marvelous passage in the Ethics of the Fathers, where a rabbi says, "Do not fool yourself into thinking that the Sheol, the other world, is an escape." People feel what difference does it make, we are all going to die. The other statement is a paradox that Rabbi Jacob makes. It says, "One hour of repentance and good deeds is to be preferred to all of the life of the world to come. On the other hand, one hour of the spiritual uplift of the world to come is worth all the life here."
>
> But I do say that there is a relationship between what we do here and the afterlife. I do not go in for any kind of a mystic reunion with God. That would involve a kind of immortality of the soul, and thus it would mean that it probably doesn't make a difference what you do here. There is a very interesting metaphor about punishment and reward. I have a feeling that I read it somewhere in Maimonides, but I have never been able to locate it again. Imagine that the reward in the next world comes . . . you are going to be studying Torah, or you are going to be listening to music if you are a music student. Imagine what a torture that would be to one who is not prepared to study Torah, or to one who must listen to music whose soul has never been attuned to music. That is the closest metaphor for the relationship. I think there is not a loss of personality, because a loss of personality would again cancel out any relationship between here and there. There is a relationship between this world and the next, but what that relationship is I have absolutely no way of knowing.

Since human relationships are the deepest and most precious experiences in life, it is not surprising that hope for reunion with loved ones would arise in thoughts about afterlife. For Jones, it will not matter whether he and his wife will know each other again after death. It will be enough for them both to be with God:

> I have such a sense of the grace of God, that he knows me and he accepts me. That goes with my son's thing you see, that the God who knows me in biological existence is himself the Lord of death. I may change but he does not. It doesn't make any difference. To be with him and to be accepted . . . you won't need anything else. My wife said, "Do you think that you will see me after death?" I said, "I don't know. I need you now but I won't need you then. I won't need my mother. I won't need my father. To be with God will be enough." You see, that will be it. That is it. You won't need any milk and honey and all of that stuff. That is it. There is nothing that you can say except that is it. Do you see my point?

Anita Caspary tells of a shift in her meditations. The importance of personal reunions or of new friendships becomes less meaningful to her in older age; she is content to dwell on life after death as an opening to something new and glorious:

> I used to think a lot about life after death and about reuniting with one's family and all of that. It might be a totally different world. It might be this world transformed. I do not think that I can imagine it. I believe in it. It is going to be a blossoming out, an opening out into something new and glorious.

The above remarks of Jones and Caspary lead us into a category of views on life after death that might be called convictions of "super-trust." In a number of opinions previously stated there is a kind of hesitancy or tentativeness concerning affirmations about an existence beyond death. It is not that the possibility and the hope are denied, but the hearer senses less than assurance or conviction about the reality of life after death. It is left shrouded in mystery; the commentators are not sure. Monihan, in contrast, speaks with assurance about life after death; he sees it as the culmination of a lifetime conversation with God, the end of a long circular movement through trials toward the full flowering of the personality:

> I am as sure of it as I am sitting here with you now. The contemplative life is the foretaste of the life after death, the down payment, as St. Paul says. The life of contemplation that hopefully the older person

has or will arrive at or will develop is the final payment, so that this conversation, communion with, or sharing with God is something that one should get in one's later years. That frequent interaction comes through a succession of trials. If you read the literature of the mystics, progress in the spiritual life is not a horizontal movement, but a circular movement—trial, trial, trial in wider and wider concentric circles, widening out to deeper realms until one has a greater wisdom or whatever you want to call it. So I can say that the life after death is a full endowment of which we have only a little bit of payoff right now. We have enough of the taste to say, "Mmmm. That is good." It is the completion of personality, the crowning of personality, the full flower of personality. We are intelligent spiritual beings, and our lives are only partly physical. The most important part of man is the dream, the personality.

Lavinia Scott maintains a similar strong belief in life after death. This tenet has been a constant throughout her life; she shows little or no doubt about its reality:

> I believe in life after death. The actual form of it I can't define. I go along somewhat with Paul, I guess, in believing in the spiritual body, but when Jesus says there's no marrying or giving in marriage, well, I wonder sometimes about these devoted couples who look forward to being together in the next life. And I just don't know; I haven't the answers. But I'm not worried about it. I think, we're with God in this life. We'll be with God in a fuller sense in a life after death. And to me it's an unfolding. And I don't know that I've changed very much in my ideas about that.

Unless he believed in the truth of afterlife in an unqualified way, affirms John Tracy Ellis, the entire gospel message would become meaningless. It is hard to imagine a more categorical statement of belief in life after death. Ellis, himself a scholar of renown, does not allow theological refinements to temper his conviction:

> I have never doubted the existence of an afterlife; nor have I ever believed other than the empty tomb on the first Easter morning. That has been a major factor—and a very consoling one—in my religious life. Some time ago I read a simple statement of Cardinal George Basil Hume of Westminster, in which he remarked, "I believe in the empty tomb." So do I, and that in an unqualified way, and without it I would find the entire Christian gospel meaningless. I respect the sophisticated research of biblical scholars, but at times their qualifications and refinements—if I understand rightly what they are writing—

seem to me more contrived than helpful. Many years ago I used to discuss questions of that kind with my friend, Fr. Roland Murphy, and if the conversation threatened to get beyond my depth, I would laughingly tell him, "Roland, leave me in simple faith!"

And as for the resurrection of the Master and the afterlife which that event implied, I do not meditate on these truths as much as I should, but I believe them with all my heart, and without them I would find life utterly absurd and meaningless.

Lawrence Jones shares such faith in an afterlife, referring to it as an immediate presence to God, who fully knows and accepts him:

There was a pastor of a church in Philadelphia by the name of Charles A. Tinsley. He wrote a song, called "Nothing Between My Soul and My Savior." It is a beautiful song. The theme of it is just that . . . I believe that life after death is not a duration, but that it is to be with God with nothing between. It is the quality of existence, a state of existence, not a linear thing. The moments in my life that have been most precious to me have been those with my wife, my children, or with my friends, when I have been fully known and fully accepted.

In the perspective of Mary Luke Tobin, the core or center of the self will surely continue when all else falls away. As a believing Christian, she has confidence that a trustworthy God will sustain us beyond death. It is also particularly interesting to note her remark toward the end of the passage to the effect that belief in life after death does not diminish her involvement in and care for the world. With this reflection, she reacts against an earlier tendency in Catholicism to stress the world-to-come over the present world:

This is where an insight of Merton's applies. The center is all that we have left when we die. This is the thing that cannot be taken away from us. So I do not think that it is just being religious or just having pious talk of prayers or something like that. To me it is an insight of who I am, which should lead me forward rather than backwards. The rest of this material is going to go. You are going to lose your body, your brains, your family. That center, that impregnable you, is going to continue. I think that if we had some sense of that, it could carry us beyond where we are going.

I am less concerned with the details of afterlife or the how of it or anything like that. As a believing Christian . . . I think I accept the fact that since I am constituted by God and of God in a very real way, I can trust myself to God after death. Because I have that trust I do not really need to know a lot about details. Maybe we will be absorbed into a total wonderful universe or something. I don't really have a lot of concern about that. But I think that I am much more turned on to life, to living, than I was some years ago. I think that we had a training that made us always do everything for the hereafter.

As a final example of "super-trust" in the promise of life after death, the following paragraphs of Albert Outler subtly explore arguments for such a belief. Of course, he realizes that he is pushing reason beyond its domain, but the reflections are, nevertheless, stimulating. He first situates himself in the overall providence of God, which he finds loving, trustworthy, and meaningful. After dismissing various teachings on rebirth into this world, he contends that life after death would be a continuation of God's giving and gratuitous way of acting. Unless all that has gone before were meaningless, he urges, there must also be meaning after death; we can extrapolate from the way God acts, freely giving meaningful existence, to the way God will act with us after our deaths. His last point provides an interesting twist on the question of whether this life is enough. The argument about the "murdered Mozarts" looks to a kind of compensatory justice in the afterlife for those whose life on earth was cut off in an untimely way:

> The notion of beforelife, life, and afterlife are three aspects of how far I am willing for my life to be from God, in God, and to God. Although I certainly couldn't claim that this has been a steady and unfaltering trust, overall it has been the only thing that I have to go on. I don't know how I got to be, but when I did know that I was, I know that whatever I was, was in and with the providence of God. As much as I know of the providence of God, it is loving, trustworthy, and meaningful. Loving, trustworthy, and meaningful are the three words that I would normally use about significant experiences anyhow.
>
> I rather think that there might very well be personal consciousness after death. Here we do not have any data, and talk about it has to be talk. Yet it is not merely wishful thinking. It is an effort at being rational that reaches beyond reason. You see I do not think that metasomatosis or metapsychosis will make an awful lot of good sense. The main thing to me is that God creates selves each in its own right, nature, and purpose. For that self there is an origin which is not its own and a destiny which is not its own. What this consists of goes quite beyond anything which I would be able to conceive. It would only seem appropriate to the kind of experiences that all of us have had. Unless this much meaning is to be cancelled and in a certain sense negated,

there must be meaning after death. What that meaning is will have to be as gratuitous and gifted as what meaning there has been in my life—all of which so far as I can see has been gifted and gratuitous.

Would it be arrogance on our part to want more than this life anyway? In a sense, yes. It would be arrogance on our part to suppose that the meaning that we have had is meaning we have made. What I am talking about is the meaning that is gifted and gratuitous and therefore likely to be a part of God's continual purpose.

Probably the crucial point would be the question of whether or not this life is enough. There is a way that you could say, "You've had enough." A long life and all of the things that mattered have happened; it has been a rounded kind of experience, something of a whole. This overlooks the fact that it is a rare, very rare experience in human existence for life to turn out as well as it has for me. The murdered Mozarts, the wasted lives, the untimely deaths, the lives without meaning . . . suggest that you can't generalize from a rather rare instance of a nearly fulfilled life and life which is so, generally speaking, unfulfilled. In principle, therefore, the question still is: What kind of meaning does God have in mind to achieve in what kind of life? There I am willing to leave it up to him, since, on the one hand, I have no other alternative, and, on the other hand, this has been a life-style which is now deeply engrained in the way that I see and feel every day's experience.

At the opposite end of the spectrum are religious people who either deny life after death or are very doubtful about its possibilities. In the following remarks of Earl Brewer, we see a meaningful participation in Christian liturgical and ethical life coupled with agnosticism about afterlife. There is also a clear admission of the impact of modern scientific thinking, in this case via sociology, on traditional beliefs; lack of empirical evidence limits his speculations about life beyond this world:

In regard to afterlife I have two responses. One is, that so far as the bodily aspect of it is concerned, both my wife and I have willed our bodies to a medical school. So we're not caught up in the theology of bodily resurrection or anything like that. I suppose I'm agnostic about a lot of features of the Christian faith. I have no difficulty in participating, and I'm an active church-goer, in the liturgy and in the practices of my faith, including statements about heaven and afterlife and resurrection and things like that. But I guess I'm too much of a social scientist to be able to go too far beyond where you have some kind of empirical evidence. This was one of the struggles that I had when I brought my faith to sociology and what I got in sociology to relate to my faith. There are whole areas of my experience where I am content with a degree of agnosticism—and of just saying, "I don't know."

With a degree of midwestern skepticism, Carroll Lemon is not able to make much sense out of belief in living beyond death. As a committed Christian, however, Lemon affirms the power of God's grace in Christ as an ability to raise people up to new graced existence within this life:

> Life after death isn't important to me. I don't understand how or where it could be. I think that life ends with death. I can't grasp any continuance of my spirit in personal or cosmic ways. Yes, I understand that the motivation has often been life eternal. I remember in my first pastorate there was a strong man in the church, a very good man who was a very good osteopath, who made the statement that he didn't see why young people, considering their conduct, didn't consider the fact of heaven and hell. And I thought at the time that it just didn't seem to make sense as a motivation. But I think sometimes at the death of our wonderful pilgrims here at Pilgrim's Place, that their life has been such that death has no sting. Some of the resurrectional dimension is in life itself, in the graced life itself. Some people are already risen in the way they live. The fact that death may be the end is not a sting.

Just as strongly as some Christians and Jews quoted above affirmed belief in a life after death, Rabbi Aaron Blumenthal denies it. He seems to conclude that life in this world is, indeed, enough, even for a believer in God. Yet this denial of life after death must be kept in a double focus in the thought of this Jewish religious professional. First, the way of the Torah is seen as God's great gift to the Jewish community; ritual, observance, and ethics continue to flow significantly from Torah. Second, there is a kind of hope for the future in the continuing life of one's own family and in the possible wellbeing of humanity at large in generations to come. Finally, Blumenthal's example of the "depersonalization of hope" in the unselfish life of his woman congregant underscores a type of goodness without personal ambitions for gratifications beyond this world:

> What aging does is that for the first time one confronts his personal death, his personal elimination from the world. Now, if you want to know anything about how I feel religiously about dying . . . to me death is the end of everything. I'm not going to heaven; I'm not going

to hell. There is no afterlife. I read something some time ago which compared a human being to a grain of sand on the beach or a drop of water in the ocean. That is what I think I am. And it's almost time for me to leave this earth. It's almost time to remove myself from the general scene. I hope it'll be done painlessly. And I'm not looking forward to an afterlife.

All personal hope merges into hope for humanity, which alone has a perennial future. In that sense there is no reason to abandon hope. It just ceases to be personal. This depersonalization of hope can be inspiring. I have a friend whose eightieth birthday we just celebrated recently. I had a congregation in Houston about thirty-five or forty years ago. She was a member of my congregation. She was the liveliest, most energetic human being you'd ever want to meet at the age of forty. She's that way at the age of eighty, now, and I think that she has no personal ambitions or hopes. She is filling her days with goodness.

NOTES

INTRODUCTION

1. U.S. Department of Health, Education, and Welfare, *Our Future Selves* by Paul A. L. Haber, Pubn. No. 78–1443 (Washington, DC: Government Printing Office, 1978), p. 3.
2. Seward Hiltner, "Discussion and Comment," *Pastoral Psychology* 24 (Winter 1975):168.
3. Roger L. Gould, *Transformations: Growth and Change in Adult Life* (New York: Simon & Schuster, 1978); and Daniel J. Levinson et al., *The Seasons of a Man's Life* (New York: Alfred A. Knopf, 1978).
4. Joel Davitz and Lois Davitz, *Making It: 40 and Beyond* (Minneapolis: Winston Press, 1979).
5. William Barrett, *The Illusion of Technique* (Garden City, NY: Doubleday & Co., 1978), see Introduction.
6. Herant A. Katchadourian, "Medical Perspectives on Adulthood," cited in *Adulthood,* ed. Erik Erikson (New York: W. W. Norton & Co., 1978), p. 57.
7. Bernice L. Neugarten, ed., *Middle Age and Aging* (Chicago: University of Chicago Press, 1968), p. 94.
8. George E. Vaillant, *Adaptation to Life* (Boston: Little, Brown & Co., 1977).
9. Donald O. Cowgill and Lowell D. Holmes, eds., *Aging and Modernization* (New York: Appleton-Century-Crofts, 1972).
10. Carl G. Jung, *The Portable Jung,* ed. Joseph Campbell (New York: The Viking Press, 1971), p. 22.

CHAPTER II

1. Daniel J. Levinson et al., *The Seasons of a Man's Life* (New York: Alfred A. Knopf, 1978), p. 242.
2. Barbara Fried, *The Middle-Age Crisis* (New York: Harper & Row, 1967), p. 70.
3. Ibid., p. 77.
4. Roger L. Gould, *Transformations: Growth and Change in Adult Life* (New York: Simon & Schuster, 1978), p. 230.
5. Ibid.
6. Bernice L. Neugarten, "Adult Personality: A Developmental View," in *Readings in Psychological Development Through Life,* ed. Don C. Charles and William R. Looft (New York: Holt, Rinehart and Winston, 1973), p. 365.
7. Elliott Jaques, *Work, Creativity and Social Justice* (New York: International Universities Press, 1970), chap. 3.
8. George E. Vaillant, *Adaptation to Life* (Boston: Little, Brown & Co., 1977).

9. Virgil, *Aeneid* 6. 126ff.

10. Adrian Van Kaam, *The Transcendent Self* (Danville, NJ: Dimension Books, 1979), p. 64.

11. Milton L. Barron, *The Aging American* (New York: Thomas Y. Crowell Co., 1961), p. 148ff.

12. Henry S. Maas and Joseph A. Kuypers, *From Thirty to Seventy* (San Francisco: Jossey-Bass, 1974), p. 173.

13. Allen Dasher, *After 45: Candid Observations on Middle Age* (New York: Exposition Press, 1952), chap. 3.

14. Edmund Bergler, *The Revolt of the Middle-Aged Man* (New York: Grosset & Dunlap, The Universal Library, 1957), p. 305.

15. W. G. Miller, "The Literature on Middle Maturity with Reference to the Psychology of Religion" (Ph.D. dissertation, Boston University, 1962), cited by M. Strommen, *Research on Religious Development* (New York: Hawthorne Press, 1971), p. 787.

16. Ronald Blythe, "Living To Be Old," *Harpers,* July 1979, p. 48; and Leslie J. Tizard and Harry J. S. Guntrip, *Middle Age* (London: George Allen & Unwin, 1959), p. 48.

17. Paul Pruyser, "Aging: Downward, Upward, or Forward?" in *Toward A Theology of Aging,* ed. Seward Hiltner (New York: Human Sciences Press, 1975), pp. 105–111.

18. A. Reza Arasteh, *Final Integration in the Adult Personality: A Measure for Health, Social Change, and Leadership* (Leiden: E. J. Brill, 1965), p. 92.

19. Literally, "In my heaviness is my love."

20. Van Kaam, *Transcendent Self,* p. 22.

21. Ibid., p. 64.

22. Leo Tolstoy, *My Confession,* trans. Leo Weiner (Boston: Dana Estes and Publishers, 1904), p. 18.

23. Ibid., p. 19.

24. Ibid., p. 21.

25. Ibid., p. 20.

26. William E. Hulme, *The Pastoral Care of Families* (New York: Abingdon Press, 1962), chap. 9.

27. Gerald O'Collins, *The Second Journey* (New York: Paulist Press, 1978), p. 75.

28. Ibid., p. 52.

29. Carl Jung, *Psychological Reflections,* ed. J. J. Jacobi (Princeton, NJ: Princeton University Press, 1971), pp. 137–138.

30. Ibid.

31. Joanne Sabol Stevenson, *Issues and Crises During Middlescence* (New York: Appleton-Century-Crofts, 1977), chap. 8.

32. Joel Davitz and Lois Davitz, *Making It: 40 and Beyond* (Minneapolis: Winston Press, 1979), p. 84.

33. Clyde B. Vedder, ed., *Problems of the Middle Aged* (Springfield, IL: Charles C. Thomas, 1965), pp. 29ff.

34. R. M. Collie, "Counseling the Middle-Yeared Pastor," *Pastoral Psychology* 22 (March 1971): 50; *see also* Ray W. Ragsdale, *Mid-Life Crisis of a Minister* (Waco, TX: Ward Books, 1978).

35. Vedder, *Problems,* pp. 44ff.

36. J. S. Slotkin, "Life Course in Middle Age," *Journal of Social Forces* 33 (1954):172–174.

37. Pat Watters, *The Angry Middle-Aged Man* (New York: Grossman Publishers, 1976), p. 179.

38. Studs Terkel, *Working* (New York: Pantheon Books, 1974), p. 23.

39. Ibid.

40. Ibid.

41. Davitz and Davitz, *Making It*, p. 151.
42. Pauline Bernice Bart, "Depression in Middle-Aged Women" (Ph.D. dissertation, University of California at Los Angeles, 1967), p. 582.
43. Gould, *Transformations*, p. 107; and Levinson et al., *Seasons*, pp. 197ff.
44. Erdman Palmore, ed., *Normal Aging*, 2 vols. (Durham, NC: Duke University Press, 1974), 2:195ff.
45. Vaillant, *Adaptation to Life*, pp. 276ff.
46. Gould, *Transformations*, pp. 231, 238.
47. See Bergler, *Revolt*.
48. Ibid.
49. Fried, *Middle-Age Crisis*, p. 59; *also* Seward Hiltner, *The Christian Shepherd* (New York: Abingdon Press, 1959), p. 169.
50. Anne Morrow Lindbergh, *A Gift from the Sea* (New York: Pantheon Books, 1955), p. 87.
51. Ibid., p. 88.
52. Ibid.

CHAPTER II

1. Grace Loucks Elliott, *Women After Forty* (New York: Henry Holt & Co., 1936), p. 36.
2. For example, see "Adult Personality: Toward a Psychology of the Life Cycle," and "The Awareness of Middle Age," in *Middle Age and Aging*, by Beatrice L. Neugarten (Chicago: University of Chicago Press, 1968), pp. 93–98, 137–147.
3. G. Stanley Hall, *Senescence: The Last Half of Life* (New York: D. Appleton & Co., 1923).
4. Daniel J. Levinson, *The Seasons of a Man's Life* (New York: Alfred A. Knopf, 1978), pp. 209ff.
5. Roger L. Gould, *Transformations: Growth and Change in Adult Life* (New York: Simon & Schuster, 1978), p. 18.
6. Ibid., p. 25.
7. Ibid., p. 88.
8. William Butler Yeats, "The Circus Animals' Desertion." *The Poems of W. B. Yeats*, Vol. 2 (London: Macmillan, 1949).
9. Levinson, *Seasons*, p. 247.
10. Bernice L. Neugarten, "A Developmental View of Adult Personality," in *Relations of Development and Aging*, ed. James Birren (Springfield, IL: Charles C. Thomas, 1964).
11. Heneage Ogilvie, ed., *Fifty: An Approach to the Problems of Middle Age* (Springfield, IL: Charles C. Thomas, 1962), p. 39.
12. William Barrett, *The Illusion of Technique* (Garden City, NY: Anchor Press and Doubleday, 1978), p. 344.
13. Alfred North Whitehead, cited by Barrett, *Illusion*, p. 269.
14. David Bakan, *The Duality of Human Existence* (Boston: Beacon Press, 1966), p. 71.
15. J. Maritain, cited by Erik Erikson, ed., *Adulthood* (New York: W. W. Norton & Co., 1978), p. 77.
16. Robert N. Bellah, "To Kill and Survive or To Die and Become," in Erikson, *Adulthood*, pp. 62ff.
17. Erikson, *Adulthood*, p. 21.
18. Pascal, *Pensées*, II, 129, in Robert M. Hutchins, ed., *The Great Books of the Western World*, Vol. 33 (Chicago: Encyclopedia Brittanica, 1952).
19. See William Johnston's *The Still Point* (New York: Harper & Row, 1970) for an interesting explication of this topic.

20. Raimundo Panikkar, "The Contemplative Mood: A Challenge to Modernity," in *Cross Currents* 31 (Fall 1981):261ff.

21. Seward Hiltner, "Personal Values in the Middle Years," in National Congress on the Quality of Life, *The Quality of Life: The Middle Years*, 3 vols. (Acton, MA: Publishing Sciences Group, 1974), 2:31.

22. Reuel L. Howe, *The Creative Years* (Greenwich, CT: The Seabury Press, 1959), p. 29.

23. Barrett, *Illusion*, p. 323.

24. Ibid., p. 344.

25. Alfred North Whitehead, *Religion in the Making* (Cleveland: World Publishing Co., 1960), p. 16.

26. William James, *Principles of Psychology* (New York: Henry Holt & Co., 1904), cited by Robert M. Hutchins, ed., *Great Books of the Western World*, 54 vols. (Chicago: Encyclopedia Britannica, 1952), 53:79.

27. Robert C. Peck, "Psychological Developments in the Second Half of Life," in Neugarten, *Middle Age*, p. 89.

28. James K. Feibleman, *The Stages of Human Life: A Biography of Entire Man* (The Hague: Martinus Nijhoff, 1975), p. 220.

29. Levinson, *Seasons*, p. 241.

30. James A. Peterson, *Married Love in the Middle Years* (New York: Association Press, 1968), pp. 107ff.

31. James Hillman, *Puer Papers* (Irving, TX: Spring Publications, 1979), p. 35.

32. Ibid., p. 36.

33. Ibid.

34. Augustine, *Enarrationes in Psalmos* 131.1, in Erich Przywara, ed., *An Augustine Synthesis* (New York: Sheed and Ward, 1945).

35. *Macbeth* v.5.19–20.

36. Augustine, *Enarrationes in Psalmos* 112.2, in Przywara, *An Augustine Synthesis*.

37. David Tracy, "Time and Aging," in *Toward A Theology of Aging*, ed. Seward Hiltner (New York: Human Sciences Press, 1975).

38. Ibid., p. 131.

39. Robert J. Lifton, "Protean Man," in *On Art and the Mind*, ed. Richard Wollheim (Cambridge: Harvard University Press, 1974).

40. W. Bouwsma, "Christian Adulthood," in Erikson, *Adulthood*, p. 87.

41. Elliott Jaques, *Work, Creativity and Social Justice* (New York: International Universities Press, 1970), p. 41.

42. Henri J. M. Nouwen and Walter J. Gaffney, *Aging* (New York: Doubleday & Co., 1974), p. 105.

43. Ibid., p. 106.

44. Ibid., p. 111.

45. Levinson, *Seasons*, pp. 148–149.

46. Howe, *Creative Years*, chap. 9.

47. Ibid.

48. Gould, *Transformations*, p. 231.

49. Ibid., p. 243.

50. Ibid.

51. Ibid.

52. J. Tizard and Harry J. S. Guntrip, *Middle Age* (London: George Allen and Unwin, 1959), p. 152.

53. Joseph Epstein, "The Virtues of Ambition," *Harpers*, October 1980, pp. 43–44.

54. Levinson, *Seasons*, p. 197.

55. Ibid., p. 224.

56. Eugene C. Bianchi, "Homo Lupus?" *Thought* 56:115.

57. Levinson, *Seasons*, p. 224.

58. *Lear* v.3: 8–19.
59. Paul Tillich, *Love, Power and Justice* (London: Oxford University Press, 1954), pp. 25–26.
60. Ibid., pp. 121–122.
61. James W. Douglass, *Resistance and Contemplation* (New York: Doubleday & Co., 1972), p. 145.
62. Ibid., p. 149.
63. Wayne Dennis, "Creative Productivity Between the Ages of 20 and 80 Years," *Journal of Gerontology* 21 (1966):1–8.
64. Alfred Lord Tennyson, "Ulysses," in *A Choice of Tennyson's Verse*, ed. Lord David Cecil (London: Faber & Faber, 1971), pp. 91–93.
65. John A. B. McLeish, *The Ulyssean Adult: Creativity in Middle and Later Years* (Toronto: McGraw-Hill Ryerson, 1976), pp. 11–12.
66. Martin Marty, "Changing Ethics and the Quality of Life," in National Congress on the Quality of Life, *The Middle Years*, p. 131.
67. Levinson, *Seasons*, p. 242.
68. Ibid.
69. W. Bouwsma, "Christian Adulthood," in Erikson, *Adulthood*, p. 92.
70. Jaques, *Work*, p. 45.
71. Howe, *Creative Years*, p. 70.
72. William H. Masters and Virginia E. Johnson, "Emotional Poverty: A Marital Crisis of the Middle Years," in National Congress on the Quality of Life, *The Middle Years*, p. 101.
73. Howe, p. 108.
74. Robert C. Peck, "Developments," in Neugarten, *Middle Age*, p. 89ff.; and Paul B. Maves, *Understanding Ourselves as Adults* (New York: Abingdon Press, 1959), pp. 146–147.
75. Lillian E. Troll, *Early and Middle Adulthood* (Monterey, CA: Brooks/Cole Publishing Co., 1975), pp. 87–88.
76. Anne Morrow Lindbergh, *Gift from the Sea* (New York: Vintage Books, 1965), pp. 80ff.
77. Howard J. Clinebell, *Growth Counseling for Mid-Years Couples* (Philadelphia: Fortress Press, 1971), chap. 2; and Robert Lee and Marjorie Casebier, *The Spouse Gap: Weathering the Marriage Crisis During Middlescence* (Nashville, TN: Abingdon Press, 1971), pp. 193ff.
78. Levinson, *Seasons*, p. 228ff.
79. Gould, *Transformations*, p. 104.
80. Eugene C. Bianchi, *The Religious Experience of Revolutionaries* (Garden City, NY: Doubleday & Co., 1972), chap. 1.
81. Eugene C. Bianchi, "From Machismo to Mutuality," in *From Machismo to Mutuality*, by Eugene C. Bianchi and Rosemary R. Ruether (New York: Paulist Press, 1976), pp. 130–131.
82. Paul Pruyser, "Aging: Downward, Upward or Forward?" in Hiltner, *Toward*, p. 103.
83. Ibid.
84. Maves, *Understanding*, pp. 146–147.
85. George E. Vaillant, *Adaptation to Life* (Boston: Little, Brown & Co., 1977), p. 29.
86. Clinebell, *Growth Counseling*, chap. 2.
87. Tournier, *Learn To Grow Old*, p. 101.
88. Gerald O'Collins, *The Second Journey* (New York: Paulist Press, 1978), p. 61.

CHAPTER III

1. *Jack S. Boozer:* born 1918, Sylacauga, Alabama; Methodist minister, army chaplain, 1944–48; Ph.D. Boston University, 1952; professor of religion, Emory University, since 1950. Coauthor of *Faith To Act,* 1967.

2. *Clarice M. Bowman:* born 1910, Mt. Airy, North Carolina; one of the first ordained women ministers in the United Methodist Church; served on National Methodist Board of Education; Jonathan Fisher Professor of Christian Education and Worship at Bangor (Maine) Theological Seminary; author of *The Living Art of Worship,* 1961.

3. *Albert C. Outler:* born 1908, Thomasville, Georgia; Methodist minister; Ph.D. Yale University, 1938; professor of theology, Southern Methodist University, 1951–79; well-known ecumenist and author of many books, including *Theology in the Wesleyan Spirit,* 1975.

4. *Earl D. C. Brewer:* born 1914, Ansonville, North Carolina; Methodist minister; Ph.D. University of North Carolina, 1951; Candler Professor of Religion and Society, Emory University (on faculty since 1946); author of many works on sociology and religion.

5. *Anne M. Bennett:* born 1903, Sandhill, Nebraska; M.R.E. Auburn Seminary, 1932; many church and seminary responsibilities (married since 1931 to John C. Bennett—see below); leader in movements for peace and for women's rights in religion.

6. *Carroll H. Lemon:* born 1908, Lincoln, Nebraska; minister, Disciples of Christ; D.D. Drake University, 1964; earlier degrees, Phillips University, 1932; served various midwestern parishes; ecumenical and educational leader with church agencies.

7. *Lavinia Scott:* born 1907, Yankton, South Dakota; M.A. Yale University, 1932; educational missionary in South Africa for 42 years with United Church Board for World Ministries; teacher and principal, Inanda Seminary, until 1969; teacher of Christian Education and Bible at ecumenical seminary in Alice, Cape Province to 1974.

8. *John C. Bennett:* born 1902, Kingston, Ontario; M.A. Oxford University, 1930; D.D. Pacific School of Religion, 1943; minister, United Church of Christ; professor of Christian Ethics at Auburn Seminary, 1930–38, Pacific School of Religion, 1938–43, Union Theological Seminary, 1943–70 (president 1963–70); returned to P.S.R. 1970–75; author of many works, including *Foreign Policy in Christian Perspective,* 1966, and *The Radical Imperative,* 1975.

9. *Benjamin Elijah Mays:* born 1895, Epworth, South Carolina; Ph.D. University of Chicago, 1935; Baptist minister; Dean, School of Religion, Howard University, 1934–40; president, Morehouse College, 1940–67; president, Atlanta Board of Education; leader in civil rights and educational movements; his seventh book, *Born To Rebel,* is an autobiographical account of three-quarters of a century of black-white relations.

10. *Lawrence Neale Jones:* born 1921, Moundsville, West Virginia; Ph.D. Yale University, 1960; minister, United Church of Christ; Dean of the Chapel, Fisk University, 1961–65; Dean of Students, Union Theological Seminary, 1965–71; Dean of U.T.S., 1971–74; Dean, Howard University Divinity School, 1975–present; his writings include *Organized Religion Among Blacks,* 1976.

11. *Anita Marie Caspary:* born 1915, Herrick, South Dakota; Ph.D. Stanford University, 1948; Dean of Graduate School, Immaculate Heart College, 1950–58; President, I.H.C., 1958–63; President, Immaculate Heart Community, 1963–73; chosen Woman of the Year by the National Coalition of American Nuns, 1976; leader of Catholic religious professionals and author of *Mauriac,* 1968.

12. *William J. Monihan:* born 1914, San Francisco, California; S.T.L. Alma College, 1946, B.L.S. University of California, 1952; Jesuit priest; Librarian, University

of San Francisco, 1947–64; Director of Library Relations, U. of San Francisco, 1964– ; specialist in rare book collecting and organizer of interdisciplinary symposia on great thinkers, writers and artists.

13. *Daniel J. O'Hanlon:* born 1919, Wallsend-on-Tyne, England; S.T.D. Gregorian University, 1958; Jesuit priest, ecumenical consultant at Second Vatican Council; professor of theology, Alma College, 1958–65; professor of theology at Jesuit School of Theology in Graduate Theological Union, 1965–present; since his Asian research, 1973–74, he has led meditative, life-integrating workshops; author of *Return to Simplicity and Wholeness,* 1979.

14. *Mary Luke Tobin:* born 1904, Denver, Colorado; Catholic nun; M.A. Notre Dame University; teacher at Loretto Heights College; administrator and then president of Sisters of Loretto, 1958–72; Director of Citizen Action, Church Women United, 1972–78; leader in peace and ecumenical movements; coauthor of *Peaceworld,* 1976, and author of *Hope Is An Open Door,* 1981.

15. *John Tracy Ellis:* born 1905, Seneca, Illinois; Catholic priest and historian; Ph.D. Catholic University of America, 1930; professor, Catholic University, 1935–64, University of San Francisco, 1964–76, Catholic University, 1977–present; leading scholar of American Catholicism, whose many volumes include *The Life of James Cardinal Gibbons,* 1952, and *American Catholicism,* 1956, revised 1969.

16. *Louisa Jenkins:* born 1898, Anaconda, Montana; Catholic; artist in Carmel, California; surgical nurse in World War I; studied art under Gonchorova in Paris; acclaimed for her mosaics, new collage techniques called "accretions," calligraphy, and scroll-making; her .vork expresses psychological and mystical themes.

17. *Aaron Blumenthal:* born 1908, Montreal, Canada; ordained rabbi Jewish Theological Seminary, 1932; army chaplain in World War II; rabbi of Congregation Emanuel, Mt. Vernon, NY; former president of Rabbinical Assembly of America; author of *If I Am Only for Myself: The Story of Hillel,* 1973.

18. *Simon Greenberg:* born 1901 in Russia; ordained rabbi 1925; rabbi of Har Zion Temple, Philadelphia, 1925–46; professor of Homiletics and Education at Jewish Theological Seminary; served as provost and vice-chancellor of J.T.S.; his works include *Foundations of a Faith,* 1967, and *Words of Poetry,* 1970.

19. *Sylvia Heschel:* born Philadelphia, Pennsylvania; M.A. Manhattan School of Music; taught piano in Cleveland and New York; gave piano recitals; married the late Abraham Heschel, professor of Jewish Religion at Jewish Theological Seminary; member of National Council of Jewish Women, and Jewish Composers Forum.

20. *Helen G. Hole:* born 1906; Quaker scholar; Ph.D. Indiana University, 1970; teacher, Westtown School, 1932–36; professor, Earlham College, 1947–69; Acting Provost at Earlham, 1970–72; author of *Prayer, the Cornerstone* and a volume on Quaker education.

21. *Ewert Cousins:* born 1927, New Orleans, Louisiana; Catholic theologian; Ph.D. Fordham University, 1966; professor of Theology, Fordham University, 1960–present; scholar of Christian spirituality from Middle Ages to the present; author of *Bonaventure and the Coincidence of Opposites,* 1978.

CHAPTER IV

1. T. S. Eliot, "The Love Song of J. Alfred Prufrock," *Collected Poems 1909–1962* (New York: Harcourt, Brace and World, 1963), pp.3ff.
2. John A. B. Mcleish, *The Ulyssean Adult: Creativity in Middle and Later Years* (Toronto: McGraw-Hill Ryesson, 1976), p. 6.
3. Simone de Beauvoir, *Old Age* (London: Andre Deutsch, 1972), p. 5.
4. Ibid.
5. *Encyclopedia of Religion and Ethics,* Vol. 1, ed. James Hastings (New York: Chase, Scribner & Sons, 1910), p. 5.

6. *The History of Herodotus* 7.46, in *Great Books of the Western World,* 54 vols., ed. Robert M. Hutchins (Chicago: Encyclopedia Brittanica, 1952), 6:225.

7. Sophocles, *Oedipus at Colonus,* 1230ff. In Hastings, ed., *Encyclopedia* 9:469.

8. *The Pastor of Hermas* 1.3.11, in *The Anti-Nicene Fathers,* ed. Alexander Roberts and James Donaldson (Grand Rapids, MI: William B. Eerdmans, 1962), Vol. 2.

9. St. Augustine, Sermon 108 (BCN), in *Select Library of Nicene and Post-Nicene Fathers of the Christian Church,* ed. Philip Schaff (Grand Rapids, MI: William B. Eerdmans, 1956), p. 440.

10. Milton, *Paradise Lost* 11.1.527–543, in Hutchins, ed., *Great Books,* 32:310–311.

11. James Boswell, *Life of Samuel Johnson,* in Hutchins, ed., *Great Books,* 44:407.

12. Chaucer, "The Reeves Prologue," *Canterbury Tales,* chap. 1, lines 3865–3897, in Hutchins, ed., *Great Books,* Vol. 22.

13. Montaigne, *Essays III,* in Hutchins, ed., *Great Books,* 25:39.

14. Richard A. Kalish, *Late Adulthood: Perspectives on Human Development* (Monterey, CA: Brooks/Cole Publishing Co., 1975), pp. 33ff.

15. Matilda W. Riley, cited by Cary S. Kart and Barbara B. Manard, eds., *Aging in America* (Washington: Alfred Publishing Co., 1976), pp. 87ff.

16. Raymond C. Kuhlen, "Personality Change With Age," in *Personality Change,* ed. Philip Worchel and Donn Byrne (New York: John Wiley, 1964), p. 554.

17. Ibid.

18. Louis Harris and Associates, *The Myth and Reality of Aging in America* (Washington, DC: National Council on the Aging, 1975).

19. This ambiguity is reflected in Harris's statement that "While these results may suggest that as people age they attach greater meaning to religion, on the other hand, those who attach the most importance to religion now may have attached that much importance to it throughout their lives. It may well be that society and the role of religion in it have changed, and not that people become more religious as they age" (Harris, *Myth and Reality,* p. 180).

20. Paul B. Maves and J. Lennart Cedarleaf, *Older People and the Church* (New York: Pierce & Smith, 1949).

21. Jean B. Abernathy, in Seward Hiltner, ed., *Toward a Theology of Aging* (New York: Human Sciences Press, 1975), pp. 49–50.

22. Jean B. Abernathy, *Old Is Not A Four-Letter Word* (Nashville, TN: Abingdon Press, 1975), p. 96.

23. Harold Geist, *The Psychological Aspects of Retirement* (Springfield, IL: Charles C. Thomas, 1968), p. 18.

24. Ronald Blythe, "Living To Be Old," *Harpers,* July 1979, p. 37.

25. Irving Kaufman, "Marital Adaptation in the Aging," in *Normal Psychology of the Aging Process,* eds. Norman E. Zinberg and Irving Kaufman (New York: International Universities Press, 1978), p. 187.

26. Jack Botwinick, *Aging and Behavior* (New York: Springer Publishing Co., 1973), p. 26.

27. Henri J. M. Nouwen and Walter J. Gaffney, *Aging* (New York: Doubleday & Co., 1974), pp. 17, 32.

28. Norman E. Zinberg and Irving Kaufman, "Culture and Personality Factors Associated with Aging," in Zinberg and Kaufman, eds. *Normal Psychology,* p. 52.

29. W. W. Meissner in "Discussion of 'Social Learning and Self-Image in Aging'" by Norman E. Zinberg, in Zinberg and Kaufman, eds., *Normal Psychology,* p. 183.

30. Richard A. Kalish, "The New Agism and the Failure Models," in *Aging and the Human Spirit,* ed. Carol LeFevre and Perry LeFevre (Chicago: Exploration Press, 1981), pp. 123ff.

31. Archibald MacLeish, "You, Andrew Marvell," *New and Collected Poems* (Boston: Houghton Mifflin Co., 1976), pp. 150–151.

32. Jonathan Swift, *Gulliver's Travels*, chap. 10, in Hutchins, ed., *Great Books*, 36:126–129.

33. Ernest Becker, *Escape From Evil* (New York: The Free Press, 1975).

34. Ibid., p. 141.

35. Alfred Lord Tennyson, "Tithonus," *Poems II* (New York: Frederick A. Stokes, 1891), p. 77.

36. Ibid.

37. *See* Alan Harrington, *The Immortalist* (Millbrae, CA: Celestial Arts, 1977); and Osborn Segerberg, *The Immortality Factor* (New York: E. P. Dutton & Co., 1974).

38. Albert Rosenfeld, *Pro-Longevity* (New York: Alfred A. Knopf, 1970).

39. Raymond A. Moody, Jr., *Life After Life* (Atlanta, GA: Mockingbird Books, 1975).

40. Henri J. M. Nouwen, "Care and the Elderly," in LeFevre and LeFevre, eds., *Aging and the Human Spirit*, p. 292.

41. Botwinick, *Aging and Behavior*, p. 105.

42. de Beauvoir, *Old Age*, p. 298.

43. Wallace Stegner, "The Writer and the Concept of Adulthood," in Erik H. Erikson, ed., *Adulthood* (New York: W. W. Norton & Co., 1978), p. 236.

44. Ibid.

45. William Butler Yeats, "What Then?" *Collected Poems* (New York: The Macmillan Co., 1940), pp. 229–300.

46. William Butler Yeats, "In Memory of Eva Gore-Booth and Con Markiewicz," *The Winding Stair and Other Poems* (London: The Macmillan Co., 1933), pp. 1–2.

47. Richard Sellers, "The Difference Between Night and Day," *The Chicago Theological Seminary Register* 63 (September 1973):39.

48. Abernathy, *Four-Letter Word*, p. 110.

49. David Hackett Fischer, *Growing Old in America* (New York: Oxford University Press, 1977), p. 77.

50. Ibid., p. 113.

51. de Beauvoir, *Old Age*, p. 6.

52. Ibid., p. 218.

53. Ernest W. Burgess, *Aging in Western Societies* (Chicago: University of Chicago Press, 1960), p. 20.

54. Robert N. Butler, *Why Survive? Being Old in America* (New York: Harper & Row, 1975), pp. 10–11.

55. Donald O. Cowgill and Lowell D. Holmes, *Aging and Modernization* (New York: Appleton-Century-Crofts, 1972), chap. 1.

56. Clark Tibbitts and Wilma Donahue, eds., *Social and Psychological Aspects of Aging* (New York: Columbia University Press, 1962), p. 455.

57. Cowgill and Holmes, *Aging and Modernization*, p. 21.

58. Ibid.

59. Tamara K. Hareven, "The Last Stage: Historical Adulthood and Old Age," in *Aging, Death and the Completion of Being*, ed. David D. Van Tassel (Philadelphia: University of Pennsylvania Press, 1979), p. 185.

60. Elaine Cumming and William E. Henry, *Growing Old: The Process of Disengagement* (New York: Basic Books, 1961).

61. Elaine Cumming, in Robert Kastenbaum, ed., *New Thoughts on Old Age* (New York: Springer Publishing, 1964).

62. Arnold M. Rose and Warren A. Peterson, eds., *Older People and Their Social World* (Philadelphia: F. A. Davis, 1965), pp. 359–366.

63. Sidney Levin, "Depression in the Aged: The Importance of External Factors," in Kastenbaum, ed., *New Thoughts*, pp. 180ff.

64. Alex Comfort, *A Good Age* (New York: Crown Publishers, 1976), p. 65.

65. Zena Smith Blau, *Old Age in a Changing Society* (New York: New Viewpoints, 1973), chap. 11.

274 · *Notes*

66. Don S. Browning, "Preface to a Practical Theology of Aging," *Pastoral Psychology* 24 (Winter 1975):151ff.

67. Robert C. Peck, "Psychological Developments in the Second Half of Life," in *Middle Age and Aging,* ed. Beatrice L. Neugarten (Chicago: University of Chicago Press, 1968), pp. 88–97.

68. Paul Pruyser, "Aging: Downward, Upward or Forward," in Hiltner, *Toward,* p. 108.

69. Irving Rosow, *Socialization to Old Age* (Berkeley, CA: University of California Press, 1974), p. 21.

70. Bernard Kutner et al., *Five Hundred Over Sixty* (New York: Russell Sage Foundation, 1956), pp. 100, 121.

71. Ibid.

72. J. J. Rousseau, *A Discourse on a Subject Proposed by the Academy of Dijon: What is the Origin of Inequality Among Men, and Is It Authorised by Natural Law?* in Hutchins, ed., *Great Books,* 38:336.

73. Anton Chekhov, *The Cherry Orchard,* trans. Constance Garnett, in *Great Russian Plays,* ed. Norris Houghton (New York: Dell Publishing Co., 1960), p. 341.

74. Ibid., pp. 360–361.

75. Edwin Arlington Robinson, "Mr. Flood's Party," *Collected Poems* (New York: Macmillan Company, 1949).

76. Arthur S. Flemming, "Spiritual Well-Being From the Perspective of the 1971 White House Conference on Aging," in *Spiritual Well-Being of the Elderly,* ed. James Thorson and Thomas Cook (Springfield, IL: Charles C. Thomas, 1980), pp. 9–10.

77. Paul Maves, "Spiritual Well-Being of the Elderly: A Rationale for Seminary Education," in Thorson and Cook, *Spiritual Well-Being,* pp. 51ff.

78. Rodney Stark, "Age and Faith: A Changing Outlook or an Old Process?" *Sociological Analysis* 29 (1968):10.

79. Ben Weininger, "Life Has No Age," in *Wisdom and Age,* ed. John Staude (Berkeley, CA: Ross Books, 1981), p. 92.

80. Ibid., pp. 93–94.

81. Sister Augustine Scheele, "Living For Real," *The Chicago Theological Seminary Register* 63 (September 1973):5.

82. Dag Hammarskjold, *Markings,* trans. Leif Sjoberg and W. H. Auden (New York: Alfred A. Knopf, 1964), p. 89.

83. Paul Tournier, cited by Blythe, "Living To Be Old," pp. 37–38.

84. Abraham J. Heschel, "The Older Person and the Family in the Perspective and Jewish Tradition," in LeFevre and LeFevre, *Aging and the Human Spirit,* p. 41.

85. Ibid., p. 42.

86. Kutner et al., *Five Hundred Over Sixty,* p. 67.

87. Augustine, "On the Good of Marriage," in Schaff, *Select Library,* Vol. 3, 24:400.

88. Alfons Deekens, *Growing Old and How to Cope With It* (New York: Paulist Press, 1972), p. 79.

89. Blythe, "Living To Be Old," p. 79.

90. Charles J. Fahey, "Spiritual Well-Being of the Elderly In Relation to God," in Thorson and Cook, *Spiritual Well-Being,* pp. 61–62.

91. Robert Havighurst, *Developmental Tasks and Education,* 2nd ed. (New York: David McKay, 1952), p. 94.

92. Augustine, "On the Good of Widowhood," in Schaff, *Select Library,* Vol. 3, 24:451.

93. Kalish, *Late Adulthood,* p. 79.

94. Blau, *Old Age in a Changing Society,* p. 53.

95. Robert F. Sayre, "The Parents' Last Lessons," in Van Tassel, *Aging, Death and Completion*, p,. 216.

96. Robert Butler, "Successful Aging and the Role of the Life Review," *Journal of the American Geriatrics Society* 27 (1974):533.

97. Ibid.

98. Ibid., p. 534.

99. Erik H. Erikson, "Reflections on Dr. Borg's Life Cycle," in Erikson, *Adulthood*, pp. 1ff.

100. Ibid., p. 26.

101. Brita Stendahl, "Honor Your Father and Your Mother," *The Christian Century*, 14 November 1979, p. 1122.

102. William Butler Yeats, "Sailing To Byzantium."

CHAPTER V

1. Henry S. Maas and Joseph A. Kuypers, *From Thirty to Seventy: A Forty-Year Longitudinal Study of Adult Life Styles and Personality* (San Francisco: Jossey-Bass, 1974), p. 173.

2. Louis Harris and associates, *The Myth and Reality of Aging in America* (Washington, DC: National Council on the Aging, 1975), p. 181.

3. Robert J. Havighurst and Ruth Albrecht, *Older People* (Chicago: University of Chicago Press and Longmans, Green & Co., 1953), pp. 203–205; *also* David O. Moberg, "Religion in the Later Years," in *The Daily Needs and Interests of Older People*, ed. Adeline M. Hoffman (Springfield, IL: Charles C. Thomas, 1970), pp. 177–186.

4. David O. Moberg, "Religiosity in Old Age," *The Gerontologist* 5 (June 1965):78–112 passim, reprinted in Beatrice L. Neugarten, *Middle Age and Aging* (Chicago: University of Chicago Press, 1968), pp. 500–508.

5. Karl R. Stolz, *Making the Most of the Rest of Life* (New York: Abingdon-Cokesbury Press, 1941), p. 189.

6. Alex Comfort, *A Good Age* (New York: Crown Publishers, 1976), pp. 23–24.

7. Quoted ibid., p. 141.

8. Carl G. Howie, "Theology for Aging," in *Spiritual Well-Being of the Elderly*, ed. James A. Thorson and Thomas C. Cook, Jr. (Springfield, IL: Charles C. Thomas, 1980), p. 69.

9. William Butler Yeats, "Death," in *The Collected Poems of W. B. Yeats* (New York: Macmillan, 1945), p. 270.

10. Robert M. Herhold, "Probing by Joseph Sittler," *The Christian Century*, 26 September 1979, pp. 915–917.

11. Leslie A. Fiedler, "Eros and Thanatos: Old Age in Love," in *Aging, Death, and the Completion of Being*, ed. David D. Van Tassel (Philadelphia: University of Pennsylvania Press, 1979), pp. 235–236.

12. Ibid.

13. John Lafarge, *Reflections on Growing Old* (Garden City, NY: Doubleday & Co., 1963), p. 28.

14. Pierre Teilhard de Chardin, *The Divine Milieu* (New York: Harper & Row, 1960), p. 67.

15. Ibid.

16. Ibid.

17. William Mountford, *Euthanasy, or Happy Talk Towards the End of Life* (Cambridge: Metcalf & Co., 1848), pp. 3–4.

18. Ronald Blythe, *The View in Winter* (New York: Harcourt Brace Jovanovich, 1979), p. 239.

19. Robert Coles, *The Old Ones of New Mexico* (Albuquerque: University of New Mexico Press, 1973), p. 46.

20. Leo O'Donovan, cited by William C. Bier, ed., *Aging: Its Challenge to the Individual and to Society* (New York: Fordham University Press, 1974), pp. 221–222.

21. O. Carl Simonton, Stephanie Matthews-Simonton, and James Creighton, *Getting Well Again* (Los Angeles: J. P. Tarcher, 1978).

22. Leo W. Simmons, *The Role of the Aged in Primitive Society* (New Haven: Yale University Press, 1945), cited by Tommy Rodgers, "Manifestations of Religiosity and the Aging Process," *Religious Education* (July-August 1976):405.

23. Robert Louis Stevenson, cited by John A. B. Macleish, *The Ulyssean Adult: Creativity in Middle and Later Years* (Toronto: Mcgraw-Hill Ryerson, 1976), pp. 242–243.

24. Quoted in Comfort, *A Good Age*, p. 42.

25. D. H. Lawrence, "Shadows," in *Last Poems*, ed. Richard Aldington and Giuseppe Orioli (Florence: G. Orioli, 1932), pp. 77–78.

26. Michael Philibert, "The Phenomenological Approach to Images of Aging," in *Aging and the Human Spirit*, ed. Carol LeFevre and Perry LeFevre (Chicago: Exploration Press, 1981), p. 160.

27. Nevitt Stanford, "Personality Development at 80 or Any Old Age," in *Wisdom and Age*, ed. John R. Staude (Berkeley, CA: Ross Books, 1981), pp. 98ff.

28. Ibid.

29. Bernice L. Neugarten, in Carl Eisdorfer and Lawton M. Powell, eds., *The Psychology of Adult Development and Aging* (Washington, DC: American Psychological Association, 1973), pp. 320ff.

30. Ibid., p. 320.

31. Jean Beaven Abernathy, *Old Is Not A Four-Letter Word* (Nashville, TN: Abingdon Press, 1975), p. 113.

32. Reuel L. Howe, *How to Stay Younger While Growing Older* (Waco, TX: Word Books, 1974), p. 125.

33. Beatrice L. Neugarten, in Eisdorfer and Powell, eds., *Adult Development*, p. 320.

34. Joanne Sabol Stevenson, *Issues and Crises During Middlescence* (New York: Appleton-Century-Crofts, 1977), pp. 28–29.

35. Richard A. Kalish, *Late Adulthood: Perspectives on Human Development* (Monterey, CA: Brooks/Cole Publishing Co., 1975), pp. 60ff.

36. Ibid., p. 65.

37. Neugarten, *Middle Age*, p. 177.

38. Henri J. M. Nouwen and Walter J. Gaffney, *Aging* (New York: Doubleday & Co., 1974), p. 137.

39. Beatrice L. Neugarten, R. Havighurst, and S. S. Tobin, "Personality and Patterns of Aging," in Neugarten, *Middle Age*.

40. M. Clark and B. C. Anderson, *Culture and Aging* (Springfield, IL: Charles C. Thomas, 1967).

41. S. Philip Brown, "Religious Needs of Older Persons," in Thorson and Cook, *Spiritual Well-Being*, p. 76.

42. Paul W. Pruyser, "Aging: Downward, Upward or Forward?" *Pastoral Psychology* 24 (Winter 1975):102–118.

43. William A. Beardslee, *A House for Hope: A Study in Process and Biblical Thought* (Philadelphia: Westminster Press, 1972), pp. 128–129.

44. Earl Brewer, "The Future of Religion and Aging as Transcending Processes," *Futurist* 4 (1980):368–370.

45. Ibid.

46. Tamara K. Hareven, "The Last Stage: Historical Adulthood and Old Age," in Van Tassel, *Aging, Death and Completion*, p. 185.

47. Walter L. Holcomb, "Spiritual Crises Among the Aging," in *Understanding*

Aging: A Multidisciplinary Approach, ed. Marian G. Spencer and Caroline J. Dorr (New York: Appleton-Century-Crofts, 1975), p. 245.

48. Ibid.
49. Carl G. Howie, "Theology for Aging," in Thorson and Cook, *Spiritual Well-Being,* p. 76.
50. William Hogan, in Bier, ed., *Aging,* p. 30.
51. Paul Tournier, *Learning To Grow Old* (New York: Harper & Row, 1972), p. 194.
52. Ibid., p. 209.
53. Charles E. Curran, "Aging: A Theological Perspective," in LeFevre and LeFevre, *Aging and Spirit,* pp. 72–73.
54. Ibid.
55. Ibid., p. 74.
56. Ibid.
57. Robert B. Hudson, "Old Age Politics in a Period of Change," in *Aging and Society,* ed. Neil G. McCluskey and Edgar F. Borgatta (Beverly Hills, CA: Sage Publications, 1980), p. 159.
58. Ibid., p. 167.
59. Minna Field, *The Aged, The Family, and The Community* (New York: Columbia University Press, 1972), pp. 204–205.
60. Marjorie H. Cantor, "The Informal Support System: Its Relevance in the Lives of the Elderly," in McCluskey and Bogatta, *Aging and Society,* p. 141.
61. Ibid., p. 143.
62. Irving Rosow, *Socialization to Old Age* (Berkeley: University of California Press, 1974), p. 167.
63. Horace Kerr, *How to Minister to Senior Adults in Your Church* (Nashville, TN: Broadman Press, 1980), pp. 29–31.
64. Robert M. Gray and David O. Moberg, *The Church and the Older Person* (Grand Rapids, MI: William B. Eerdmans Publishing Co., 1977), pp. 122–126.
65. Ibid., pp. 141ff.
66. Phillip E. Hammond, "Churches and Older People," in LeFevre and LeFevre, *Aging and the Human Spirit,* p. 232.
67. Richard Wiseman, "The Aging Genius," in Staude, *Wisdom and Age,* p. 165.
68. Ibid.
69. Leon Edel, "Portrait of the Artist as an Old Man," in Van Tassel, *Aging, Death and Completion,* p. 207.
70. Quoted Ibid., p. 208.
71. William Butler Yeats, "Sailing To Byzantium."
72. William Butler Yeats, cited by Richard W. Wiseman, "The Aging Genius," in Staude, *Wisdom and Age,* p. 163.
73. Rilke, "Sonnets to Orpheus," cited by Wiseman, "The Aging Genius," in Staude, *Wisdom and Age,* p. 166.
74. Gay Gaer Luce, "SAGE and Wisdom," in Staude, *Wisdom and Age,* p. 44.
75. Joseph Meeker, "Wisdom and Wilderness," in Staude, *Wisdom and Age,* p. 67.
76. Sophocles, *Oedipus at Colonus* as cited in Christine Downing, "Your Old Men Shall Dream Dreams," in Staude, *Wisdom and Age,* p. 176.
77. Ibid., p. 177.
78. T. S. Eliot, *Four Quartets* (New York: Harvest Books, 1943), p. 59.
79. Louis J. Novick, "How Traditional Judaism Helps the Aged Meet Their Psychological Needs," in LeFevre and LeFevre, *Aging and the Human Spirit,* p. 332.
80. Gino K. Rovesana, "The Aged in Chinese and Japanese Cultures," in Bier, *Aging,* p. 16.
81. M. J. Levy, Jr., *The Family Revolution in Modern China* (Cambridge: Harvard University Press, 1949), pp. 63–64.
82. From the *Manu Smitri,* as cited in Drew Christiansen, "Dignity in Aging:

Notes in Geriatric Ethics," in LeFevre and LeFevre, *Aging and the Human Spirit*, p. 308.

83. Ibid.

84. Edward Fischer, "Aging as Worship," *Worship* (March, 1978):100–103.

CHAPTER VI

1. *Mildred W. Cranston:* born 1898, Adrian, Michigan; Ph.D. Boston University, 1930; Methodist missionary in China, 1922–27; many responsibilities with church agencies (e.g. YWCA), educational groups (e.g. Board of Education, Pasadena, California), and civic associations (e.g. City Council, Redlands, California).

INDEX